GW00514826

PORTUGAL

SPIRALGUIDE

AA Publishing

Contents

Written by Tony Kelly
Where to…sections by Andrew Benson
Revised and updated by Emma Rowley Ruas

Project Editor Sandy Draper
Project Designer Alison Fenton
Series Editor Karen Rigden
Series Designer Catherine Murray

Published by AA Publishing, a trading name of AA Media Limited,
whose registered office is Fanum House, Basing View, Basingstoke,
Hampshire, RG21 4EA. Registered number 06112600.

ISBN: 978-0-7495-6596-1

The contents of this publication are believed correct at the time of
printing. Nevertheless, AA Publishing accepts no responsibility for
any errors, omissions or changes in the details given, nor for the
consequences of readers' reliance on this information. This does
not affect your statutory rights. Assessments of the attractions,
hotels and restaurants are based upon the author's own experience
and contain subjective opinions that may not reflect the publisher's
opinion or a reader's experience. We have tried to ensure accuracy,
but things do change, so please let us know if you have any
comments or corrections.

A CIP catalogue record for this book is available from the British
Library.

Cover design and binding style by permission of AA Publishing
Colour separation by AA Digital Department
Printed and bound in China by Leo Paper Products

Find out more about AA Publishing and the wide range of travel
publications and services the AA provides by visiting our website at
theAA.com/shop

A04026
Maps in this title produced from mapping © MAIRDUMONT /
Falk Verlag 2010 (except p185)
Transport map © Communicarta Ltd, UK

The Magazine

A great holiday is more than just lying on a beach or shopping till you drop — to really get the most from your trip you need to know what makes the place tick. The Magazine provides an entertaining overview to some of the social, cultural and natural elements that make up the unique quality of this engaging country.

21st-century PORTUGAL

Visit Portugal today and you are just as likely to indulge in café culture, play on some of the best golf courses in Europe or shop in the chic Chiado quarter of Lisbon as you are to sit on a beach or watch the procession of a religious festival.

Portugal in the 21st century is changing fast. This dynamism can be partly traced to entering the European Union in 1986, when Portugal broke with its more traditional past. Since then, they have adopted the euro as currency (in 2002), hosted Europe's biggest football competition (Euro 2004) and enjoyed a number years as one of the fastest-growing economies in Europe. All this, despite the fact that Portugal has the longest working hours in the European Union (apart from the UK) with some of its lowest

salaries, and 2007 saw mass demonstrations against economic reforms. Today the government still faces the difficulty of sustaining the country's growth rate and curbing rising unemployment.

But you'll be able to see the pull between old and new that still goes on: brand new developments in cities standing cheek-by-jowl with low-cost housing, particularly on the outskirts of Lisbon; and in Porto, where young Portuguese business women wearing international labels stand next to widows who are still expected to wear the traditional black mourning outfit.

Changing Frontiers

But discovering all of this for yourself has certainly got easier. Portugal is located in southwest Europe, bordering the Atlantic Ocean, and to the west of Spain, and its main city airports and railway stations welcome around 7 million people from all over the world each year. For much of the 20th century, the country was far from accessible for your average traveller, and even in 1985, hardy visitors would have been faced with just one motorway that ran between Porto and Lisbon, and very few ways of exploring any further afield. Today there are dozens of new roads, financed by European Union grants, opening up the interior and linking previously inaccessible regions with Lisbon and Spain.

The staging of Expo'98 in Lisbon (► 58–59) on the 500th anniversary of Portuguese explorer Vasco da Gama's epic journey to India unleashed a building boom in the capital, bringing about new bridges, Metro lines, skyscrapers and shopping malls. Similarly, hosting Euro 2004 meant vast sums of money were spent on building new stadia and upgrading hotels, all of which are enjoyed by visitors today. And the building continues – the lively city of Guimarães in northern Portugal is destined to be European Capital of Culture in 2012, which is expected to further boost investment and the local economy in the area.

Vasco da Gama bridge at Parque das Nações in Lisbon
Page 5: The fishing fleet at Albufeira

Breaking with the Past

The first seeds for this intense period of change came with the Carnation Revolution of 1974, when the people of Lisbon stuffed carnations down the barrels of soldiers' guns, bringing to an end more than 40 years of dictatorship under António Salazar. At the same time, the end of the colonial wars and the granting of independence to the former African colonies brought thousands of Angolans, Cape Verdeans and Mozambicans to Lisbon, creating a vibrant, racially diverse, tolerant city.

> "Catholic priests are no longer seen as the guardians of public morality in Portugal"

Over the next decade, Portugal slowly moved into the European mainstream, and some of its more entrenched social and family traditions began to wane; the influence of the Catholic church, for example, is in decline, and although over 84 per cent of the population declared themselves to be Catholic at the last census in 2001, and religious festivals are as popular as ever, Sunday attendance is at a record low. Catholic priests are no longer seen as the guardians of public morality in Portugal, and contraception is widely available. Sex outside marriage is no longer taboo, and homosexuality is more widely accepted, with a growing gay scene in cities such as Lisbon and Porto.

Portuguese Heroes

Portugal is also making a bigger impact outside of its borders. Portuguese novelist and man of letters José Saramago won the Nobel Prize for Literature in 1998, Paula Rego is an internationally feted artist whose painting of Germaine Greer hangs in the National Portrait Gallery in London and Alvaro Siza Vieira is a Pritzker Prize-winning architect. More popularly, both Luis Figo and Cristiano Ronaldo are regularly feted among the world's best footballers, and coach José Mourinho has not only won the Champions League, but also coached FC Porto, England's Chelsea and Italy's Internazionale.

SPEAKING PORTUGUESE

Today, the population of Portugal stands at around 10.7 million, with a further three million citizens living abroad. Portuguese is spoken by more than 200 million people worldwide and is the official language of five African nations, as well as Brazil in South America (in fact, in May 2008, parliament controversially voted to bring the spelling of "Portuguese" in its home country in line with that in Brazil). This makes Portuguese the world's seventh most spoken language and more common than French.

Portugal in a glass
PORT AND WINE

Portugal's wine industry has long ceased to be about port and Matheus Rosé. Inspired by indigenous grape varieties and helped by the warm sunny weather, winemakers are now making rich, smooth red wines and crisp, fresh whites, which compete with other quality wine regions.

It takes grit to make wine in much of the country. Many of the vines grow on sharp, heat-baked schist rocks that can only be cared for by hand because of steep slopes that sit at around 700m (2297 feet) above sea level. Nowhere is this more evident than the beautiful Douro Valley in the north of Portugal, which has long been famous for its production of grapes destined for port and is the oldest demarcated wine region in the world. Today it is also producing well-structured, powerful red wines that have deservedly been getting more and more international attention – perfect for pairing with a rich steak sauce.

The mild and sunny Portuguese climate creates the perfect conditions for winegrowers

Fruity Reds and Crisp Whites

Heading further south, halfway between Porto and Lisbon, the pretty Beiras region with its Roman ruins and fairy-tale castles produces the full-bodied reds of the Dão and the fruity reds of Bairrada. And further still, between Lisbon and the Algarve, the Alentejo is probably the fastest-growing wine region in the country, with new producers bringing in outside investment, and fresh ideas.

"Alentejo is probably the fastest-growing wine region in the country"

White wine lovers shouldn't dismiss the vibrant, slightly sparkling Vinho Verde which comes from northwest Portugal. It has managed to shake off much of its old-fashioned image in recent years, and is the perfect aperitif; order it on a shaded terrace in the hot sunshine, or pair it with an appetiser of grilled sardines.

Port – Perfect Anytime

While the vineyards of Portugal develop, port still remains symbol of the local drinks industry. In its home country, port is a drink to be enjoyed at any time – not just after dinner – a white port and tonic as an aperitif, or an aged tawny with chocolate cake to round off a meal.

Wine has been made in the 100km (62-mile) stretch of the Douro Valley since Roman times, but the origins of port lie in the 17th century, when British traders, cut off from their supplies of claret by wars with France, developed a taste for strong Portuguese wines. The Methuen Treaty of 1703 lowered the duty on Portuguese wine coming into Britain in return for concessions for British textile merchants in Portugal. But the wines did not travel well, so the port shippers began adding brandy to fortify them

---

VISITING THE PORT HOUSES

Both the Douro vineyards and Vila Nova de Gaia are UNESCO World Heritage Sites, and a new wine tourism movement in both areas has meant that many port houses open for visitors, plus there are a variety of car, boat and train trips that can take you out to explore the terraced vines. The town of Porto (➤ 80–83) is a perfect weekend destination, with its narrow winding streets and large handsome squares. Climbing to the highest point of Porto, you get a beautiful view over the river to Vila Nova de Gaia (➤ 84–85), with the neon signs for famous names of port flashing like a tiny Hollywood Hills. Over in Gaia itself, there are increasing numbers of wine bars and restaurants opening up, and extensive restoration work has been done on the waterfront. Some of the best port houses to visit include Ramos Pinto and Taylor's (➤ 85). Or for a wide range of ports by the glass, visit the Solar do Vinho do Porto in Lisbon (➤ 72) where there are more than 300 varieties to choose from.

STYLES OF PORT

White: Dry or sweet, and served chilled as an aperitif
Pink: Light and fruity style of port designed to appeal to younger drinkers.
Ruby: Dark, full-bodied and fruity
Tawny: Amber-coloured, aged in wood for ten years or more
Colheita: Complex, spicy, single-harvest tawny aged for at least seven years
Late Bottled Vintage (LBV): Smooth and light-bodied port from a single-harvest wine aged in wood for four to six years.
Vintage: In exceptional years, a vintage may be declared and the very best wine will be transferred into bottles after two years in the cask. it will age in bottle for at least 10 years, developing a dark colour, a heady aroma and a crusty sediment. Vintage port should be decanted before being served, and unlike other ports, it needs to be consumed within a day of being opened.

during their long sea voyage. Port was born, and with it the household names (Croft, Dow and Taylor) that still control much of the trade.

The grapes – usually Tinta Roriz and Touriga Nacional – are harvested by hand in autumn, and crushed in stone vats or (more usually) fermented in steel tanks. After two days, the fermentation process is stopped by the addition of grape spirit and the wine is transferred into wooden casks (known as pipes). The following spring the casks are transported down river to mature in the port lodges at Vila Nova de Gaia (➤ 84–85). It is no longer essential to ship direct from Vila Nova de Gaia, which has led to emergence of smaller houses that sell direct from the Douro.

A few of the famous port lodges lining the river bank in Vila Nova de Gaia

Nautical NATION

On the edge of the Atlantic and at odds for much of its history with Spain, its only land neighbour, the coastline defines Portugal's identity as a seagoing nation, and its influence is seen in everything from architecture to food.

The Age of Discovery

The Portuguese like to look back to the golden age when their explorers sailed uncharted waters in search of new lands. The greatest of all Portuguese heroes is Henry the Navigator (1394–1460), Grand Master of the Order of Christ and architect of the descobrimentos (discoveries).

Henry took part in the capture of Ceuta on the Moroccan coast in 1415, but never sailed again, instead he retired to Sagres (➤ 156) where he established a school of navigation to train the nation's best minds. Here, new forms of navigational instruments were developed and a design for a new type of ship, the caravel, a cross between a traditional Douro cargo boat and an Arab dhow. The caravel revolutionised sea travel. Its triangular sails allowed sailors to take advantage of side winds and travel much faster and were used by Columbus (1451–1506) in voyages to the New World.

Great Explorers

During Henry's lifetime, Madeira and the Azores were discovered and the explorer Gil Eanes rounded the Cape Bojador in West Africa – believed at the time to be the end of the known world, beyond which were thought to

lurk sea monsters and unknown perils.

The holy grail was the discovery of a sea route to India by Vasco da Gama in 1498, which allowed Portugal to control the trade of oriental spices, silks and carpets that crossed Asia, and establish colonies in Angola and Mozambique as well as trading posts in Goa, Timor and Macau. The Vasco da Gama bridge in Lisbon is a fitting tribute to the great man; it crosses the Rio Tejo and at 17.2km (11 miles) is the longest bridge in Europe.

Statue of Henry the Navigator in Lagos

Fishing boats at Setúbal harbour, fishing remains one of Portugal's major industries

In the meantime, Pedro Álvares Cabral had discovered Brazil, awarded to Portugal under the 1494 Treaty of Tordesillas, which divided the thus far known world into Spanish and Portuguese spheres of influence. The country's naval influence declined during the 17th century as the Dutch and English fleets grew in strength, particularly in the trade with the East Indies and Asia, although Portugal's last overseas colony, Macau, was handed back to China only in 1999.

Portuguese Fishing Industry
In the 20th century Portugal still had one of the world's largest fishing fleets and cod fishing off the coast of North American and Canada became

---

PORTUGAL'S GREAT VOYAGES OF DISCOVERY

1419 Madeira
1427 The Azores
1460 Cape Verde
1482 Diego Cão reaches the mouth of the Congo, leading to the Portuguese conquest of Angola
1488 Dias rounds the Cape of Good Hope, South Africa
1498 Vasco da Gama discovers a sea route to India
1500 Pedro Álvares Cabral discovers Brazil
1519 The Portuguese sailor Fernão de Magalhães (Ferdinand Magellan) leads the first circumnavigation of the world, though he is killed in the Philippines en route (the journey was completed under the leadership of Juan Sebastian del Cano, a Spanish voyager).

To learn more about Portugal's relationship with the sea, visit the Museu de Marinha in Belém (➤ 48–49) which is devoted to Portugal's maritime history.

The Monument to Discoveries, Lisbon, built to commemorate Portugal's great explorers

the driving force of the Portuguese economy, with elaborate ceremonies held to wave the men off on fishing voyages. In recent years, however, the Portuguese fishing fleet has declined due to overfishing, and stringent rules aimed at conserving the world's deep-sea fish stocks. But fishing is still an important industry and brightly coloured wooden boats remain a familiar sight in ports like Peniche and Nazaré on the west coast, and Lagos and Olhão in the Algarve.

These days, the sea is yielding a different but still lucrative harvest, as hordes of tourists from around the world are attracted to the superb beaches of the Algarve, Costa de Lisboa, Costa de Prata and Costa Verde. And in one maritime area at least, Portugal in still leading the world; just off the coast of northern Portugal, in Agucadoura, the world's first commercial wave farm went into production in October 2008, generating renewable energy that will be enough to power 15,000 homes.

MANUELINE ART

King Dom Manuel I is known as Manuel the Fortunate as it was during his reign (1495–1521) that the sea route to India was discovered, bringing riches to Portugal in the form of spices, ivory and gold. The king has lent his name to a uniquely Portuguese version of late Gothic architecture, inspired both by the florid forms of Indian art and by the discoveries themselves. The most typical symbols of Manueline art are the armillary sphere (a navigational device consisting of a celestial globe with the earth at the centre, which became the emblem of Manuel I), the cross of the Order of Christ, seafaring imagery such as anchors and knotted ropes, and exotic fauna and flora from the newly discovered lands. The finest examples of Manueline art are the monastery and tower at Belém (► 47–49), the cloisters and unfinished chapels of the abbey at Batalha (► 112–113) and the windows of the Convento do Cristo at Tomar (► 116–118).

POUSADAS
and Solares

A traditional Portuguese guest house makes for a great way to experience some of the local traditions. Choose between a *pousada* (historic buildings turned into hotels) and a *solar* (usually a manor house run like an upmarket family B&B).

On 19 April 1942 the first *pousada* opened in the border town of Elvas to cater for travellers from Spain. The price of a double room was 80 escudos (€0.40). The *pousadas* were state-run inns along the lines of the Spanish paradores, offering simple hospitality and regional cuisine, and were the brainchild of the minister for popular culture and tourism, António Ferro. "At the current time, nearly all construction in Europe is intended for war," he said at the opening ceremony, "*pousadas* will be fortresses of peace, refuges of grace and quiet."

Pousadas Today
Sixty years later, there are 40 *pousadas* in Portugal, but they are no longer state-owned. All of them are housed in historic buildings, such as a restored castle in Óbidos (➤ 124) or Estremoz (➤ 144), or situated in places of natural beauty (a village house in Monsanto (➤ 124) or Marvão (➤ 143), or both (try a convent in Évora (➤ 143) or Beja (➤ 144).

Convento dos Lóios is a 15th-century monastery converted into a *pousada* in Évora

Perhaps the finest of all the *pousadas* is Pousada de Santa Marinha, a 12th-century convent overlooking the historic city of Guimarães (➤ 97). The bedrooms are in former monks' cells around the cloisters, with gorgeous tile-lined stairways and corridors filled with antiques. By contrast, the simple pousada at Ourém, just outside Fátima (➤ 123), is a tasteful modern conversion of a group of medieval houses attractively set in the centre of the walled village.

António Ferro wanted the *pousadas* to be "small hotels where people could feel at home". For Ferro, rustic furniture and local crafts were part of the experience, which was summed up as "comfort without ostentation".

Ironically, as levels of service rise ever higher in response to customer demands, the *pousadas* are in danger of moving away from their roots and Ferro's ambition to make guests feel truly at home: "If a guest walks into one of our *pousadas* and feels as if he has returned to his own house, then we will have achieved what we were striving for".

Solares de Portugal

If you really want to feel at home, you could stay in a family home, known as a *solar*. This is hardly a low key option, as many *solares* are manor house that have been converted into guest houses, where a Portuguese family will welcome, feed and possibly entertain you.

The Count of Calheiros, president of the Solares de Portugal (➤ 35), has been welcoming guests to his ancestral home (Paço de Calheiros, tel: 258 947 164, www.pacodecalheiros.com) since 1985. The house, built in the 17th century, stands at the end of an avenue of magnolia trees with a stone fountain in the yard. Chestnut ceilings are weighed down with chandeliers, and family portraits hang on the walls. The chapel has a carved 17th-century altarpiece and a vault where the last count is buried. The old stables have been turned into apartments and there is a swimming pool and tennis court in the grounds. From the terrace there

The elegant and comfortable interior of the Hotel Pousada Flor de Rosa in Crato

Many *pousadas* are converted historic buildings, such as this castle in Palmela

are views over the vineyards to Ponte de Lima, the headquarters of Solares de Portugal and the town with the largest concentration of manor houses in the scheme.

A few hours east in Trás-os-Montes, Brazilian artist Maria Francisca Pessanha introduces visitors to Solar das Arcas (tel: 278 400 010, www.solardasarcas.com), a 17th-century mansion built for the descendants of a Genoese navigator who arrived in Portugal in the 14th century at the invitation of Dom Dinis. The library has shelves of antique books. The apartments have wooden furniture, granite fireplaces and Maria Francisca's modern art on the walls. From your room, the only sounds you can hear are church bells and horses' hooves on the village street. The Pessanhas offer guests their own wine and home-cured sausages, and advice on walking, cycling and horse-riding in the area.

> "From your room, the only sounds you can hear are church bells and horses' hooves"

Solares de Portugal offers around 100 properties, from manor houses and country estates to rustic farmhouses and cottages. Most are in the Minho, but others are scattered across Portugal, right down to the Alentejo and the Algarve. Most are in quiet rural locations and many have swimming pools. However, what makes this experience really special is that guests enjoy a real insight into Portuguese family life.

Useful Addresses

■ Pousadas de Portugal, Rua Soares de Passos 3, Alto de Santo Amaro, 1300-314 Lisbon, tel: 218 442 001, www.pousadas.pt (➤ 35)
■ Solares de Portugal, Praça da República 4990, Ponte de Lima, Lisbon, tel: 258 741 672, http://www.solaresdeportugal.pt (➤ 35)

ON THE TILES
The art of Azulejos

If a single image defines Portuguese style, it is the Azulejo tile. You see them at stations, churches and shops, palaces and backstreet bars, and covering entire buildings in Lisbon.

Azulejos are not unique to Portugal, but it is perhaps here that they have achieved their finest expression. Similar glazed and painted tiles are found across the Arab world and in the Spanish region of Andalucía, from where azulejos originally came.

The name probably derives from an Arabic phrase meaning "azure polished stone" and they were first introduced to Portugal in the late 15th century when Manuel I imported Hispano-Arabic tiles from Seville for his royal palace at Sintra (➤ 60).

Early Tiles
These early tiles were called alicatados and were made of monochrome pieces of glazed earthenware that were cut into shapes or separated by strips to form mosaic-like geometric patterns.

The majolica technique was introduced from Italy during the 16th century. This involved coating the clay in a layer of white enamel onto

WHERE TO SEE AZULEJOS

- Museu Nacional do Azulejo, Lisbon (➤ 65)
- Palácio Nacional, Sintra (➤ 60)
- Sé Velha, Coimbra (➤ 108)
- Igreja dos Lóios, Évora (➤ 133)
- Nossa Senhora da Consolação, Elvas (➤ 141)
- Museu Regional, Beja (➤ 142)

which the artist could paint directly. In the 17th century, the fashion was for tapetes (carpet tiles), painted blue and yellow and resembling Moorish tapestries and rugs.

Mass Production

The first mass-production tile factory was set up after the 1755 earthquake in Lisbon, which also saw the development of the familiar blue and white tiles, heavily influenced by Chinese porcelain.

The custom of covering entire house- and shopfronts with azulejos began in Lisbon during the mid-19th century and came from Brazil, where Portuguese settlers used it as a way of keeping out the tropical rain. Today, azulejos continue to be a popular decoration, brightening up patios and courtyards, parks and gardens, and several of Lisbon's Metro stations.

Cloisters of the Sé Cathedral, Porto (left); Jardim Zoologico de Lisboa, Lisbon (right)

FADO
Lisbon's urban blues

You may never have heard of *fado* before coming to Portugal, but even first-timers are struck by how this traditional music evokes the worldwide tradition of folk and blues music, telling stories of melancholy and loss.

A traditional *fado* evening can be dramatic – all eyes are on the musicians, one with a guitarra (a Portuguese guitar like a mandolin), the other with a viola (acoustic Spanish guitar). There is silence as a woman dressed in black rises to sing. She sings of love and death, of triumph and tragedy, of destiny and *fado* (fate). Above all she sings of *saudade*, that Portuguese notion best translated as a longing for that which has been lost, from a broken love affair to the days when Portugal was great seafaring nation.

Fado Clubs
There are singers today who are renewing *fado* and finding new audiences both in Portugal and internationally, but a lot of musicians are happily stuck in their old, pleasurable ways. *Fado* is a great night out, although watch out for being overcharged for meals at some events, but mainly the music is taken very seriously, and the *fado* clubs in Lisbon are wonderful places to go. For the most authentic experience, try the clubs of Alfama and Bairro Alto. At Parreirinha de Alfama, *fado* legend Argentina Santos continues to sing in her backstreet cellar club, with black-and-

---

ORIGIN OF FADO

Fado has its origins in the working-class bairros of Lisbon in the early 19th century. At first, it was played in taverns and brothels, then, in the 1920s, the first casas de fado opened, with professional singers making recordings and putting on shows for tourists. It is only now that *fado* is making a comeback among young Portuguese as a genuine art form. It is melancholic, dramatic and heart-wrenching – think of the blues born in the poor neighbourhoods of America. All female fadistas wear a black shawl in memory of Maria Severa (1810–36), the first great fado singer, whose scandalous affair with a bullfighter and tragically early death are the subject of many songs.

A traditional *fado* singer in a restaurant in the Biarro Alto area of Lisbon

white photos of *fadistas* on the walls. A few streets away, guitarist Mário Pacheco plays every night in his intimate Clube de Fado, one of the newest of Lisbon's *fado* clubs. These places have a minimum charge but beyond that there is little commercialism and most of the customers are Portuguese. Outside of Lisbon, the other *fado* centre is in Coimbra.

For a more spontaneous experience, head for the bars and clubs where *fado amador* is played, where there are house musicians, but any one can turn up and sing. In Bairro Alto, Adega do Ribatejo is a popular meeting place, where waitresses Sara Cristina and Maria Raquel can be seen swapping aprons for black shawls and turning into *fadistas* for the night.

Modern *Fado*

Other modern singers include Ramana Vieira (American Portuguese), and Lisbon native Raquel Tavares, who won the biggest song contest dedicated to Fado in Portugal: 'Grande Noite Do Fado', and sings regularly at Bacalhau De Molho, one of the most famous houses in Lisbon.

LISBON'S FADO CLUBS

- Parreirinha de Alfama, Beco de Espírito Santo 1, tel: 218 868 209
- Clube de Fado, Rua São João da Praça 92, tel: 218 882 694, www.clube-de-fado.com
- A Baiúca, Rua de São Miguel 20, tel: 218 867 284
- Adega do Ribatejo, Rua do Diário do Notícias 23, tel: 213 468 343
- Adega Machado, Rua do Norte 91, tel: 213 224 640, www.adegamachado.web.pt
- Bacalhau de Molho, Casa de Linhares Restaurante, Beco dos Armazens do Linho 2, tel: 218 865 088, www.casadelinhares.com

BEYOND THE BEACHES

Portugal has 960km (600 miles) of beaches, but a few days exploring the interior will reveal traditional villages, vast acres of cork trees and breathtaking mountain ranges that offer excellent walking, hiking and adventure sports.

The highest mountains in Portugal are concentrated in the north and east – known as Terra Fria (cold lands) – and have a climate which is often described as "nine months of winter and three months of hell". Until fairly recently, these regions were very difficult to reach, but a new highway from Porto to Bragança has opened up the route to northern Spain, which passes through many of them. Today you can easily reach the spectacular Douro Valley (► 176–177), with its terraced vineyards and craggy peaks that cover 250,000 ha (617,763 acres), the bleakly beautiful Trás-os-Montes (► 76) and Serra da Estrela (► 119–120), the highest range in

Portugal. For a gentler experience, explore the Peneda-Gerês ranges in Vinho Verde, a stunning national park that has several camping sites, and plenty of activities, including walking trails and waterfalls (▶91–92).

Behind the Mountains

In Tras-os-Montes (which translates literally as Behind the Mountains, giving you some idea of how cut off the region has been), cars and tractors are replacing horse-carts and bullock-ploughs, and the emigrants who abandoned the area for lack of work opportunities are returning to build chic new houses (casas de emigrante) with the money they have made in France, Germany, Luxembourg and the United States, bringing with them cosmopolitan values and a taste for fast food.

But the sense of other-worldliness has not entirely left Tras-os-Montes, making it a fascinating place to explore. Until recently, when people were ill, they used folk remedies or consulted the local witch and the winter solstice is still marked by masked dancers running through the village with cowbells round their waists in a ritual that dates to pagan times.

Vines growing on the terraced slopes in the Douro Valley

Tranquil scenery in Parque Nacional da Peneda-Geres

As you move further down the country, the mountains may lose a little height, but that doesn't mean you can't find excellent walking and exploring opportunities. Near Lisbon, check out the dinosaur footprints near the village of Bairro in the Serras de Aire natural park, the oldest of their kind in the world, while children will love the many donkeys that live around here. Limestone is the dominant rock in both the Serras de Aire and Candeeiros natural park, and you can visit the dramatic caves and gullies.

For beach lovers who want to take a day off, there are one or two very good walking opportunities in Serra de Monchique (▶ 154–155). This low-lying mountain range is within an hour's drive of the Algarve coast and is blanketed with cork, chestnut and eucalyptus trees.

INTO THE WILD

Some of the wildest parts of Trás-os-Montes are in the Parque Natural de Montesinho, between Bragança and the Spanish border. The heather-clad uplands rise to 1,480m (4,855 feet) while the lower slopes support chestnut and holm oak. Golden eagles hover above the hills, wolves hide in the forests, and at weekends the local farmers go hunting for partridge, deer and wild boar. At least 90 villages are scattered about the park, with horseshoe-shaped dovecotes and slate-roofed houses where the oxen sleep downstairs and a granite staircase leads to the living quarters above.

The village of Rio de Onor, right on the border, is half-Spanish, half-Portuguese. The only sign that you are crossing from one country to another is a stone block marked with the letters "E" (España) and "P" (Portugal) and the change to a tarmac road on the Spanish side. A study by the Spanish anthropologist António Jorge Dias in 1953 found that the people of Rio de Onor lived a communal existence, sharing land and cattle with their Spanish neighbours quite independently of the State and speaking a dialect common to them both, Rionorês. Although the village has become depopulated in recent years, some of these traditions still survive.

Trás-os-Montes Folk Traditions

To find out more about Trás-os-Montes folk traditions, visit the local museums in Bragança (▶ 94–95) and Miranda do Douro (▶ 95).

Portuguese
PASSIONS

There is probably a festival going on somewhere in Portugal every day of the year. Outside the festivals Portuguese culture is full of drama, from the national obsession of football to the traditional spectacle of running with the bulls.

Festa!

Nothing quite matches the colour and spectacle of a Portuguese festa. Every town and village has its own saint's day, marked by religious processions, music, dancing and parades. Many of these festivals combine Christian and pagan elements, and all provide an excuse for partying, drinking, flirting and fireworks.

The biggest of the year centre around Holy Week in March or April, where there are candlelit processions. Another excellent evening's entertainment is the Festa de São João in June for the summer solstice in Porto and Vila Nova de Gaia where the streets on either side of the Douro River are full of people hitting each other on the head with leeks or plastic hammers, and fireworks are set off over the city late into the night. Food plays an important part of almost all Portuguese festivals, and tiny stalls set up along the roads selling grilled sardines and sweet treats.

Traditional costume of Costa Verde (left); Festival of Tabuleiros, Tomar (right)

Football...the beautiful game

There are plenty of secular pleasures to enjoy in Portugal also, and football is the true modern-day obsession. Football has been played in the country since the 19th century, and the main competition is the Portuguese Liga. This highly popular league usually comes down to a play-off between the red Benefica and the green Sporting, both Lisbon teams, and FC Porto who are both national and former European champions.

Portugal hosted the European football championships in 2004 for which new stadia were built all over the country and the host nation managed to make the final, eventually losing to Greece.

Best Annual Festivals

Carnival (Feb/Mar): Masked dances, fancy-dress costumes and processions of floats mark the end of winter and the arrival of Lent. Some of the most colourful parades are in Loulé and Elvas.

Holy Week (Mar/Apr): Torchlit processions of hooded and barefoot penitents take place on the Thursday and Friday before Easter in Braga.

Festa das Cruzes (first weekend in May): A country fair in Barcelos, with processions of crosses along flower-strewn streets.

Festas dos Santos Populares (12–29 Jun): Three weeks of merrymaking takes place in Lisbon to mark the feasts of the "popular saints". On 12 June, the bairros of Lisbon are decorated and people pour into Alfama to eat grilled sardines at tables set up on the street.

Festa de São João (23–24 Jun): Bonfires and fireworks mark the summer solstice in Porto with a regatta on the River Douro.

Romaria de Nossa Senhora da Agonía (weekend nearest 20 Aug): A huge, traditional romaria (religious festival) in Viana do Castelo with bullfights, fireworks, folk dancing and the blessing of fishing boats.

Germany and Portugal soccer fans (2006 World Cup) (left); Festival celebrations (right)

RUNNING WITH THE BULLS

Especially over the summer months, you are likely to see a bullfight taking place somewhere in Portugal. The biggest difference with Spanish bullfights is that in Portugal bulls are not killed in the ring (though don't be fooled by the large declarations on posters, as they are invariably mortally wounded and dispatched out of sight after the fight).

The spectacle during a fight is certainly dramatic, with bullfighters in 18th-century costumes and scarlet cummerbunds leaping onto the bull and wrestling it to the ground, but a less controversial tradition is bull-running. This takes place in the streets at Vila Franca de Xira, north of Lisbon, during the Festa do Colete Encarnado (Festival of the Red Waistcoat) in early July and the Feira de Outubro in early October. As in Pamplona in Spain, this event involves members of the public running through the streets with bulls, and although not without its dangers, is fun to watch.

Romaria de Nossa Senhora da Nazaré (8 Sep): Religious processions, folk dancing and bullfights take place in the fishing village of Nazaré.
Feiras Novas (third weekend in Sep): There's a large market and fairground with fireworks, brass bands and parades in Ponte de Lima, a centre of traditional Minho culture.
Festa dos Rapazes (25 Dec–6 Jan): Christmas in Portugal is a family affair, a time for eating bacalhau (salt cod) and bolo rei (fruit cake) – except in the villages around Bragança, where young men put on masks, cowbells and suits of ribbons and run through their villages in an ancient rite of passage which dates back to pre-Christian times.

Dignitaries assemble in front of a large crucifix during the Festas das Cruzes, Barcelos

FOOD traditions

The Portuguese like to eat, and not only is there an enormous variety of traditional ingredients and cooking styles, but these are being interpreted and highlighted by an increasing number of young, world-class Portuguese chefs.

Grilling fresh sardines in Portimão

Seafood Delights

With its long relationship with the sea, no prizes for guessing that there is plenty of fresh fish at many Portuguese restaurants. Depending on region and season, you can find pretty much every kind of fish you can imagine, but among the most sought after are sardines, red mullet (salmonete) and swordfish. If you can't decide on your favourite fish, try a *cataplana*, which is a mixed seafood dish of shellfish cooked with onions and potatoes, or a fish stew, known as *caldeirada*, a delicious blend of fish, onions, garlic, potatoes, peppers and usually copious amounts of wine.

Regional Dishes

There are also many regional dishes that give clues to the history of the individual areas. In the Tras-os-Montes, for example, you often find a chicken sausage on the menu known as an *alheiras*. This dates back to the 15th century, when Jews fled to the remote mountainous region from the Spanish Inquisition. The chicken sausage was first made as a way of fooling the Inquisitors that they had renounced their Jewish ways and started to eat pork, and are still eaten today.

The Portuguese love to eat meat, and vegetarians may find a rather limited selection on offer. Meat eaters, however, will discover a succulent array of hams, sausages, salamis (in fact 40 per cent of meat eaten in Portugal is pork). One of the best of these cured hams come from

Alentejo's acorn-fed black pigs and is known as "presunto de porco preto bolata". These pigs have grazed in the gentle Montados countryside and are said to offer the same benefits to your heart as olive oil.

Cheese

The regional cheeses are also found in a seemingly endless array of varieties. Most cheeses are either from ewes or goats, or a combination of both. The best known is probably 'Queijo da Serra da Estrela', from Portugal's highest mountain range. This is a delicious mountain sheep cheese that is rich and creamy, and usually eaten straight out of the pot after six weeks of ripening.

> "the locals can't resist a sweet start to the day, or end to a meal"

And just as there are more and more single quinta wines from new quality-conscious producers, so there are also many new single-quinta olive oils from the Douro, Tras-os-Montes, Alentejo and Ribatejo.

Order of Play

All meals in Portugal are likely to start with soup (and again, vegetarians beware, as even vegetable soups usually have bits of meat lurking within them). Typical soup of the north is the *caldo verde*, with cabbage, onions and potatoes, while a chilled Alentejo soup is made of bread, egg and garlic. And many dishes have spicy touches that contain flavours of cumin, cinnamon, paprika and sweet peppers brought back from former Portuguese outposts in Brazil, Goa, the Azores and further afield.

But the Portuguese really come into their own with the sweet specialities. All over the country, you'll find that the locals can't resist a sweet start to the day, or end to a meal. Among the stickiest treats on offer are the *doces conventuais*, little egg-yolk sweets. Look out also for *marmelada* – not marmalade as the name suggests, but a quince paste – and jams made from the delicious Elvas plums. And towns large and small can be counted on to contain at least one or two bakeries, where you should ensure you stock up on egg custard *natas*.

BACALHAU

The Portuguese passion for *bacalhau* (dried salted cod) has its origins in the fishing fleets that sailed the waters off Newfoundland in the early 16th century. At that time there was an abundance of cod, but it had to be preserved for the journey back to Portugal. Despite the presence of numerous fresh fish off the coast, *bacalhau* remains a Portuguese favourite and there are said to be 365 different ways of cooking it.

Best of Portugal

Portugal has so much to offer – from markets and festivals to beaches and landscape – this is just a few of its highlights.

Ten Memorable Experiences

- A blustery morning at Belém (➤ 46–49), feeling the ocean breeze as you recall the voyages of Portugal's explorers.
- An evening at one of Lisbon's fado clubs (➤ 20–21).
- Touring the port lodges of Vila Nova de Gaia (➤ 84–85).
- Exploring the Douro Valley by road, river or rail, or taking the scenic train line from Tua to Mirandela (➤ 176–178).
- Joining the crowds to pick up a bargain at the busy Thursday market in Barcelos (➤ 94).
- The view from the summit of Serra da Estrela (➤ 119–120).
- A boat trip from Lagos or Carvoeiro in summer to explore the cliffs, caves and cove beaches of the Algarve (➤ 159–161).
- Standing on the cliffs at Cabo de São Vicente (➤ 157–158) to watch the magnificent sight of the sun setting over the Atlantic.
- Spending the night in the medieval town of Evora, capital of the Alentejo (➤ 132–135).
- A walk in Parque Natural da Ria Formosa (➤ 162).

If You Only Visit One Market...

...make it the Thursday market at Barcelos (➤ 94), which has the atmosphere of a fair. There are other markets at Estremoz (➤ 140) and Loulé (➤ 163).

Best Castles in the Air

Portugal has a wealth of romantic ruined castles, many in hilltop towns along the Spanish border. Among the best are Castelo de São Jorge, Lisbon (➤ 52–53) and the castles at Sintra (➤ 60–62), Guimarães (➤ 93), Bragança (➤ 94–95), Silves (➤ 165) and the walled villages of Óbidos (➤ 121–122) and Marvão (➤ 138–139).

Best for People-Watching

The terrace of Café Nicola (➤ 174) or Pastelaria Suiça (➤ 174) in Lisbon.

Best for Kids

- Algarve beaches, boat trips and waterparks (➤ 159–161).
- Oceanário, Lisbon (➤ 58), Europe's largest aquarium.
- Portugal dos Pequenitos, Coimbra (➤ 106).

The golden sweep of sand and sandstacks at Praia de Rocha in the Algarve

Finding Your Feet

First Two Hours

Arriving by Air
There are international airports at Lisbon, Porto and Faro. All three have tourist offices, post offices, currency exchange facilities and car hire outlets.

Lisbon
- **Portela Airport** (www.ana.pt) is 7km (4.3 miles) north of the city centre. Tel: 218 413 500 (enquiries), tel: 218 413 700 (arrivals/ departures).
- The **Aerobus** (inexpensive; free for passengers flying with TAP, the Portuguese national airline) departs for central Lisbon from outside the arrivals hall every 20 minutes 7:40–8:45 daily. The route takes in Avenida da Liberdade, Rossio, Praça do Comércio and Cais do Sodré (for trains to Estoril and Cascais). Tickets are also valid for one day on Lisbon's buses, trams and funiculars.
- A **taxi** to central Lisbon should cost around €15–€20, with supplements for extra luggage or night travel. Fares are metered, so make sure that the meter is switched on. An alternative is to buy a pre-paid taxi voucher from the tourist office in the arrivals hall.
- By **metro,** there is no direct connection from the airport but the nearest metro station, Parque das Nações, is 10 minutes from the airport by taxi (www.metrolisboa.pt).

Porto
- **Francisco Sá Carneiro Airport** is 11km (6.8 miles) north of the city centre. Tel: 229 432 400; www.ana.pt.
- **Buses** 87 and 601 (www.stcp.pt) run daily from 5:13am–9pm every 30 minutes and the fare is €1.30.
- On the **Metro** (www.metrodoporto.pt) take the Violeta Line, 6am–1am every 20 minutes (€1.25), which takes 20–35 minutes to the centre.
- A **taxi** to central Porto should cost around €15–18, with supplements for extra luggage or night travel.

Faro
- **Faro Airport** is 6km (3.7 miles) west of the city centre (tel: 289 800 800; www.ana.pt).
- From the airport take buses No 16 and No 14 into Faro.
- **Taxi** fares to Faro and the various resorts are listed in the arrivals hall, but it is worth checking the price with the driver before you set off.

Tourist Information Offices
Most tourist office staff speak excellent English, and have maps and information in English. There are tourist offices in all main towns and cities.
- **Lisbon:** The main office (daily 9–7), **Lisboa Welcome Center**, Rua do Arsenal 15, tel: 210 312 700; www.visitlisboa.com. There are tourist offices on Praça dos Restauradores (daily 9–8) and information kiosks at Belém, Rua Augusta and Castelo de São Jorge.
- **Porto:** The main tourist office is at Rua Clube dos Fenianos 25, near the top of Avenida dos Aliados (tel: 223 393 470; www.portoturismo.pt).
- **Faro:** The tourist office is at Rua da Misericórdia 8 (near the entrance to the old town), tel: 289 803 604. There is also an office at the airport.
- **The Algarve:** There are also tourist offices at Albufeira, Alcoutim, Carvoeiro, Lagos, Loulé, Monchique, Monte Gordo, Portimão, Praia da Rocha, Sagres, Silves and Tavira.

Getting Around

Portugal's compact size makes it easy to get around. There are excellent bus and train connections between the major cities in Portugal, but to get to the more out-of-the-way places you will need a car.

Driving

- Drivers **bringing their own cars** into Portugal need to carry their driving licence, registration document, insurance certificate and display a nationality sticker on their car.
- **Car rental** is available at all airports and in major towns and resorts. To rent a car you must be aged over 21 and have a passport, driving licence and credit card. You can book in advance through the major international car rental agencies (see below). Local firms offer competitive rates, but you should check carefully the level of insurance cover and excess. Keep the car-rental documents and your driving licence with you at all times.
  Avis: tel: 218 435 550 (Lisbon Airport); www.avis.com
  Europcar: tel: 218 401 176 or 800 201 002 for reservations (Lisbon Airport); www.europcar.com
  Hertz: tel: 218 438 660 (Lisbon Airport); www.hertz.com
- Theft from rental cars is common. Never leave items on display in the car, and take all valuables with you or lock them out of sight.

Driving Essentials

- Drive on the **right**.
- **Seat belts** are compulsory for the driver and all passengers.
- The legal **alcohol** limit is 0.05 per cent.
- **Speed limits** are 120kph (74mph) on motorways, 90kph (56mph) on main roads, 50kph (31mph) in urban areas, unless otherwise indicated.
- **Driving standards** are generally poor and Portugal has one of the highest accident rates in Europe. The N125 across the Algarve is notorious for its high number of accidents. If you are involved in an accident, use the orange SOS phone on a motorway to call the police.
- A network of **motorways** and **main roads** connects Lisbon, Porto and the major cities. Motorways are prefaced with A and incur tolls. Other main roads are prefaced with IP or IC, or N (for *nacional*).
- **Check regulations before you travel** – www.theAA.com has comprehensive European driving information.

Buses and Trains

- Bus and train services connect the main towns and cities. On both, children under 4 travel free, under-12s travel half fare, and over-65s receive a discount.
- **Bus** services are operated by **private companies**.
- **Train** services are operated by **Caminhos de Ferros Portugueses** (**CP**, tel: 808 208 208; www.cp.pt). Tickets can be purchased in advance from stations. **CP** also sells a rail pass valid for 7, 14 or 21 days.
- The Alfa Pendular from Lisbon to Porto via Coimbra or to Faro will save you time, because it is a **fast train service**.
- There are five main **railway stations** in **Lisbon**. Trains depart from Sete Rios for Sintra, from Cais do Sodré for Estoril and Cascais, Obidos and the west coast from Santa Apolónia or Oriente for Porto and Madrid and from Entrecampos for Faro and Evora.

City Transport

- **Lisbon** has an excellent network of buses, trams, Metro trains and *elevadores* (funiculars).
- **Single tickets** can be bought on buses or at Metro stations and validated at the machines behind the driver or at the station barriers. Less expensive options include a two-journey ticket or a one-day or three-day pass, valid on buses and trams, from the Carris ticket booth on Praça da Figueira. You can also buy a four-day or seven-day *passe turístico*, valid on Metro, buses and trams, on production of your passport. Metro stations sell 10-ticket *cadernetas*, which are good value for multiple journeys. Tourist offices sell the **Lisbon Card**, valid for up to three days, which gives unlimited travel on public transport and free or discounted admission to more than 20 museums and places of interest.
- **Porto** has a good metro system with seven different lines (named A–G), which covers most of the city, including the main part of Porto, over the bridge to Gaia and out to the airport (www.metro-porto.pt). There is also good network of local **buses**. Single-journey tickets and one-day passes can be bought on the bus. Tourist offices sell one- or two-day passes called the **Porto Card**, which include discounts at museums and on river cruises, and free travel on buses, trams and the Metro.

Admission Charges

The cost of admission for museums and places of interest featured in the guide is indicated by the following price categories.

Inexpensive = under €3   Moderate = €3–€6   Expensive = over €6

Accommodation

Especially outside Lisbon and the Algarve, accommodation in Portugal is very good value. Independent travellers can choose from a wide range of places and the luxury end of the market is refreshingly informal.

Booking

- Advance booking is vital in the **high season** (July and August) or if your stay coincides with events such as local festivals or pilgrimages. In quiet periods rates can drop to 40 per cent of the high-season price, but beware that in coastal resorts places may shut completely in the winter.
- **Tourist offices** have comprehensive lists of official accommodation or the addresses of *dormidas* or *quartos* (rooms for rent).
- Many hotels and tourist complexes in the Algarve are **block booked** throughout the summer; either reserve months ahead or choose a guesthouse, *pousada* or *estalagem* instead.

Hotels

- Hotels are invariably **clean and safe**, but you might find alternative types of accommodation (➤ oppposite) more attractive and welcoming than budget hotels, especially in cities.
- An **official price list** must be displayed inside the door of every room.
- **IVA** (VAT) or sales tax must be included in the advertised room rate; breakfast tends to be included and varies from continental to a buffet.

- You may be **charged extra** for using a garage or gym.
- **Extra beds** are often supplied for a small fee.
- **Children** (usually under four years) can stay free or at a discount.

Pousadas and Accommodation with Character

- *Pousadas* (which means "a place to rest") are privately owned hotels located throughout the country (many in the Alentejo), aimed at tourists looking for somewhere special to stay, usually near centres of interest.
- They are set in **fabulous surroundings** and have elements of traditional architecture and furnishing, as well as good to excellent restaurants – open to non-residents – where you can sample Portuguese specialities and wine, often in highly atmospheric dining rooms.
- **Standards of comfort** are reliably high.
- Numbering 44 in all, there are four categories: historical *pousadas*, converted castles and monasteries; historic design *pousadas*, as above but with modern boutique-style elements; nature *pousadas,* in spectacular natural settings; charm *pousadas,* often in converted village houses. All *pousadas* are good value for money and even the most expensive, such as those at Estremoz (➤ 144) and Guimarães (➤ 97), cost less than the equivalent luxury establishments in most other countries.
- *Pousadas* are popular with honeymooners, who receive special treatment, and they also offer discounts to families, the under-30s and those aged 60 or over.
- The *pousadas* described in this guide are not necessarily the best, but form part of a balanced selection of accommodation for each region. For a complete listing and detailed information, including promotions and booking facilities, contact **Pousadas de Portugal**, Rua Soares de Passos 3, Alto de Santo Amaro, 1300-314 Lisbon; tel: 218 442 001; www.pousadas.pt
- On a more intimate scale, the **Solares de Portugal**, and other similar schemes, offer a huge choice of alternative accommodation across the whole country in the mid-budget range. Government-approved but privately owned, these tend to be farmhouses and country houses with around 12 rooms, sometimes with facilities such as swimming pools but seldom offering meals other than breakfast.
  A complete list is available from the following:
  - **Solares de Portugal**, Praça da República 4990, Ponte de Lima; tel: 258 741 672; www.solaresdeportugal.pt
  - **Privetur**, Largo das Pereiras, 4990 Ponte de Lima; tel: 258 743 923; www.privetur.co.uk
  - **CENTER** (Centro de Turismo no Espaço Rural), Praça da República 4990, Ponte de Lima; tel: 258 931 750; www.center.pt
- Also look out for the official green tree symbol awarded to government-approved country guesthouses often advertised as a *turismo rural*. These also offer charming accommodation in manors and farms, usually on a bed-and-breakfast basis, plus facilities such as horse-riding.
- Traditional Alentejo farmhouses, known as *montes*, have grouped together to form **Turismo Montes Alentejanos,** Avenida da Liberdade 115, 7400-217 Ponte de Sôr (tel: 242 291 226; www.montesalentejanos.com.pt).

Pensões and Residencials

- In addition to rooms for rent, at the lower end of the budget range is the *residencial*. These are nearly always clean and comfortable, if basic, but do not provide any meals, except possibly breakfast. The *pensão* is another alternative, sometimes offering no meals at all, or sometimes breakfast and an evening meal. Alternatively, there is the *hospedaria*, the lowliest of all. Some rooms have their own bathroom, sometimes at a far higher rate than if you share facilities. In value terms, these are often better value than a low- to mid-budget hotel, and some of these places have wonderful character.

Youth Hostels
■ *Pousadas de Juventude* (youth hostels) are good on the whole and some are excellent – clean, safe and friendly.
■ In **high season** you should book ahead, either through your local youth hostel association or the **Portuguese Youth Hostel Association** (Movijovem), Rua Lúcio de Azevedo 27, 1600-146 Lisbon, tel: 707 203 030 (reservations); www.pousadasjuventude.pt; reservas@movijovem.pt
■ Of all the 30 or so hostels, the one in **Leiria** has the best reputation, while the most expensive are in the big cities and the Algarve (where the favourite is at Alcoutim). The hostels in Lagos, Portimão, Coimbra and Penhas da Saúde are all acclaimed. Expect to pay around €9–€43 a night, depending on location, room type and time of year.

Camping
■ *Parques de Campismo* (campsites) are usually well run, with facilities ranging from basic to quite luxurious, again at relatively low prices.
■ The best ones in **prime seaside locations**, especially in the Algarve where there are several, are crowded in high season – and be warned that theft can be a problem.
■ Only a few require an **international camping carnet**, available from national organisations. Charges hover around the €5 per person mark.
■ Sites belonging to **ORBITUR** are more expensive but slightly better: ORBITUR, Rua Diogo Couto 1/8°, 1149-042 Lisbon; tel: 218 117 070, fax: 218 117 034; www.orbitur.pt
■ For more details contact the **Portuguese Camping Federation**, Avenida Coronel Eduardo Galhardo 24 D, 1199-007 Lisbon, tel: 218 126 890, www.fcmportugal.com, or **Roteiro Campista**, Rua do Giestal, 5-1° Fte, 1300-274 Lisbon, tel: 213 642 370, fax: 213 619 284 for the invaluable booklet of the same name (www.roteiro-campista.pt).

Self-Catering
■ Self-catering apartments and villas are found mostly along the **south coast**, though they can be found throughout Portugal.
■ **Facilities** range from a basic refrigerator and cooker to fully equipped kitchens, swimming pools, large gardens and a regular maid service.
■ It's worth **booking privately** rather than through a tour operator to get better value for money.
■ Local and national **tourist offices** should be able to supply contact names and addresses.
■ Also try www.ownersdirect.co.uk or www.holidaylettings.co.uk

---

Accommodation Prices
The symbols refer to the average cost of a double room per night in high season. Singles often cost more than half the double rate.
€ = under €60
€€ = €60–€120
€€€ = €121–€180
€€€€ = over €180

Food and Drink

There are said to be 365 ways of preparing the national favourite, *bacalhau* (salt cod, the traditional staple, ➤ 29) so you are sure to find it on the menu. Be adventurous and seek out other specialities and, given the subtle regional variations, the advent of several imaginative chefs, plus some remarkably low prices, you can enjoy some memorable meals without breaking the bank.

Eating Out – A Practical Guide
■ Strict **dress codes** are almost non-existent, though Sunday best is still customary in the provinces. Jacket and tie is *de rigueur* in only a handful of restaurants in Lisbon and Porto.
■ A notch up the scale and mostly found in cities, *cervejarias* (beer houses) also serve food. *Marisquerias* specialise in *marisco* (seafood), where *gambas* (prawns), lobster and luxury fish, served by weight, are expensive.
■ **Restaurant terraces** (as opposed to café *esplanadas*) are a rarity, so the coolness of deep cellars where some dining rooms are located may prove welcome in the height of summer.

Portuguese Cuisine
■ **Seafood**, usually top rate and priced accordingly, is served all along Portugal's long coasts, while inland, lamb, pork and game (in season) are the features.
■ Portugal's answer to **"surf and turf"** is *carne de porco à alentejana* (pork simmered with clams and fresh coriander).
■ *Bacalhau* (salt cod, soaked to remove most of the salt) is a favourite. There are several different recipes, such as à Gomes de Sá (with hard-boiled egg, boiled potatoes and black olives), *à brás* (stir-fried with eggs, onions and potatoes), *à minhota* (with fried potatoes) and *com natas* (baked in a rich cream sauce).
■ *Churrasco* (barbecued meat), sometimes served Brazilian-style (*rodízio*), is the house speciality of many roadside grills and can be great value.
■ *Leitão* (suckling pig) is the speciality of the region between Lisbon and Coimbra, but is considered a delicacy nationwide.
■ **Vegetarians** have a fairly hard time in Portugal – ask for salads or side orders such as spinach. Although rice and potatoes are frequently on the menu, the only true concession to vegetarians will be omelettes.

Practicalities
■ All but the most modest places now accept **credit cards**, but check first in case you don't have enough cash on you.
■ **Lunch** is over by 2, maybe 3 in the south. **Dinner** is served around 8 and you may find it hard to find a kitchen open after 10 or 11, especially in rural areas.
■ In Lisbon, fashionable places serve until very late into the night, while *cervejarias* (beer houses) may stay open all afternoon too. Some establishments may close Sunday evening, many more are closed all day Monday.
■ Standard servings are **enormous**, except in chic restaurants: you can often ask for *meia dose* (half portion) for one person.
■ **Service** is rarely included and never compulsory, but a 10 per cent tip will always be welcome even in cafés and tea-rooms.
■ The *ementa turística* (daily set menu) can be very good value (as little as €5–€6), but is normally only available at lunchtime.

Snacks and Sweets

- The Portuguese are great on **snacks** (*petiscos* are the local answer to *tapas*), while *lanche* (afternoon tea) is faithfully observed.
- With a good breakfast (coffee or tea, bread and jam or cheese, cold meats and eggs) you can probably survive until the evening by eating in cafés, *confeitarias* and *pastelerias* (cake shops), and *casas de chá* (tea-rooms).
- **Coffee** is good and popular and a few sumptuous cafés have survived modernisation in towns and cities. *Bica* (*um café* in Porto and Lisbon) is a strong espresso, while *galão* is a milky coffee served in a glass, perfect with a *torrada* (thick slices of toasted bread dripping with butter).
- In addition to *sandes* (sandwiches), *pregos* (bread rolls with hot slices of beef) and *bifanas* (like *pregos* but with pork), try *rissóis* (deep-fried meat or prawn patties) and *pastéis de bacalhau* (mini cod fishcakes).
- Portuguese **cakes** (*pastéis* or *bolos*) are very sweet. The main ingredient is sugar, followed by almonds, honey and egg yolks, and sometimes all four. The regional and local variations on these themes are countless. The best are the cheese-based *queijadas* from Sintra and custard-filled *pastéis de nata* (especially the fabulous ones at Belém, ➤ 69).
- **Dessert** fans will appreciate *arroz doce* (rice pudding with cinnamon), *pudim flan* (crème caramel) and a whole range of nut and chocolate concoctions. Baked apple (*maçã*) and quince (*marmelo*) are delicious.

Cover Charges and Starters

- In nearly every restaurant there's a **cover charge** – ostensibly for the bread – and in more expensive places this can be quite high.
- ***Acepipes*** – an array of olives, ham, cheese (traditionally served before rather than after meals) and pickles – can keep you going until the main course arrives but, even if unsolicited, they will be itemised on your bill if you so much as touch them. Politely but pointedly refuse them if you don't want to be charged.
- ***Entradas*** (starters) come in the form of vegetable soups (such as *caldo verde*, containing strips of kale cabbage) or seafood, or maybe a salad.

Drinks

- **Mineral water** is inexpensive – ask for *agua sem gas* (still) or *agua com gas* (sparkling) served *fresca* (chilled) or *natural* (room temperature).
- Apart from **vinho do Porto** (port, ➤ 10) and **Mateus Rosé**, there are excellent **wines** to sample, the best coming from the Dão and Douro valleys, plus full-bodied reds from Bairrada and the Alentejo. Or there's *vinho verde* – slightly sparkling young wine from the Minho (mostly whites).
- **Beer** is popular in big cities and on tap should be ordered by the *imperial* (in the south) or *fino* (in the north).
- There are some good **brandies** (*conhaque*) as well as *aguardente*, *bagaço* and *medronho*, made in the Algarve from arbutus berries. Cherry-based *ginginha* is a popular tipple, especially in Lisbon.

Restaurant Prices

The following symbols indicate the average price per person for a three-course meal excluding drinks and tips.

€ = under €12
€€ = €12–€24
€€€ = €25–€36
€€€€ = over €36

Shopping

Traditional markets across Portugal can be colourful spectacles as well as great places to shop. Ceramics are often on sale along with foods, but the finest items are only sold during local fairs (*feiras*). With its juxtaposition of extravagant boutiques and dusty groceries alongside state-of-the-art shopping malls and beguiling bookstores, Lisbon is Portugal's undisputed shopping capital, though Porto does its best. Every town and city has a busy commercial street or two where you can pick up bargains. Perhaps the best gifts are food or wine related, though sometimes you can come across interesting arts and crafts. Footwear and other leather goods are also good value.

Opening Hours
- Shops usually open daily 9–7, except Sunday, with a two-hour lunch break – *sestas* (siestas) are rare outside the rural interior.
- Modern shopping centres open 10am–midnight, seven days a week.

Clothes and Footwear
- Items such as belts, bags, wallets, shoes, jackets and purses are less expensive than in the rest of western Europe. Leather gloves are also a bargain, still sold in old-fashioned booth-like shops.
- **Home-grown designers** are worth investigating, though few have branches outside Lisbon.

Food and Wine
- In addition to wine and port, brandy, *aguardente* (firewater) and, in the Algarve, *medronho* (➤ 169) make good gifts. Decanters and other wine-connoisseur paraphernalia can be interesting – some are designed by fashionable artists.
- The easiest foodstuffs to transport include olive oil (try and get "luxury" oil – 0.1 or 0.2 per cent acidity, packaged in smart, corked bottles), cheese (some of it at astronomical prices, so beware), *bacalhau*, and non-perishable cakes and biscuits.
- Pine nuts, almonds and dried and candied fruit are very good value compared with prices in most other countries.

Art and Crafts
- Ceramics, basket- and wicker-ware, and copper pans tend to be the traditional items appealing to all tastes. Pottery and porcelain can be more of an acquired taste.
- The yellow-dotted brown earthenware dishes from Barcelos are universally popular with tourists– as is the "Galo" (rooster) commemorating a folk legend originating in the eponymous northern town, and now a national symbol (➤ 94).

Souvenirs
- *Azulejos* (traditional glazed tiles) range from mass-produced souvenirs to whole sets of antique tiles. Measure up before you come to Portugal and you can have a set tailor-made, to your own design.
- *"Scissor chairs"* are distinctive seats from Monchique in the Algarve.
- *Cataplanas* are metal cooking pans used to make seafood dishes.
- *Arraiolos carpets* are exquisite (and expensive) rugs made in the picturesque town of the same name, to ancient designs.
- *Fado* (➤ 18) – a CD or cassette of Portuguese "blues".

Entertainment

Portugal is noted for its traditional festivals – the calendar is packed with them – *Fado* and, of course, football so there's usually something to suit every taste.

Information
■ In the Algarve there are three monthly **English-language publications**: *Essential Algarve*, *Welcome to the Algarve* and *Algarve Guide*, all available from tourist offices and hotels. In Lisbon you can find *Follow Me* for the Greater Lisbon area, and for Sintra and Cascais *What's In Sintra* and *What's in Cascais*. Elsewhere you'll have to rely on weekly English-language newspapers *The Portugal News* and *The Resident*, Portuguese-language publications, such as the daily press, tourist office information and posters and flyers. Or check out the various websites (► 188).

Music and Other Cultural Entertainments
■ Having both served as European Capital of Culture, Lisbon and Porto are better equipped with dance, music and other performing arts than ever before (► 44, 80). Provincial centres such as Faro, Évora, Braga and Coimbra are no cultural deserts either; elsewhere classical concerts are held in churches and monasteries – look out for posters.
■ *Fado* (► 20–21) is the most famous musical form – the better-known Lisbon version is performed in special *casas* in the capital, most of them aimed at tourists, but internationally famed stars sing in venues across the country. The folksier, academic variant unique to Coimbra is harder to track down, though a couple of places in the city stage regular sessions.
■ **Ballet, opera and jazz** are mostly confined to big cities, though some music clubs in the Algarve resorts cater to highbrow tastes.

Festivals
■ The most important festivals are covered in the regional listings, but look out for others – it's important to know if only because accommodation can be scarce. Check at local tourist offices.

Spectator Sports
■ Luís Figo and Cristiano Ronaldo are the most prominent Portuguese **footballers** since Eusébio. Porto and Lisbon's rival teams, Benfica, Boavista, FC Porto and Sporting, have the national championship stitched up between them and fans might like to see them play at home (► 74).
■ **Roller-hockey** is the only sport at which Portugal regularly excels internationally (► 74), while **bullfighting** (*touradas*) – less cruel than in Spain but still not a sight for animal-lovers (► 27) – is making a comeback in some areas.

Sport and Outdoor Pursuits
■ The Algarve is a sports paradise, and some of Europe's best **golfing** fairways, **tennis courts**, **watersports** and **diving clubs** are to be found along Portugal's warm southern coast (► 170).
■ The western seaboard – where wind and rollers are perennially reliable – is better for **surfing**, **windsurfing** or just a refreshing dip.
■ Inland unspoiled mountain scenery lends itself to **hiking**, **mountain-biking**, **hang-gliding** and **horse-riding** – ask at local tourist offices for outfits.
■ **Boating**, **fishing** and other **watersports** can be practised at sea or on inland waterways; many places hire equipment (► individual chapters).

Lisbon and Around

Getting Your Bearings

The capital of Portugal since around 1255, Lisbon (Lisboa) is one of Europe's smallest and most atmospheric capitals. Built in a rambling heap on seven hills on the north bank of the Tagus (Tejo) estuary, it has a vibrant, multicultural appeal that stems from the large number of immigrants from its former African and Asian colonies. One in ten of Portugal's population live here, creating a lively, Latin atmosphere.

The best way to arrive in Lisbon, and to get a sense of the city's layout, is on one of the ferries across the River Tagus. In front of you is Praça do Comércio, the former parade ground and symbolic entrance to the city. Ahead, beyond a triumphal arch, Rua Augusta leads through the Baixa (lower town), the downtown business and shopping district. To one side stands the Bairro Alto (upper town); to the other, Alfama, crowned by a splendid Moorish castle. Across the water, beyond Ponte 25 de Abril, a giant statue of Christ gazes down from the south bank.

The present-day shape of Lisbon is largely the result of the most traumatic incident in the city's history, the earthquake of 1755. It struck on All Saints' Day, when most of the population were at church, causing a tidal wave and hundreds of fires as buildings full of lighted candles collapsed in ruins. At least 40,000 people were killed. The subsequent rebuilding of the Baixa on a grid plan was largely the work of one man, the chief minister, Marquês de Pombal.

Two buildings that mostly survived the destruction were the Manueline tower and monastery at Belém, inspired by the discoveries and built on the riches that made Lisbon great – spices from India and gold from Brazil.

In the last few years, Lisbon has seen another transformation, with new dockside leisure facilities, one of Europe's longest bridges and European Union funding for new façades. Perhaps, at last, Lisbon is once again looking to the future rather than harking back to a golden age.

CA
REST
PEDROUÇOS
Belém

**Page 41:
Torre Vasco
da Gama, at
Parque das
Nações in
Lisbon**

Mosaic pavement at Parque Eduardo VII

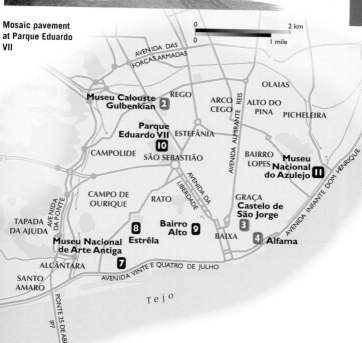

AVENIDA DAS FORÇAS ARMADAS

OLAIAS

Museu Calouste Gulbenkian 2 REGO ARCO CEGO ALTO DO PINA PICHELEIRA

AVENIDA ALMIRANTE REIS

Parque Eduardo VII 10 ESTEFÂNIA

CAMPOLIDE SÃO SEBASTIÃO

BAIRRO LOPES **Museu Nacional do Azulejo** 11

CAMPO DE OURIQUE RATO

AVENIDA DA LIBERDADE

GRAÇA **Castelo de São Jorge** 3

AVENIDA INFANTE DOM HENRIQUE

TAPADA DA AJUDA

AVENIDA DA PONTE

Museu Nacional de Arte Antiga 8 **Estrêla** **Bairro Alto** 9 BAIXA 4 **Alfama**

ALCÂNTARA 7

SANTO AMARO

AVENIDA VINTE E QUATRO DE JULHO

PONTE 25 DE ABRIL

IP7

Tejo

0 ——— 2 km
0 ——— 1 mile

In Four Days

If you're not quite sure where to begin your travels, this itinerary recommends a practical and enjoyable four days out in Lisbon and Around, taking in some of the best places to see using the Getting your Bearings map on the previous page. For more information see the main entries.

Day 1

Morning
From Praça do Comércio, take tram No 15 to 🚇 **Belém** (➤ 46–49) to savour the glories of Portugal's maritime past. Walk along the waterfront to the Torre de Belém, then visit the Museu de Marinha and Mosteiro dos Jerónimos, built to celebrate the achievements of Portuguese explorers. Unwind at the Antiga Confeitaria de Belém (➤ 69).

Afternoon and Evening
Return by tram as far as the Alcântara docks and climb the steps to the 🔟 **Museu Nacional de Arte Antiga** (➤ 63) to explore this fine collection of Portuguese art. If clubbing is your thing, head back down to the revitalised docks area and take your pick from the clubs on and around Avenida 24 de Julho (➤ 74). Otherwise return to Belém to take in a concert at the **Centro Cultural de Belém** (➤ 74) – as well as three auditoria, there are free concerts on weekday evenings at the terrace bar.

Day 2

Morning
Take the Metro to São Sebastião for the 🔟 **Museu Calouste Gulbenkian** (➤ 50), then stroll through the sculpture park for lunch at **Centro de Arte Moderna** (➤ 51).

Afternoon and Evening
Walk downhill to central Lisbon through 🔟 **Parque Eduardo VII** (right, ➤ 64) and along the tree-lined Avenida da Liberdade. Continue by taking Tram 28 through the narrow streets of Alfama. Climb up to the 🔟 **Castelo de São Jorge** (➤ 52–53) to watch the sun set over the River Tagus, then wander back down to Alfama and spend the evening in one of its *fado* clubs (➤ 20).

Day 3

Morning

Take the Metro to Oriente for the
5 Parque das Nações (➤ 58–59).
Visit the oceanarium (left) and ride
the cable-car along the waterfront,
then have lunch at one of the
riverside restaurants.

Afternoon and Evening

Shop for souvenirs in the Centro
Comercial Vasco da Gama, then take
the Metro to Rossio for a drink at a
pavement café. Take the Elevador
da Glória up to the Bairro Alto –
perhaps an apéritif at the **Solar do
Vinho do Porto** (➤ 71), followed by
a meal at **Água do Bengo** (➤ 69),
then try one of the wine bars around
9 Bairro Alto (➤ 64).

Day 4

Morning and Afternoon

Take the train from Cais do Sodré to **12 Estoril** (➤ 65) and stroll along the
seafront to **12 Cascais** (below, ➤ 65). After exploring this fishing port, get
on a bus to **6 Sintra** (➤ 60–62) and have lunch at **Tulhas** (➤ 72). Hop on
the bus for the climb to Castelo dos Mouros and Palácio da Pena. Walk
back through the pinewoods to Sintra or take the bus to the station to
return to Lisbon by train.

❶ Belém

More than anywhere else in Portugal, it is at Belém that you feel the pull of the Atlantic and the excitement of the great Age of Discovery. For more than a century, Portuguese ships left from Belém in search of new worlds, bringing back untold riches from unknown lands. Add to that its status as Lisbon's museum district, along with the crowning glories of Manueline architecture, and there are plenty of attractions here.

The best way to reach Belém is on the No 15 tram that clatters along the waterfront from central Lisbon.

On arrival, head for the **Padrão dos Descobrimentos** (Monument to the Discoveries), built in 1960 to mark the 500th anniversary of Prince Henry the Navigator's death. A *padrão* was a stone cairn surmounted by a cross, built

The Torre de Belém is Lisbon's most emblematic building

by Portuguese explorers to mark their presence on new territory; this modern version neatly combines the form of a caravel, a cross and a sword. The prow of a ship faces out to sea with an image of Prince Henry at the helm. Behind him are other heroes of the discoveries, including Gil Eanes, Vasco da Gama, Pedro Álvares Cabral and poet Luís de Camões, who celebrated the Age of Discovery in his epic work *Os Lusíadas* (*The Lusiads*).

Take the lift to the top of the tower, which is 52m (171 feet) high, for views over the harbour, then wander around the marble map of the world at its base, with dates showing Portuguese conquests in Africa, Asia and America.

Portuguese heroes are carved in stone

Manueline Masterpiece

Just along the waterfront is the **Torre de Belém**, built by Dom Manuel I between 1515 and 1520 to guard the entrance to Lisbon harbour. This elegant fortress is a good example of what has come to be called the Manueline style, a Portuguese version of late Gothic architecture inspired by the discoveries and particularly associated with Dom Manuel.

The hallmark of this architectural style is the extravagant use of seafaring imagery, with windows and doorways decorated with stone carvings of knotted ropes, anchors, globes, exotic fauna and flora and other maritime motifs. Two symbols which are ever present in Manueline architecture are the armillary sphere (emblem of Dom Manuel) and the Cross of the Order of Christ.

You can go right inside the tower and up onto the terrace for closer views.

The Place to Go

The other main sights of Belém are across the railway line, around the Praça do Império gardens.

On one side is the **Centro Cultural de Belém**, conceived as a showpiece for Portugal's presidency of the European Union in 1992. Built out of the same limestone as the Mosteiro dos Jerónimos, it was initially controversial as it was a modern building right beside the monastery, but it has now been widely accepted and blends in surprisingly well with its surroundings. Already it has become one of Lisbon's most vibrant cultural centres, with art galleries, concerts, bookshops and trendy cafés.

A Long History

However, the sight that really takes your breath away is the **Mosteiro dos Jerónimos**, begun in 1502 on the site of a former hermitage founded by Prince Henry the Navigator. It was here in 1497 that Vasco da Gama spent his final night before setting off to discover a sea route to India, and Dom Manuel vowed that he would build a great church to the Virgin if the voyage was successful. The monastery, begun by French architect Diogo de Boytac and continued by Spaniard João de Castilho, is full of Manueline flourishes, especially the south portal, with its stonework saints and figure of Prince Henry on a pedestal. Immediately inside the church are the tombs of Vasco da Gama and Luís de Camões. Go through a separate entrance to the two-storey cloister, a masterpiece of Manueline art. It was here that the treaty of accession for Portugal's entry to the European Union was signed in 1986.

Carving at the cloisters of Mosteiro dos Jeronimos, Belem

Maritime History

A 19th-century wing of the monastery houses the **Museu de Marinha**, devoted to Portugal's maritime history. Among the large collection of model boats, maps, navigational instruments and Oriental art, there is graffiti, carved onto the African rocks by Portuguese explorer Diogo Cão in 1483. Other highlights are the model of Vasco da Gama's flagship, maps of the known world and the reconstruction of the state rooms from the royal yacht *Amélia*, right down to the king's private piano and roulette table.

A separate building contains the royal barges, including the sumptuous gilded barge built for the wedding of João VI in 1780, rowed by 78 oarsmen and last used to transport Britain's Queen Elizabeth II on the River Tagus in 1957.

Travelling by Coach

Museu Nacional dos Coches is one of the most visited museums in Portugal. Housed in an attractive 18th-century building by the Balem Royal Palace, the museum features coaches and carriages from the 17th to 19th centuries. The museum is set to increase in size on a new site just opposite the current one in 2010, designed by Brazilian architect Paulo Mendes da Rocha.

TAKING A BREAK

Treat yourself to a coffee and a custard tart at the **Antiga Confeitaria de Belém** (➤ 69).

🚗 196 off A1 🚋 Tram 15 🚃 Belém (Lisbon to Cascais line)

Padrão dos Descobrimentos

✉ Avenida de Brasília ☎ 213 031 950; www.padraodescobrimentos.egeac.pt
🕐 May–Sep daily 10–6:30; Oct–Apr 10–5:30 💷 Inexpensive

Torre de Belém
✉ Avenida de Brasília ☎ 213 620 034; www.mosteirojeronimos.pt 🕐 Oct–Apr Tue–Sun 10–5; May–Sep Tue–Sun 10–6:30. Last entry 30 mins before closing 💶 Moderate (free Sun 10–2)

Mosteiro dos Jerónimos
✉ Praça do Império ☎ 213 620 034; www.mosteirojeronimos.pt 🕐 Oct–Apr Tue–Sun 10–5; May–Sep Tue–Sun 10–6 💶 Church free, cloisters moderate (free Sun 10–2)

Museu de Marinha
✉ Praça do Império ☎ 213 620 010; http://museu.marinha.pt 🕐 Oct–Apr Tue–Sun 10–5; May–Sep Tue–Sun 10–6 💶 Moderate

Museu Nacional dos Coches
✉ Praça Afonso de Albuquerque ☎ 213 610 850; www.museudoscoches-ipmuseus.pt 🕐 Tue–Sun 10–6. Last entry 30 mins before closing 💶 Moderate (free Sun 10–2)

The ornate facade of the Museu de Marinha in the Belem area

Centro Cultural de Belem
✉ Praça do Império ☎ 213 612 400; www.ccb.pt 🕐 Mon–Fri 8–8, Sat–Sun 10–7 💶 Free entry; workshops moderate; concerts prices vary

BELÉM: INSIDE INFO

Top tip Visit Belém on a Sunday morning when many of the museums and sights have free entrance. Avoid Mondays when almost everything is closed.

In more depth The **Museu da Electricidade** (www.fundacao.edp.pt; Sun–Sat 10–6), housed inside the thermo-electric power station at the eastern end of Belém contains original generators and energy-themed exhibitions.

2 Museu Calouste Gulbenkian

The most significant museum in Portugal is the result of one man's passionate collecting, encompassing the entire history of both Eastern and Western art. What makes it all the more enjoyable is that although each piece is worth seeing, the small size of the collection means that it can be thoroughly explored in a visit of a couple of hours.

Calouste Gulbenkian (1869–1955) was an Armenian oil magnate who earned his nickname "Mr Five Per Cent" when he negotiated a five per cent stake in the newly discovered oilfields of Iraq.

The Mirror of Venus, **1870–76 by Sir Edward Burne-Jones**

He spent much of his wealth acquiring works of art, from Roman coins to old masters. During World War II he moved to Portugal, and bequeathed his fortune and his art collection to the Portuguese. The foundation, established after his death, is now one of the largest cultural institutions in the world, which supports museums, orchestras and charitable projects.

Treasures from around the world

The **Museu Calouste Gulbenkian** was opened in 1969 and contains the most precious objects from Gulbenkian's collection. Your tour of the museum begins with a small room devoted to ancient Egyptian art, including funerary statues, bronze sculptures and an alabaster bowl dating from 2700BC. The next room contains superb classical art from Greece and

A 14th-century mosque lamp

Rome, together with an impressive life-size relief of an Assyrian warrior from the ninth century BC.

Some of the greatest treasures are found in the **Gallery of Islamic and Oriental Art**, which features Persian rugs, Ottoman ceramics, enamelled glassware and a beautiful late 13th-century glazed ceramic *mihrab* (a prayer niche indicating the direction of Mecca) from a Persian mosque. Also in this room is a small case of illuminated gospel manuscripts from Gulbenkian's native Armenia.

This leads into the **Far East Gallery**, which has porcelain, jade, lacquered boxes and screens.

European art

The largest part of the museum is devoted to **European art** from the 13th to the 20th centuries. It begins with early illuminated gospels and a 14th-century French triptych depicting scenes from the life of the Virgin.

Among the paintings to look out for are *Portrait of an Old Man* by Rembrandt and *Flight Into Egypt* by Rubens (which features a terrified Mary clutching Jesus to her breast as the beasts of the forest surround her). From the Impressionist period there is *Self-Portrait* by Degas and *Boy Blowing Bubbles* by Manet. Other prominent European artists represented in the museum include Gainsborough, Turner, Renoir and Monet, along with some superb marble sculptures by Rodin.

The Gulbenkian Foundation is also responsible for the **Centro de Arte Moderna** (same hours as the museum), devoted to 20th-century Portuguese art. Walk through the attractive sculpture gardens and past an amphitheatre where open-air concerts are held in summer.

TAKING A BREAK

Take a **picnic** to the sculpture gardens or visit the café of the **Centro de Arte Moderna,** Rua dr Nicoalau de Bettencourt, (tel: 217 823 474), which has a good lunchtime cold buffet.

➕ 196 off A5 ✉ Avenida de Berna 45 ☎ 217 823 000; www.museu.gulbenkian.pt ⏰ Tue–Sun 10–5:45 Ⓜ São Sebastião or Praça de Espanha 🚌 16, 726, 56, 718, 742 🎟 Moderate (free on Sun)

MUSEU CALOUSTE GULBENKIAN: INSIDE INFO

Top tips The Gulbenkian Foundation has its own **orchestra and choir** and also hosts concerts by visiting musicians. Ask for a programme at the museum reception desk or contact the box office (tel: 217 823 000).

■ As well as paintings and sculpture, the European art galleries contain fine examples of **decorative arts**, including 18th-century Louis XV furniture from France and a set of gorgeous Italian tapestries depicting children playing in the woods.

Hidden gem Don't miss the **René Lalique Gallery** at the end of the European Art section, with stunning art nouveau jewellery by the French decorative artist, René Lalique, who was a friend of Calouste Gulbenkian.

3 Castelo de São Jorge

Dominating the skyline above the Alfama district, the Castelo de São Jorge (St George's Castle) has a long and chequered history. Yet despite its bloody past this is now one of the most peaceful spots in Lisbon. The gardens make a pleasant place to escape for an hour or two, and there are fine views over the city and the river from its walkways and terraces.

The castle occupies the site where Phoenician traders set up their first camp when they occupied Lisbon during the eighth century BC. It was fortified by the Romans and again by the Visigoths, and the Moorish rulers built their palace here.

The castle was taken for the Christians in 1147 by Afonso Henriques, Portugal's first king, who captured it after a 17-week siege, with the help of British and French crusaders. The victorious battle saw the death of the Portuguese knight Martim Moniz, who is honoured in the name of a Metro station and a nearby square.

After the Christian conquest, the Portuguese kings used the *Moorish palace* as their royal home until Dom Manuel I moved it to Terreiro do Paço, on the site of Praça do Comércio.

You enter the outer walls through the Arco de São Jorge, where a niche houses an image of the saint. This leads you

Climb on to ramparts for the best views

The superb views from Castelo de São Jorge

into the *bairro* of **Santa Cruz**, a village-like quarter of medieval houses around the 18th-century church of Santa Cruz do Castelo. A separate gateway leads into the castle proper, and a parade ground dominated by a statue of Afonso Henriques.

From the castle terrace, there are wonderful **views** and photo opportunities to be enjoyed over the River Tagus, named the *mar de palha* (sea of straw) by locals because of the way it shimmers like gold in the sun.

Walkways lead around the walls, and you can climb up onto the battlements and the roofs of the ten towers for more superb views. In summer, peacocks strut around the gardens and artists set up their stalls beneath the ramparts.

Part of the old royal palace now contains **Olisipónia**, a multimedia exhibition. The video sequence takes you on a tour of Lisbon's history, including a simulation of the 1755 earthquake, with commentary and sound effects.

The other attraction here is the fascinating **Câmara Escura**, housed in one of the inner towers, a device that provides live 360° images of the city and people below going about their daily business.

TAKING A BREAK

There is a good café and a restaurant within the castle if you want to stop for a meal, or for something different try a Goan curry at **Arco da Castelo** (➤ 70).

🔂 197 E4

Castelo
☎ 218 800 620; www.castelosaojorge.egeac.pt 🕐 Mar–Oct 9–9; Nov–Feb 9–6 🚌 37; tram 12, 28 💶 Moderate

Olisipónia
🕐 As castle, above 💶 Included in castle entry

Câmara Escura
🕐 Nov–Feb 10–5:30; Mar–Oct 9–8:30 💶 Included in castle entry

CASTELO DE SÃO JORGE: INSIDE INFO

Top tips The castle can be reached by a short, steep climb from the **Miradouro de Santa Luzia**, but if you want to avoid the walk, **bus 37** goes all the way to the outer walls.

■ The castle terrace is a great place from where to watch the **sunset**.

■ A fado festival is held inside the castle on summer weekend evenings.

4 Alfama

The oldest quarter of Lisbon is also its most charming. Alfama sprawls across a hill between the Castelo de São Jorge and the River Tagus, a maze of cobbled lanes, alleyways, staircases and secret gardens whose Moorish streetplan has largely survived the damage caused by the 1755 earthquake.

This is a district for aimless strolling through lanes where you will be rewarded with endless surprises as you discover a pretty courtyard, a public washing place or a statue of the Virgin in a niche high on a wall. Although Alfama is undergoing some changes, it is still primarily a working-class *bairro*, with a densely populated community of fishermen – who spend their spare time in local *tascas* (bars) – and their wives, who set up stalls on the street. The scent of charcoal and grilled sardines is ever present as the life of the community goes on in dilapidated houses with wrought-iron balconies and *azulejo* panels on the walls.

View from Portas do Sol over the rooftops of Alfama

Cathedral and Teatro Romano

The name Alfama probably derives from the Arabic *al hama* (fountain) and there is evidence of Roman and Moorish settlements here. The Christians built their *sé* (cathedral) on the site of the main mosque, soon after Afonso Henriques captured the city in 1147. Built in Romanesque style and closely resembling a fortress, it has twin towers either side of a

rose window on the main façade. The Gothic cloisters contain
the excavated remains of the Roman city.

Just above the cathedral, the **Teatro Romano** is a partly
excavated Roman theatre, built during the reign of Emperor
Augustus and rebuilt under Nero in the first century AD.
The theatre itself is found in a shed on Rua de São Mamede,
and there is a small museum across the street displaying
archaeological finds.

Miradouro de Santa Luzia

Walk (or take tram 28) uphill from the cathedral to reach
Miradouro de Santa Luzia, a pretty garden with fine views
over Alfama and the River Tagus. Notice the tiled panels on the
south wall of the nearby church, one depicting Lisbon before
the earthquake, the other showing Christian soldiers with
helmets, swords and shields attacking the Castelo de São Jorge
(► 52–53), which is defended by turbanned Moors.

Museu de Artes Decorativas

Around the corner is the **Museu de Artes Decorativas**,
containing the applied arts collection of the Portuguese banker
Ricardo do Espírito Santo Silva. The collection is particularly
rich in Portuguese furniture, as well as ceramics, clocks, fans
and guns, all displayed in a re-creation of a 17th-century
aristocratic home. Don't miss the *Giraffe Parade*, a colourful
16th-century Flemish tapestry in the main hall. The museum
also has workshops where artisans reproduce traditional skills
such as bookbinding and woodcarving.

**An aristocratic
drawing room
in the Museu
de Artes
Decorativas**

There are more views over the Alfama rooftops from the
terrace at **Largo das Portas do Sol**, opposite the museum.
Notice here the statue of São Vicente, Lisbon's patron saint,
bearing the city's symbol, a boat with two ravens (the relics of
the saint were said to have been brought to Lisbon by Afonso
Henriques in a boat piloted by ravens).

Two Churches

Looking east from the terrace, the skyline is dominated by two white marble churches, the vast bulk of **São Vicente de Fora** and the domed church of **Santa Engrácia**. You can hop back on the tram to visit both of them.

São Vicente de Fora means "St Vincent Beyond the Wall" as the church was originally outside the city walls. The first church was built on this site soon after the Christian conquest, though the current one dates from 1629. Go through a side entrance to visit the monastery and cloisters. There is a fine 18th-century sacristy with walls of inlaid polychrome marble and a set of *azulejo* tiles depicting the fables of the 17th-century French satirist La Fontaine.

The former monks' refectory is now the pantheon of the House of Bragança, containing the tombs of monarchs from Catherine of Bragança (Queen of England) to the assassinated Dom Carlos I and his son, Dom Manuel II, who died in exile in England in 1932.

The superb illuminated dome of Santa Engracia

The baroque church of **Santa Engrácia**, by contrast, has become the national pantheon, with monuments to Portuguese heroes such as explorers Vasco da Gama and Luís de Camões, as well as the *fadista* Amália Rodrigues. You can take the lift up to the rooftop for fabulous views over the River Tagus and the city.

The open ground between the two churches, **Campo de Santa Clara**, is the setting for Lisbon's liveliest flea market, the Feira da Ladra (Thieves' Market) which takes place on Tuesday and Saturday mornings.

Fado

Alfama is the true home of the traditional music of *fado* (► 20–21), and there are several clubs in the back streets where you can hear it performed each night.

To find out more about this uniquely Portuguese music, visit the **Museu do Fado**, on the southern edge of Alfama, close to the river. This excellent museum describes the history and traditions of *fado* and of the Portuguese guitar, a mandolin-type instrument that was introduced by British traders in the 18th century. There are frequent live performances, and the shop sells *fado* books and CDs..

TAKING A BREAK

The largest concentration of restaurants is at the foot of Rua de São Pedro, on and around Largo do Chafariz de Dentro. Try **Os Corvos** (Beco do Alfurja 4, tel: 218 884 508, €€) for traditional Portuguese cuisine fresh from the market, or **Lautasco** (Beco de Azinhal 7A, tel: 218 860 173, €€) for seafood *cataplana* (steamed with strips of ham).

Narrow cobbled streets in Alfama, Lisbon's oldest quarter

🔲 197 F3 ✉ Tram 12, 28, bus 37

Sé
🔲 197 E2 ✉ Largo da Sé ☎ 218 876 628 🕐 Museum daily 10–5; cloisters 10–6; cathedral daily 9–7 💷 Church free, cloisters inexpensive

Museu de Teatro Romano
🔲 197 E2 ✉ Pátio de Aljube 5, Rua Augusto Rosa ☎ 217 513 200
🕐 Tue–Sun 10–1, 2–6 💷 Free

Museu de Artes Decorativas
🔲 197 E3 ✉ Largo das Portas do Sol 2
☎ 218 881 991; www.fress.pt 🕐 Daily 10–5 💷 Moderate

São Vicente de Fora
🔲 197 off F4 ✉ Largo de São Vicente
☎ 218 824 400 🕐 Church Tue–Sat 9–4, Sun 9–12:30; cloisters Tue–Sat 10–5, Sun 19–11:30 🚌 Bus 37 💷 Free

Santa Engrácia (Panteão Nacional)
🔲 197 F4 ✉ Campo de Santa Clara
☎ 218 854 820 🕐 Tue–Sun 10–5
🚌 Bus 34 💷 Inexpensive (free Sun 10–2)

Museu do Fado
🔲 197 F2 ✉ Largo do Chafariz de Dentro
☎ 218 823 470; www.museudofado.egeac. pt 🕐 Tue–Sun 10–6. Last entry 30 mins before closing 💷 Inexpensivet

ALFAMA: INSIDE INFO

Top tips Come here on **weekday mornings** when the street life is at its most lively and a fish market is set up along Rua de São Pedro.
■ Alfama is a poor area with a reputation for **petty crime**, so avoid flaunting anything valuable and take care when wandering at night.

Hidden gems One particularly charming spot is the **courtyard** at the top of **Escadinha de Santo Estêvão**, between Rua dos Remédios and Santo Estêvão.

Igreja de Santo André e Santa Marinha is one of the oldest convents in Lisbon. Parts of the convent are closed to the public, but the church is open and the views over the city and river from the courtyard are stunning.

5 Parque das Nações

The former Expo'98 site has become an open-air playground where Lisboetas flock at weekends to enjoy its many restaurants, bars, sculpture gardens and riverside walks. With stunning modern architecture and a range of high-tech attractions, a day out at "the invented city" offers a completely different experience of Lisbon.

The hosting of the World Exposition in 1998 gave Lisbon the opportunity for a major project in urban renewal. A derelict area of warehouses and oil refineries, 5km (3 miles) east of the city, was transformed into a riverside park for the exhibition. When Expo'98 closed, the site was renamed Parque das Nações and turned into a business and residential zone – in effect a new city with cultural and sporting facilities. The project is now complete and already more people are visiting this area than when Expo'98 was in full swing.

Most visitors arrive at the **Estação do Oriente**, an airy, light, steel-and-glass Metro station. This leads into the Vasco da Gama **shopping mall**. Walk through the mall to emerge on the waterfront.

Shops and restaurants in the Vasco da Gama mall

Portugal's Most Popular Attraction

The **Oceanário** is one of the largest aquariums in Europe, and receives one million visitors per year. It is based around a huge tank, the size of four Olympic swimming pools, with windows at two levels that allow you to watch the sharks swimming near the surface and flatfish on the seabed.

Ranged around this are four separate tanks devoted to the ecosystems of the North Atlantic, South Atlantic, Pacific and Indian oceans. More than 15,000 marine animals and birds are on show, including puffins, penguins, sea otters and spider crabs, together with some superb examples of coral reefs.

From here you can walk or take the cable-car along the banks of the River Tagus, passing the Garcia de Orta gardens. The ride ends close to **Torre Vasco da Gama**, Lisbon's tallest building, which rises 145m (476 feet) above the river.

The River Tagus is spanned by the extraordinary 18km (11-mile) bridge, **Ponte Vasco da Gama**, which passes directly over water for 10km (6 miles) of its length and almost seems to be floating.

TAKING A BREAK

There are more than 40 restaurants in the area, offering a choice of fast food, Brazilian, Cuban, Chinese, Italian, Spanish and Portuguese cuisine. You'll find everything from ice-cream parlours, pizza houses and *tapas* bars to traditional restaurants serving Portugese dishes.

The ultra-modern and extraordinary Wall of Water Fountain

➕ 200 B2 ☎ 218 919 333; www.parquedasnacoes.pt

Oceanário
☎ 218 917 002; www.oceanario.pt 🕐 Nov–Mar daily 10–7; Jun–Sep daily 10–8. Last entry one hour before closing. 💰 Expensive

Teleférico (cable-car)
☎ 218 956 143; www.parquedasnacoes 🕐 Jun–Sep Mon–Fri 11–8, Sat–Sun 10–9; Oct–May Mon–Fri 11–7, Sat–Sun 10–8 💰 Moderate

The waterfront area is a pleasant place to relax

PARQUE DAS NAÇÕES: INSIDE INFO

Top tips If you have small children with you, you can get around the various attractions on a **miniature road train** that makes regular circuits of the park.
- The **Cartão do Parque**, valid for two days, gives free entry to the Oceanário and cable-car, as well as discounts at other attractions, and is good value if you intend doing them all.

In more depth Try the bowling alley **BIL (Bowling Internacional de Lisboa)** if the weather is unfavourable (Mon–Thu 12–2am, Fri 12–4am, Sat 11–4am, Sun 11am–2am, moderate) and also the **Pavilhão do Conhecimento** (Tue–Fri 10–6, Sat–Sun 11–7, moderate), an interactive science museum (www.pavconhecimento.pt).

6 Sintra

If you only have time for one excursion, you should make it Sintra. Once the summer residence of the kings of Portugal, this UNESCO World Heritage site is where wealthy *Lisboetas* come to escape the city, in whitewashed *quintas* set on green hillsides among palaces, pinewoods and granite crags.

Palácio Nacional

The centre of the town is dominated by the **Palácio Nacional**, with its two enormous conical chimneys. This royal palace was begun by João I in the late 14th century and completed by Manuel I in the Manueline style.

Look out for the **Sala dos Cisnes** (Swan Room) and **Sala das Pegas** (Magpie Room), named after the birds in the ceiling frescoes. The **Sala dos Brasões** (Arms Room) has *azulejo* walls depicting hunting scenes and a coffered gilded ceiling with the coats of arms of 72 noble families.

Also in the palace is the **bedchamber of Afonso VI**, the deranged king held prisoner here by his brother Pedro II, who added insult to injury by marrying his queen.

The Castle

The other main sights of Sintra are found on the hills above the town. The **Castelo dos Mouros** (Moors' Castle) was built in the ninth century and captured by Afonso Henriques in 1147. You can walk around the ramparts, with views stretching

The Palácio Nacional's conical chimneys are hard to miss

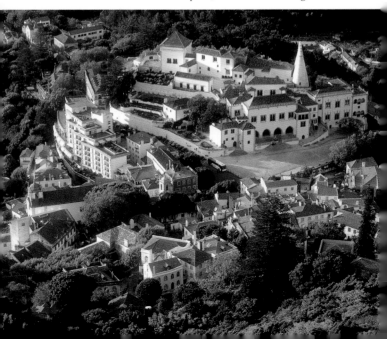

The fantasy facade of Palacio da Pena

beyond Lisbon and out to sea, to reach the royal tower, where there is a fine view of the Palácio da Pena, on a granite peak.

Palácio da Pena

The climb to the **Palácio da Pena** takes you through the woodlands of Parque da Pena, dotted with lakes and follies. With its minarets, towers and golden domes, the palace is one of the best-known images of Portugal. This intricate fantasy was built in the 1840s by Prince Ferdinand of Saxe-Coburg-Gotha, husband of Dona Maria II and honorary king of Portugal, on the site of a monastery established by Manuel I to give thanks for the sighting of Vasco da Gama's fleet returning from India.

This was the last royal palace to be built in Portugal and the German architect, Baron Eschwege, ran riot with his imagination. Gargoyles gaze down from the doorways and chandeliers are held up by life-size statues. The queen's antechamber is decorated entirely in Meissen porcelain, and the Arabic Room features playful *trompe-l'œil* walls. Everything is preserved as it was when Dom Manuel II went into exile in 1910. From the belvedere you can look out to Cruz Alta, the highest point of the Serra de Sintra, marked by a stone cross and a statue of Baron Eschwege.

Toys, Science and Modern Art

There are three museums worth visiting in the centre of town. The **Museu do Brinquedo** (Toy Museum), in the old fire station, contains the collection of João Arbués Moreira, gathered over 50 years. Among the toys are Egyptian marbles, Roman bronze figures, toy soldiers and model cars.

The **Sintra Live Science Museum** has recently opened a Planetarium that is proving popular.

The **Museu de Arte Moderna**, in the old casino, features rotating exhibits from the Berardo Collection of 20th-century art, including works by Dalí, Miró, Picasso and Warhol.

TAKING A BREAK

Try *Queijadas*, sweet cheese and cinnamon pastries, at **Fábrica das Queijadas da Sapa** near the Palácio Nacional at Volta da Duche.

The rugged battlements of the Castelo dos Mouros are worth the climb

➕ 200 A2

Tourist Information Office
✉ Praça da República 23 ☎ 219 231 157; www.cm-sintra.pt

Palácio Nacional
✉ Largo Rainha D Amélia ☎ 219 106 840; www.ippar.pt 🕐 Thu–Tue 10–5:30 (last entry 5)
💶 Moderate (free Sun 10–2)

Castelo dos Mouros
☎ 219 237 300; www.parquesdesintra.pt
🕐 Oct–Mar, daily 9:30–5; Apr–Sept, daily 9:30–8 (last entry 7) 🚌 434 💶 Moderate

Palácio da Pena
✉ Estrada da Pena ☎ 219 105 340; www.ippar.pt 🕐 May–Sept, Tue–Sun 10–7, Sept–Apr, Tue–Sun 10–5.30 🚌 434 💶 Moderate

Museu do Brinquedo
✉ Rua Visconde de Monserrate ☎ 219 242 171; www.museu-do-brinquedo.pt 🕐 Tue–Sun 10–6 💶 Moderate

Sintra Live Science Centre
✉ Old Tramway Garage, Estrada Nacional 247, Ribeira de Sintra ☎ 219 247 730 🕐 Tue–Fri 10–6, Sat–Sun 11–7; Planetarium: Sunday 4–7. Or by appointment (minimum 10 people) during the week 💶 Moderate

Museu de Arte Moderna
✉ Avenida Heliodoro Salgado ☎ 219 248 170; www.cm-sintra.pt or www.berardocllection.com 🕐 Tue–Sun 10–6 (last entry 5:30) 💶 Moderate

SINTRA: INSIDE INFO

Top tips The main sights are connected by a **circular bus route** (No 434) that links the station, old town, Castelo dos Mouros and Palácio da Pena. A single ticket is valid for any number of journeys in a day. If you are coming from Estoril or Cascais, buy a Day Rover ticket (*bilhete turístico diário*), which includes travel within Sintra.

■ The **Sintra Music Festival**, which takes place in June and July, is one of Portugal's top classical music festivals. Details from Sintra tourist information office.

■ A tram runs direct between Praia das Maçãs beach and the Museu de Arte Moderna in Sintra every weekend in summer

In more depth Another of Portugal's elaborate royal palaces, **Palácio de Queluz** (tel: 214 343 860, Wed–Mon 10–4:30, moderate), lies close to the Sintra train line and can be visited on the way back to Lisbon.

At Your Leisure

7 Museu Nacional de Arte Antiga

It may not have the treasures of the Museu Calouste Gulbenkian (➤ 50), but the National Museum of Ancient Art does have the most complete collection of Portuguese art, together with the cultures that influenced it. Among the items to look for are Indo-Portuguese furniture, Sino-Portuguese ceramics, a carved ivory salt cellar from Africa, and 16th-century lacquer screens showing the arrival of Portuguese explorers in Japan. Many of the religious paintings, such as Nuno Gonçalves' 15th-century *St Vincent Altarpiece*, were confiscated from churches following the dissolution of the monasteries in 1834. The museum also contains a complete baroque chapel from the Carmelite convent that once stood on this site, with gilded woodwork and outstanding *azulejo* tiles.

➕ 196 off A1 ✉ Rua das Janelas Verdes, Lapa ☎ 213 912 800; www.mnarteantiga-ipmuseus.pt ⏱ Wed–Sun 10–6, Tue 2–6 🚌 60, 713, 714, 732; tram 15, 18, 25 💷 Moderate (free Sun 10–2)

The Museu Nacional de Arte Antiga

LISBON FOR KIDS

- **Parque das Nações** (➤ 58–59): the former Expo'98 site, now offering the Oceanário and Pavilhão do Conhecimento Virtual, with hands-on exhibits, and there's even a mini road train to take you round.
- **Planetário Calouste Gulbenkian**: the planetarium next to the Museu de Marinha (➤ 48–49) has special children's shows at weekends.
- **Museu da Carris**: take tram No 15 to the tram museum (Mon–Sat 10–4:30; www.carris.pt).
- **Jardim Zoológico**: take the Metro to Jardim Zoológico to visit Lisbon's zoo (Oct–Mar daily 10–6 (last entry 5); Apr–Sep 10–8, tel: 217 232 900; www.zoo.pt).

8 Estrêla

The No 28 tram ride ends in Estrêla, a well-to-do neighbourhood some 2km (1.2 miles) west of Bairro Alto.

The area is dominated by the **Basílica da Estrêla**, a late 18th-century baroque church whose white dome is visible from across the city. Across the street, **Jardim da Estrêla** is one of Lisbon's prettiest public gardens, with a bandstand, play area and a small pond. Walk through the gardens to reach St George's Anglican church (service: Sun 11:30) and the **Cemitério Inglês**, where the novelist Henry Fielding is buried.

➕ 196 off A3 🚃 Tram 25, 28

Basílica da Estrêla
✉ Praça da Estrêla ☎ 213 960 915 ⏱ Mon–Sat 8:30–12, 1–7, Sun 10–11:45, 3–6:45 💷 Free

Cemitério Inglês
✉ Rua de São Jorge à Estrêla ☎ 213 906 248 ⏱ Mon–Sat 9–5, Sun 9–1 🚌 709, 720, 738 💷 Free

🟨 Bairro Alto

The grid of 16th-century lanes which makes up the Bairro Alto (upper town) is best known as Lisbon's nightlife quarter, where the plaintive strains of *fado* compete with African and Latin vibes.

Traditionally a working-class area, Bairro Alto has seen gentrification in recent years, with art galleries, cocktail bars and alternative fashion shops giving the area a bohemian appeal. If you like port, don't miss the Solar do Vinho do Porto (➤ 71).

Near here is the Jesuit **Igreja de São Roque**, whose plain façade belies the richness of its interior, especially its lavish side chapels. The Capela de São João Baptista, fourth on the left, is a riot of marble, alabaster, lapis lazuli, amethyst, mosaic, silver and gold, built in Rome and taken to Lisbon on the orders of Dom João V.

Just down the hill, on the edge of the chic shopping district of Chiado, the **Museu Arqueológico do Carmo** occupies the old Carmelite convent, destroyed in the earthquake of 1755 and now a Gothic shell. Among the items on display are Egyptian and Peruvian mummies, Roman mosaics and a stone bust of Afonso Henriques dating from the 12th century.

➕ 196 A3 🚃 Tram 28 or Elevador da Glória

Igreja de São Roque

➕ 196 A4 ✉ Largo Trindade Coelho

FOUR BEST VIEWPOINTS

■ **Castelo de São Jorge** (➤ 52): standing at the top of Alfama, there are fine views from the castle ramparts.

■ **Miradouro de Santa Luzia**, Alfama (➤ 55): views over the River Tagus and Alfama.

■ **Miradouro de São Pedro de Alcântara**, Bairro Alto (➤ 63, 174): views from the top of the Elevador da Glória over the Baixa and River Tagus.

■ **Ponte 25 de Abril** (➤ 43): Stretching across the River Tagus, the views from the bridge are breathtaking.

The atmospheric streets of the Barrio Alto area at night

☎ 213 235 380 🕐 Church daily 8:30–5; museum Tue–Sun 10–5 💷 Church free; museum inexpensive

Museu Arqueológico do Carmo

➕ 196 B3 ✉ Largo do Carmo ☎ 213 478 629 ; www.museusportugal.org/AAP/html/historia.htm 🕐 May–Sep Mon–Sat 10–6; Oct–Apr Mon–Sat 10–5 💷 Inexpensive (free Sun 10–2)

🔟 Parque Eduardo VII

This large, formal park was laid out at the end of the 19th century and named after the English king, Edward VII. The best reason for coming here is the magnificent view from the terrace at the top of the park, where a stone monument commemorates the 1974 revolution. From here you look down over sweeping lawns and along the broad Avenida da Liberdade all the way to the River Tagus. Near here is a garden dedicated to the *fado* singer Amália Rodrigues. On one side of the park is a pavilion, named after the 1984 Olympic marathon champion Carlos Lopes; on the other side is the Estufa Fria greenhouse, with delightful lakeside walks and hothouses full of tropical plants.

➕ 196 off A5 🚇 Marquês de Pombal, Parque, São Sebastião 🕐 Daily 9–sunset

Walkways intersect lengths of grass with manicured hedges at Parque Eduardo VII

Ⅺ Museu Nacional do Azulejo

It's worth making the short trek out of the centre of Lisbon to visit the National Tile Museum, housed in the former convent of Madre de Deus. The museum traces the development of *azulejo* tiles (➤ 19) from the 15th century onwards, in the setting of a lovely baroque church with Manueline cloisters and tiled walls. The highlight is an 18th-century panel of more than 1,300 tiles, which gives a panoramic view of pre-earthquake Lisbon. The 20th-century galleries show how *azulejos* have moved out of monasteries and into shopping malls, Metro stations and the realms of abstract art.

➕ 197 off F2 ✉ Rua Madre de Deus 4
☎ 218 100 340; www.mnazulejo-ipmuseus.pt
🕐 Wed–Sun 10–6, Tue 2–6 🚌 718, 742, 794
💰 Moderate (free Sun 10–2)

Ⅻ Estoril and Cascais

These twin resorts, linked by an attractive seafront promenade, lie at the heart of the Lisbon coast. Estoril is more cosmopolitan and chic, with a casino, golf course, racetrack and a mock castle on the beach.

The busy resort at Praia do Tamariz is popular with tourists and locals

During World War II, when Portugal remained neutral, Estoril was a refuge for diplomats, spies and exiled royalty – King Juan Carlos of Spain spent his childhood here.

Although a growing resort, Cascais retains its fishing village charm, with daily fish auctions beside the beach, Praia da Ribeira.

Beyond Cascais, a coastal corniche leads past Boca do Inferno (Hell's Mouth), where waves crash energetically against the cliffs, to the windswept dunes at Praia do Guincho, a popular windsurfing beach, and Cabo da Roca, mainland Europe's westernmost point.

This area makes a good base for a short stay near Lisbon, combining a beach holiday with a city break. Trains to Lisbon follow a scenic line along the coast, via the resorts of São Pedro do Estoril and Carcavelos.

🚉 200 A2

🔢 Palacio de Mafra

The pink marble Palácio-Convento de Mafra, 40km (25 miles) northwest of Lisbon, was built by Dom João V in 1717 to give thanks to God for the birth of a royal heir. Like El Escorial in Madrid, it served both as a royal palace and a monastery.

Financed by profits from Brazilian gold, the palace employed 50,000 workers in its construction; originally intended to hold 13 monks, it ended up accommodating 300 monks and

A corridor in the spectacular Palacio-Convento de Mafra

the entire royal family. You can visit the basilica and the palace on guided tours, including the monks' cells, the pharmacy, and the baroque library. There are also tours of the royal hunting ground, now a wildlife park.

🚉 200 A3 ☎ 261 817 550; www.ippar.pt/english/monumentos/palacio_mafra 🕐 Wed–Mon 10–5 (last entry 4:30) 💰 Moderate

---

LISBON RIDES
It is fun (and has the advantage of being much cheaper) to join the locals on public transport.

■ **Ferries:** Commuter ferries cross the Tagus to Barreiro and Cacilhas. The boats for Barreiro depart from Terreiro do Paço, with superb views of the city.

■ **Trams:** A ride on one of Lisbon's antique wooden trams is an experience in itself. The most enjoyable route is No 28, which rattles up and down the steep streets of Alfama on its way from Graça to Estrela.

■ *Elevadors*: These ancient lifts and funiculars are part of Lisbon's public transport system. Take Elevador da Glória from Praça dos Restauradores to Bairro Alto, or Elevador de Santa Justa for views over Baixa.

Where to...
Stay

Prices
Expect to pay for a double room per night in high season

€ under €60	€€ €60–€120	€€€ €121–€180	€€€€ over €180

LISBON

Albergaria Senhora do Monte €€–€€€

The gorgeous pink and white décor and marble bathrooms in this modern hotel complement the romantic location, high up in the quiet *bairro* of Graça. The panoramic restaurant-bar (open to non-guests for drinks) is a wonderful place to linger over breakfast. More expensive rooms with south-facing terraces also have air-conditioning – ask for one when booking. It's a short tram ride into downtown Lisbon.

🚏 197 E5 🖂 Calçada do Monte 39 ☎ 218 866 002; www.maisturismo.pt/sramonte 🚋 Tram 12, 28

Hotel Bairro Alto €€–€€€

Chic, luxurious and in a great neighbourhood, this restored 18th-century townhouse makes for a memorable stay in Lisbon. Every detail has been thought about here – generous beds in sleekly designed bedrooms, 24-hour concierge, a good café-bar, a small gym and spa. The sixth-floor terrace offers views over the rooftops of Bairro Alto and down to the Tagus River. Everything suggests understated luxury, but

it can all get rather expensive. If you want to experience the hotel without quite the same price tag, the loft rooms are smaller, but are well designed and offer excellent value.

🚏 196 A2 🖂 8 Praça Luís de Camões ☎ 213 408 288; www.bairroaltohotel.com 🚇 Baixa/Chiado

Hotel Heritage Av Liberdade €€–€€€

This hotel is the most recent addition to this small chain of renovated historic buildings that have been turned into luxury boutique hotels in key areas of Lisbon. Renovated by Portuguese architect Miguel Cancio Martins, this 18th-century townhouse was the winner of the Historic Rehabilitation Prize 2008 of the Portuguese Real State Oscars. The hotel feels chic and intimate, with good-sized bedrooms, large marble bathrooms and a heated lap pool in the basement. No restaurant, but there's a cosy, well-decorated

bar downstairs, where breakfast is served and bar snacks in the evenings. Even better, it's an easy walk into the centre of town. Babysitting services are available, and there's WiFi in all rooms.

🚏 196 A5 🖂 28, Avenida da Liberdade ☎ 213 218 200; www.heritage.pt/heritage_av_liberdade.htm 🚇 Estacao do Rossio

Jerónimos 8 €€–€€€

Situated directly opposite to the magnificent Jerónimos monastery in Belém, this contemporary and cleverly designed hotel is perfectly placed for exploring the many monuments, museums and waterfront of Belém. Discreet from the outside, the public areas of the hotel are sleek and modern, with low-level sofas in bright colours and large artworks hanging on the walls. Outside, there are several terraces on higher floors for enjoying a drink on warm days. The bedrooms are reasonably sized, uncluttered and comfortable – ask for one with a view of the monastery. A lively and popular bar serves a range of drinks and cocktails (including a house wine made in the vineyards of a sister hotel), together with a range of simple but well cooked bar food. Recommended.

➕ 196 off A1 ⊠ 8, Rua dos Jerónimos ☎ 213 600 900; www.jeronimos8.com 🚌 15

Pensão Londres €€

This simple, reliable *pensão* is superbly located for exploring the sights in the Príncipe Real district, and many of the rooms command fabulous views across the rooftops to the Ponte 25 de Abril or Castelo São Jorge (▶ 52). The 40 rooms, ranging from well-appointed singles, doubles, triples and suites, all have their own bathrooms. The largest doubles have attractive period furniture. A full breakfast is served in a charming dining room, which also has a fine view. And it's gay-friendly.

➕ 196 off A4 ⊠ Rua Pedro V 53/1-2 ☎ 213 462 203; www.pensaolondres.com.pt 🚋 Elevador da Glória, Bus 58

Residencial Santa Catarina €-€€

The simple Santa Catarina is located along a quiet, cobbled street, not far from the top of the ancient Bica funicular. The upper floor rooms of this charming family guesthouse are comfortably appointed and have superb views across to the River Tagus. The Santa Catarina viewpoint (▶ 80) and the nightlife and restaurants of the Bairro Alto are only a short walk away.

➕ 196 off A2 ⊠ Rua Dr Luís de Almeida e Albuquerque 6 ☎ 213 466 106 🚋 Tram 28, Elevador da Bica

Sé Guesthouse €€

The well-appointed Sé Guesthouse is a relaxing place to stay and is in fact two guesthouses in the same building – one with five bedrooms and the other with four. In a good location, just behind the *sé* (cathedral), and on the edge of Alfama, Lisbon's old town, this nine-room *pensão* is on the first floor of a beautiful townhouse.

Tastefully furnished with African artefacts and antique furniture, the rooms are large and comfortable but some don't have their own bathrooms, so book early if you want an en suite room. Breakfast is copious. The owners speak English.

➕ 197 E2 ⊠ Rua de São João da Praça 97/1 ☎ 218 864 400 🚋 Tram 12 and 28

Hotel Olisseppo Oriente €€

This is one of the newer hotels in this area, and on a street lined with plenty of smart places to stay. The comfortable, if functional, rooms have kitchenettes so that you can self-cater if you choose. You also have the Parque das Nações, the former Expo'98 site (▶ 58), on the doorstep, with its shopping, eating and entertainment opportunities and all rooms have staggering views of its futuristic buildings, the "Sea of Straw" (River Tagus) and the Ponte Vasco da Gama (▶ 59).

➕ 200 B2 ⊠ Avenida Dom João II, Parque das Nações ☎ 218 929 100; www.olissippohotels.com 🚇 Metro Oriente

Veneza €€-€€€

This well-run Venetian-style palace, built in 1886, is one of the few townhouses on the Avenue da Liberdade that has managed to escape the demolition trucks. The interior is lavishly decorated in a traditional style with wrought iron, polished wood and stained glass, while murals of Lisbon by Portuguese artist Pedro Luís Gomes adorn the monumental staircase, guarded by kitsch, torch-bearing statues. The 38 *en suite* rooms are stylish, with an understated décor.

➕ 196 A5 ⊠ Avenida da Liberdade 189 ☎ 213 522 618; www.3khoteis.com 🚇 Metro Avenida

York House €€€-€€€€

A tranquil and elegant place, for many this is the best spot to stay in Lisbon, so book well in advance. In a discreet Lapa location, accessed by a shady stairway, this 17th-century Carmelite convent was first turned into a guesthouse in the late 19th century by two ladies from York in England – from whom it gets its oddly un-Portuguese name. In fair weather you can breakfast under the huge palm in the flower-filled courtyard. Inside there are welcoming sitting rooms and labyrinthine corridors decorated with religious art, and a fine dining room serving refined Portuguese cuisine. The 32 rooms are decorated either in a traditional or minimalist chic style.

∰ 196 off A1 ⊠ Rua das Janelas Verdes 32 ☎ 213 962 435; www.yorkhouselisboa.com ☐ Tram 25, Train Santos

SINTRA

Hotel Central €€

Recently renovated, this well priced 1920s hotel is located in the centre of town, within walking distance of most of Sintra's attractions, and has a beautiful exterior covered in traditional *azulejo* tiles. Inside it has a Grand Epoque feel, with high ceilings, carvings and mirrors everywhere – and more *azulejo* tiles

on the walls. The hotel is a little functional, but the rooms offer great value for the location, and there is a good quality restaurant too.

∰ 200 A2 ⊠ Praça da República ☎ 219 230 963; www.sintracentralhotel.com

Lawrence's Hotel €€€€

This beautiful house near to central Sintra, Lawrence's claims to be the oldest hotel in Iberia and is highly recommended. The exquisitely decorated 11 rooms and five suites have the latest facilities, including air-conditioning and satellite TV; some have Jacuzzis in the huge bathrooms, and open fireplaces. At the top-class restaurant you can sample some of the best cooking in Sintra – even if you're not a hotel guest. A refined cellar backs up the Portuguese-influenced cuisine. Golfing packages are also offered, with discount rates at the best local golfcourse links.

∰ 200 A2 ⊠ Rua Consiglieri Pedroso 38–40 ☎ 219 105 500; www.lawrenceshotel. com

Where to...
Eat and Drink

Prices

Expect to pay per person for a three-course meal, excluding drinks and tips
€ under €12   €€ €12–€24   €€€ €25–€36   €€€€ over €36

LISBON

Antiga Confeitaria de Belém €

Although you can order a range of delicious sandwiches and cakes, most people come here for the *pastéis de nata*. You can find these crisp tartlets filled with egg-custard in *pastelarias* across the country, but those made here are unanimously regarded as superior – and they are noticeably less sweet.

∰ 196 off A1 ⊠ Rua de Belém 84–88 ☎ 213 637 423; www.pasteisdebelem.pt ☐ Tram 15, Train Belém ☺ Nov–Apr Mon–Sat 8am–11pm, Sun 8am–10pm; May–Oct daily 8am–midnight

Arco do Castelo €€

If you're hungry for something a bit different from the usual Portuguese cuisine, try this Goan restaurant in Alfama. Portugal's colonial influence is clear – both pork and beef feature on the menu, with coconut, ginger and cardamom dominating. Try *balchão de porco* (pork and shrimp curry) or *sarapatel* (pork with ginger). If you're baffled by the word *chamuças* on the menu, just say it out loud: it's the Portuguese spelling of *samosas*.

∰ 197 E3 ⊠ Rua Chão da Feira 25 ☎ 218 876 598 ☐ Tram 12 and 28 ☺ Mon–Sat 12:30–3:30, 6–10:30

A Bica do Sapato €€€€

Leading light Manuel Reis – who owns Lux, the nearby nightclub (▶ 74) – has an eye for location and impeccable taste in décor. Right on the waterfront at up-and-coming Santa Apolónia, this three-in-one temple to good food is currently the place to eat and be seen, whether in the stylish café-bar, the sushi section or the restaurant. In the latter you can sample clever concoctions dreamed up by Joaquim Figueredo, Lisbon's chef of the moment, who uses seafood as nobody else in the country dares.

🔠 197 E2 ⊠ Avenida Infante Dom Henrique, Armazém B ☎ 218 810 320; www.bicadosapato.com 🚌 Bus 9, 28, 35, 81, 82, 90 Ⓖ Restaurant: Tue–Sat 12:30–2:30, 8–11.30. Sushi Bar: Mon–Sat 9:30pm–1:30am. Café: Mon 5pm–1am, Tue–Sat 12:30–3:30, 7:30–1am. Closed Sun

A Brasileira €

Few old-style cafés have survived in Lisbon, but this one thankfully has – the timeless atmosphere is enhanced by a handless clock at the far end of the mirrored salon. It's not only a meeting place for students, intellectuals and other regulars drawn by the excellent coffee and *pastéis*, it is also a shrine to Fernando Pessoa who frequented it – witness the bronze statue on the small esplanada, next to which many tourists have their picture taken, often without having heard of the great 20th-century poet. It is a bit touristy, and not the cheapest place, but a real institution.

🔠 196 B3 ⊠ Rua Garrett 120 ☎ 213 469 541 🚇 Metro Baixa-Chiado Ⓖ Daily 8–2

Café Martinho da Arcada €€

Superbly located at the foot of the Alfama district, under the arcades and on one of the city's main squares, this is one of Lisbon's oldest cafés, with more than 200 years of service, and a dining experience that should not to be missed. The wine list is excellent and the very friendly waiters are more than happy to offer suggestions for dishes that have been sourced that morning from fishing boats or local markets.

🔠 196 C1 ⊠ 3 Praça do Comércio ☎ 218 879 259 🚋 Tram 15 Ⓖ Mon–Sat 8–10:30pm

Casa da Comida €€€€

Tucked away in a side street above the Rato, not far from the Amoreiras shopping centre, this restaurant is one of Lisbon's finest and with prices to match. Inside it has the atmosphere of a noble mansion house with a beautiful patio and sophisticated decor. The cuisine is superb and perfectly combines French flair with traditional Portuguese dishes using local crab and clams, pheasant and partridge. Desserts are fabulous too and there's an excellent wine cellar. This is the perfect place for an celebration or an expensive treat.

🔠 196 off A4 ⊠ Travessa das Amoreiras ☎ 213 885 376; www.casacomida.pt 🚇 Metro Rato Ⓖ Tue–Fri 1–3, Mon–Sat 8–11. Closed Sunday

Casa do Alentejo €–€€

Behind a run-of-the-mill façade and up a gloomy staircase, there's a fantastic, if slightly decadent, patrician mansion, with Moorish *patios* and beautiful skylights, decorated with carved wood, gleaming *azulejos* and huge palms. The reliably good and well-priced food served in two dining rooms, one more subdued, the other lined with bright tiles, gives you a taste of the Alentejo, with classic dishes such as *carne de porco à alentejana* (pork with coriander and clams). Exhibitions and other events are also held in this house dedicated to "a people, a region and a culture".

🔠 196 B5 ⊠ Rua das Portas de Santo Antão 58 ☎ 213 405 140 🚇 Metro Restauradores Ⓖ Daily 12–3, 7–11

Cerverjaria Trindade €–€€

This boisterous but cheerful beerhouse (*cerverjaria*) also serves seafood, and is popular with artists and locals. Once a convent, the Trindade has beautiful vaulted ceilings and a splendid display of *azulejos*. Draught Portuguese beer is served ice-cold and is the perfect accompaniment to the simple, but delicious, seafood dishes.

🞢 196 B3 ⊠ Rua Nova da Trinidade 20 ☎ 213 423 506; www.cervejariatrindade.pt 🚇 Metro Rossio 🕙 Daily 10–2am

Chafariz do Vinho €–€€

Located in a very attractive traditional building that also houses an interesting water museum (with exhibitions on the history of aqueducts), you'll find a good choice of wines here, all chosen by award winning Portuguese wine writer João Paulo Martins. Good food too, with tapas and other food/wine tasting plates.

🞢 196 off A5 ⊠ Chafariz da Mãe d'Água, Rua da Mãe d'Água à Praça da Alegria ☎ 213 422 079; http://chafarizdovinho.com 🚇 Avenida 🕙 Tue–Sun 6–2am

Comida de Santo €€–€€€

Of the many Brazilian restaurants in Lisbon, this one has the most

reliably good food, served with a smile in tropical surroundings, including a stylised jungle fresco. It can get very busy, especially on Sundays when nearly everywhere else is closed, so book. The *caipirinhas* (lime and white rum cocktails) are expertly prepared, as is the delicious Bahia-dominated cuisine. The portions of thick *vatapás* (spicy shrimp purée) and succulent chicken *muquecas* (cooked in coconut milk) are easily enough for two, as is the *feijoada* (pork and black bean stew) with its trimmings of toasted manioc and orange slices. Fresh mango and papaya round off your meal.

🞢 196 off A4 ⊠ Calçada Engenheiro Miguel Pais 39 ☎ 213 963 339 🚇 Metro Rato 🕙 Daily 12:30–3:30, 7:30–1am

Cultura do Cha €

A neighbourhood institution, this lovely teashop has a calming atmosphere, friendly staff and plenty of character. Choose from a range of herbal and black teas

from all over in world, plus coffees, healthy smoothies and juices, hot chocolates and good snacks. There is plenty to look at inside, because the walls are covered with works from local artists.

🞢 196 A3 ⊠ 38 Rua das Salgadeiras, Bairro Alto ☎ 213 430 272 🚇 Baixa-Chiado 🕙 Daily 8–9:30

Mercado de Santa Clara €–€€

One of the few places in Lisbon which is open for Sunday lunch, this wonderful spot, perfectly located above the market hall, gets packed out with customers for its special *feijoada* (bean stew) buffets and the *cozido à portuguesa* (a regional dish of mixed meats and sausages with vegetables). The rest of the week you can taste refined cuisine using superbly fresh produce from the local market: a range of *bacalhau* dishes, steaks and another local favourite, *iscas com elas* (fried liver in white wine). There are also great views of the Panteão Nacional and the river.

🞢 197 F4 ⊠ Campo Santa Clara 7 ☎ 218 873 986 🚊 Tram 28 🕙 Tue–Sat 12:30–3, 8–10:30, Sun 12:30–3

Pap'Açorda €€€

This Bairro Alto haunt of the rich, famous and glamorous never seems to go out of fashion. Humorous but professional waiters give diners an attentive service, while the lavish decor of crystal chandeliers, plentiful plants and a lively atmosphere explain the restaurant's popularity. But people also come for the expertly prepared food. The emphasis is on mussels, clams and other seafood. The house speciality is the Lisbon delicacy, *açorda*, a concoction of bread, oil, egg and coriander that tastes far better than it sounds or looks. The *açorda real*, with lobster and prawns, is truly "regal". To round off a delicious meal, the chocolate mousse is famous for being the best in town.

🞢 196 A3 ⊠ Rua da Atalaia 57–59 ☎ 213 464 811 🚇 Metro Baixa-Chiado. Bus 58, 790 🕙 Tue–Sat 12–2, 8–11

Pavilhão Chinês €

A classy tearoom and cocktail bar combined on the edge of the Bairro Alto, the Chinese Pavilion must also be one of the most eccentric bars in the world, let alone Lisbon. The walls, cabinets and ceilings of its three red lacquer salons are crammed with ornaments, including fans and oriental porcelain, statues and dolls, lead soldiers and iron helmets, all collected by Lisbon celebrity Luís Pinto Coelho, also responsible for the aptly named Paródia (Rua do Patrocínio 26) in Campo de Ourique. Both are unusual places for an aperitif.

⊞ 196 off A4 ⊠ Rua Dom Pedro V 89 ☎ 213 424 729 ⬚ Metro Restauradores and Elevador da Glória ⊙ Mon–Sat 6–2am, Sun 9–2am

Primeiro de Maio €€

With friendly service and a loyal clientele of journalists, intellectuals and bohemian types, this favourite restaurant dishes up very tasty Portuguese specials. This is one of the best places to try starters such as *pastéis de bacalhau* (bite-sized cod cakes), *peixinhos da horta* (green bean fritters) or *favas com enchidos* (broad beans and sausage). As an *adega* (wine cellar), one of the few traditional ones left in the Bairro Alto, it also has decent house wine and bottled vintages. Recommended.

⊞ 196 A3 ⊠ Rua da Atalaia 8 ☎ 213 426 840 ⬚ Metro Baixa-Chiado ⊙ Mon–Fri 12–3, 7–10:30, Sat 7–10:30

Solar do Vinho do Porto €–€€

A cosy but modern place, furnished with comfortable sofas and a dimly lit bar, Solar do Vinho d Porto is the perfect place to taste your way through a bewildering list of more than 300 ports. It's the ideal way to find out which ones are to your taste – and which ones are within your budget range. Vintage ports, however, can only be sampled by the bottle, so come with other port fans so you can share the bill. Incidentally, there's another solar in port's home city of Porto, housed in the Museu Romântico, Rua de Entre Quintas (▶ 81).

⊞ 196 A4 ⊠ Rua de São Pedro de Alcântara 45 ☎ 213 475 707; www.ivp.pt ⬚ Metro Baixa-Chiado ⊙ Mon–Sat 11–12

Tágide €€€€

For reliable, classic Portuguese cuisine with a pronounced French influence, Tágide remains at the pinnacle of gastronomic Lisbon and well worth the pricey bill. If you want a window seat – book well ahead and specify this requirement – you are also treated to incredible views of the city and river that would distract you from the food were it not so delicious. Not surprisingly the wine cellar is one of the most refined in the city, and you can choose a suitable wine to accompany different regional dishes. The baked *bacalhau* is the omnipresent house special and the cheese board is first class. Recommended for a fine, albeit expensive, dining experience.

⊞ 196 B2 ⊠ Largo da Academia Nacional de Belas Artes 18 ☎ 213 404 01 ⬚ Metro Baixa-Chiado ⊙ Mon–Sat 12–2:30, 7:30–10:30

SINTRA

Tulhas €€

A charming restaurant located right in the centre of Sintra (▶ 60–62), and close to the tourist office, Tulhas is in a beautiful rustic building that used to be a barn. The food is varied, with both fish and meat dishes on the menu, and you should certainly try the house special, *lombos de vitela com vinho de Madeira* (medallions of veal in Madeira sauce). An *ementa turística* (set menu of the day) makes this an ideal place for a quiet and relaxing authentic lunch during a day's sightseeing in this beautiful hilltop town.

⊞ 200 A2 ⊠ Rua Gil Vicente 4–6 ☎ 219 232 378 ⊙ Thu–Tue 12–3:30, 7–10

Where to...
Shop

MARKETS AND SHOPPING MALLS

Feira da Ladra (Campo de Santa Clara, São Vicente, Tuesday morning and Saturday) is Lisbon's flea market. Mercado da Ribeira (Cais do Sodré, Avenida 24 de Julho, closed Sunday) is the most interesting traditional market.

Visit the modern mall of Armazéns do Chiado (Rua do Carmo), for independent shops and international chain stores.

The landmark towers of Amoreiras (Avenida Engenheiro Duarte Pacheco), Centro Comercial Colombo (Avenida Lusiada, Benfica) and Centro Comercial Vasco da Gama (Avenida Dom João II) out at the Parque das Nações, are great places to window shop.

CLOTHES AND FOOTWEAR

In the hip Bairro Alto, Eldorado (Rua do Norte 23), Fátima Lopes (Rua da Atalaia 36) and Manuel Alves & José Manuel Gonçalves (Rua das Flores 105/1D) are three fashion boutiques, the first specialising in retro clothing.

In Chiado, Ana Salazar (Rua do Carmo 87) is still one of the leading names of local couture, while Atelier Gardénia (Rua Nova do Almada 96 and Rua Garrett 54) sells great clothes by Luis Buchinho, Nuño Gama and others. José António Tenente (Travessa do Carmo 8) is the place for suits.

In the Baixa and around the Rossio head for Hamrou in Chiado (Rua Augusta 250) for bespoke tailoring. Suitably for "Gold Street",

Araújos (Rua do Ouro, also known as Rua Aurea, 261) is a top jeweller and Azevedo Rua (Praça Dom Pedro IV 69) is the best milliner in the capital.

ANTIQUES AND CRAFTS

Religious statues are worth a look at Galeria da Arcada (Rua Dom Pedro V 49). António Trindade (Rua do Alecrim 79) has antiques. You can find delicate lead crystal at Atlantis Cristal (Centro Colombo and branches). Another excellent Portuguese design shop is Alma Lusa (363 Rua de Sao Bento). There are branches in Lisbon and at Lisbon Airport.

For azulejos try Ratton (Rua Academia das Ciências 2C, São Bento) for modern designs, Sant'Ana (Rua do Alecrim 95, Chiado) for reproductions, Solar (Rua Dom Pedro V 68) for antiques, and Viúva Lamego (Calçada do Sacramento 29, Chiado) for made-to-order specials. Casa dos Tapetes

Arraiolos (Rua da Imprensa Nacional 116) sells hand-made carpets from Arraiolos (▶ 146).

FOOD AND DRINK

Manteigaria Silva (Rua Dom Antão de Almada 1C-D) is best for bacalhau, while Manuel Tavares (Rua da Betesga 1A-B) has an array of sausages and candied fruit. A great deli is Martins & Costa (Rua Alexandre Herculano 34). The Garrafeira Nacional (Rua dos Dourados 149–157) and Pasteleria San Roque in Bairro Alto (57 Rua Dom Pedro V) is where it is rumoured that Lisbon's best bread is sold. The shop also won Wine Merchant of the Year and has a wine museum. Wine connoisseurs should not miss Coisas do Arco do Vinho (Centro Cultural de Belém) for speciality corkscrews and fine vintages. At the Antiga Confeitaria de Belém (Rua de Belém 84–88, ▶ 69), you can buy boxes of fresh pastéis.

Where to...
Be Entertained

INFORMATION

Get tickets for football matches, concerts and events at the **Agência Alvalade** (Alvalade Shopping, Praça de Alvalade 6, tel: 217 955 859), at the **ABEP booth** (Praça dos Restauradores, tel: 213 475 823/4) or FNAC stores in shopping malls.

ARTS AND CULTURE

You can hear chamber, choral and orchestral music at the **Fundação Calouste Gulbenkian** (▶ 50–51). The **CCB (Centro Cultural de Belém**; ▶ 47) stages exhibitions, theatre and dance events.

Movie fans should check out the programme at the **Cinemateca** (Rua Barata Salgueiro 39, box office tel: 213 596 266; www.cinemateca.pt) and the **Monumental** (Praça Duque de Saldanha, tel: 213 142 223), Lisbon's best art-house cinema.

Teatro Camões (tel: 218 923 470; www.cnb.pt) is now home to the superb Companhia Nacional de Bailado (National Ballet).

SPECTATOR SPORTS

Footballs fans won't be disappointed and might like to try and attend a match at either of the capital's top teams' home grounds: **Sporting** (Estádio de Alvalade, Edifício Visconde de Alvalade, Rua Professor Fernando da Fonseca; tel: 217 516 000) and **Benfica** (Estádio da Luz, Avenida General Norton de Matos, tel: 217 219 500).

For a game of **roller-hockey** at weekends go to **Paço d'Arcos** (Pavilhão Gimnodesportivo, Avenida Bonneville Franco, tel: 214 432 238).

MUSIC

The tiny **Hot Clube** (Praça da Alegria 39) is still Lisbon's best jazz venue, while **Ateneu Café** (Rua das Portas de Santo Antão, 110, tel: 917 231 484) is a lively restaurant and bar with live jazz sessions. It's carnival every night (except Sundays) at **Brazilian Bruxa Bar** (Rua São Mamede 35). The **Teatro Nacional de São Carlos** (Rua Serpa Pinto 9) has excellent acoustics.

FAMILY FUN

The best **beaches** near Lisbon are at Caparica, across the River Tagus or between Carcavelos and Guincho on the city side of the Tagus. World **windsurfing** championships are held at Guincho.

The **golf course** at Estoril is one of Portugal's best.

NIGHTLIFE

Lux (Avenida Infante Dom Henrique, Armazém A, Santa Apolónia) and **Frágil** (Rua da Atalaia 126) are both popular.

Santos and the **Avenida 24 de Julho** are home to Lisbon's club scene: **Indústria** (Rua do Instituto Industrial 6), **Kapital** (Avenida 24 de Julho 68) and **Kremlin** (Escadinhas da Praia 5) are three good ones.

GAY NIGHTLIFE

Many of Lisbon's gay venues are located in the **Príncipe Real** district. **Frágil** (▶ above) is gay at weekends, and **Harry's** (Rua São Pedro de Alcântara 57, Bairro Alto). Lesbian bars include **Memorial** (Rua Gustavo Matos Sequeira 42A), **Sabath Café** (14 Rua Quintinhas De Fora) and **Tejo Bar** (Beco Do Vigário, 1a).

Northern Portugal

Getting Your Bearings

The north is the cradle of Portugal and Guimarães was Portugal's first king, Afonso Henriques, inherited Portucale and, from here, extended it south during the Reconquest from the Moors. It was the north, too, that produced Portugal's last and longest ruling dynasty, the dukes of the house of Bragança, who came to the throne in 1640 and ruled until the foundation of the republic in 1910.

Porto, the biggest city of the north, grew rich when merchants travelled to Brazil, returning with gold and diamonds, which financed the city's extravagant churches and palaces. Later, it profited from the port wine trade, which continues to dominate Vila Nova de Gaia and the valleys of the Upper Douro.

The north is divided into two contrasting regions. The Minho, which occupies the historic boundaries of Portucale between the Douro and Minho rivers, is a land of lush, green countryside fed by the highest rainfall in Portugal. Much of the land is given over to smallholdings, though there also manor houses, many of which take in guests. This densely populated region hosts some of Portugal's biggest country markets and fairs. It also contains two important historical towns – Portugal's first capital, Guimarães – to be European City of Culture in 2012 – and its religious centre, Braga. .

Trás-os-Montes is a wild and rugged region of mountains and remote villages with a harsh climate. Few crops survive except the hardiest vines, and the region grows some of the grapes for Mateus Rose, as well as for port wine production.

Above: Statue in the gardens at Casa de Mateus

Page 75: 25 April celebrations in the Gaia area of Porto

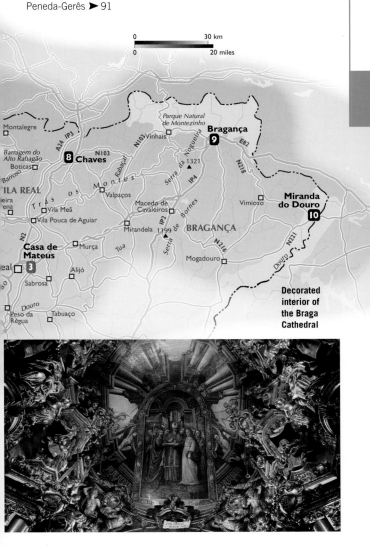

Decorated interior of the Braga Cathedral

In Three Days

If you're not quite sure where to begin your travels, this itinerary recommends a practical and enjoyable three days out in Northern Portugal, taking in some of the best places to see using the Getting your Bearings map on the previous page. For more information see the main entries.

Day 1

Morning
Spend the morning exploring the old town of **1 Porto** (➤ 80–83). Start by climbing Torre dos Clérigos for an overview of the city, then wander around the Bolhão market and have a coffee at **Café Majestic** (➤ 98) before walking uphill to the cathedral. Drop down to the Ribeira district (above) to admire the opulence of the Bolsa (Stock Exchange) and São Francisco church before lunch in one of the riverside cafés.

Afternoon and Evening
Walk across Ponte Dom Luís I to **2 Vila Nova de Gaia** (➤ 84–85). Spend the afternoon touring the wine lodges and tasting port. In summer you can take a boat cruise on the River Douro. Return to the north bank for dinner on Cais da Ribeira at **Filha de Mãe Preta** (➤ 98), overlooking the quayside.

Day 2

Morning
Leave Porto on the IP4/A4 to Amarante and Vila Real, to visit the **3 Casa de Mateus** (➤ 86–87). After a stroll around the gardens, take the N2 south to Peso da Régua for lunch by the river.

Afternoon and Evening

From here you can do a shortened version of the Port Country tour (➤ 84), travelling through the steeply terraced vineyards (left) between Peso da Régua and Pinhão on a beautiful stretch of the Douro Valley. Returning to Vila Real, take the IP4 to Amarante and head north on the N101 to **6 Guimarães** (right; ➤ 93). Follow the signs to the castle (right), where Portugal's first king was born, then wander down to the old town for a drink at one of the cafés on Largo da Oliveira. Stay at Pousada de Santa Marinha (tel: 253 511 249, €€€–€€€€), in a 12th-century convent on a hill overlooking Guimarães. One of the finest of all the *pousadas*, this one has fountains and *azulejo*-tiled cloisters.

Day 3

Morning

Make an early start to visit the cathedral in **4 Braga** (➤ 88) and the sanctuary at **4 Bom Jesus** (➤ 89). From here, drive north on the IP1/A3 to the attractive town of Ponte da Lima for a walk along the river and a drink in one of the cafés by the Roman bridge. Follow the N203 along the Lima Valley to enter the **5 Parque Nacional da Peneda-Gerês** (below; ➤ 91–92).

Afternoon

Allow plenty of time to explore the national park. Tour through the villages of Soajo and Lindoso before briefly entering Spain on the way to the spa town of Caldas do Gerês. Take the N103 to **8 Chaves** (➤ 94), If time, visit **9 Braganca** (➤ 94), and take the motorway back to Porto.

◻Porto

Portugal's second city enjoys a magnificent position, tumbling down the steep slopes on the north bank of the River Douro. A workaday, rough-and-ready port city, frayed at the edges but wonderfully charismatic, Porto makes a good introduction to the many delights of northern Portugal.

Porto (whose English name, Oporto, derives from *o porto*, "the port") has been occupied for at least 3,000 years. The Romans built a harbour here at *Portus*, an important river crossing on the route from Lisbon to Braga. The settlement on the south bank, where Vila Nova de Gaia now stands, was called *Cale*. These two towns gave their names to the county of Portucale, brought by Teresa of Castile as her dowry when she married Henry of Burgundy in 1095. When their son, Afonso Henriques, captured the rest of the country from the Moors, he named his new kingdom Portugal. In more recent history, Porto was named European Capital of Culture in 2001.

The Modern City

The heart of Porto is **Avenida dos Aliados**, whose central promenade, with flowerbeds and a mosaic pavement, leads up to the town hall. From the foot of the avenue, on Praça da Liberdade, you can see the baroque church and tower of **Clérigos** to the west. Designed by the Italian architect Nicolau Nasoni, this was the first oval church in Portugal. The tower, 75m (246 feet) high, is one of the tallest in the country and you can climb it for views over the city and the wine lodges of Vila Nova da Gaia (➤ 84–85).

East of Avenida dos Aliados, **Baixa** is the main shopping district, centred around the covered Bolhão market. You can buy vegetables upstairs, while downstairs there are stalls offering maize bread, fresh fish, live chickens, pigs' ears and tripe. Across the street are several *confeitarias* (pastry shops) featuring Porto's other speciality, *bacalhau*, large slabs of salt cod (➤ 29).

Rua de Santa Catarina is lined with leather and jewellery shops and the old-world Café Majestic (➤ 98), and leads to Praça da Batalha.

The **sé** (cathedral) is clearly visible from here, built on a rocky outcrop overlooking the Douro. Begun in the 12th century as a Romanesque fortress church, it was remodelled in Gothic style. The 14th-

Above: The Ponte Dom Luís I bridge crosses the River Douro from Ribeira to Porto

Left: View of Ribeira area of Porto

century cloisters are decorated with *azulejos* depicting the life of the Virgin. A grand staircase by Nicolau Nasoni leads to the chapter house and an upper gallery that has fine views. There are more good views from the terrace in front of the cathedral, and a street market most weekdays.

The area between the cathedral and the waterfront was declared a Unesco World Heritage Site in 1996. Walk down through the **Bairro da Sé**, the oldest quarter, similar to Alfama (➤ 54–57) in Lisbon. The daily life of the district mingles with ancient churches and *azulejo*-tiled walls as housewives gather at the public washhouse and shop in the local market.

ART VERSUS PORT

The **Museu Nacional Soares dos Reis** (Rua Dom Manuel II, tel: 223 393 770; www.ipmuseus.pt, Tue 2–6, Wed–Sun 10–6, moderate; Sun 10–2; free) is Portugal's oldest national museum, dedicated to Portuguese art, including the work of the 19th-century sculptor António Soares dos Reis. The **Museu Romântico** (Quinta da Macieirinha Palace, Rua de Entrequintas 220, tel: 226 057 033, Tue–Sat 10–12:30, 2–5:30, Sun 2–5:30, inexpensive; Sat–Sun free), is a re-creation of a 19th-century aristocratic home. The same building houses the Solar do Vinho do Porto (➤ 71).

ART, MUSIC AND BEACHES
Take the bus to Serralves to the **Museu de Arte Contemporânea** (Rua Dom João de Castro 210, tel: 808 200 543; www.serralves.pt) a modern art museum that opened in 1999, designed by Álvaro Siza Vieira. It is situated in the gardens of the art deco Casa de Serralves, with a rose garden, arboretum, tea-house, lake and sculpture park. Continue on the bus to **Foz** where you can stroll along the promenade. The main Avenida da Boavista, which runs from the centre to the beach at Foz do Douro has recently been renovated with shops and houses the new Casa da Música, by Dutch architect Rem Koolhas (610 Avenida da Boavista, tel: 220 120 220; www.casadamusica.com).

A statue of Henry the Navigator stands on **Praça do Infante**, near the former customs house where it is believed he was born. Also on this square is **Palácio da Bolsa**, the Stock Exchange built in 1834 over the ruins of the São Francisco convent. The highlight here is the Arabian Room, whose carved wood, gold leaf and Arabic inscriptions were modelled on the Alhambra in the Spanish city of Granada. There is a restaurant in the Palacio da Bolsa, called O Comercial, to honour the spirit of the building.

Behind the building, the **Igreja de São Francisco** is richly ornamented with gilded baroque carvings. Before the church was ransacked by Napoleon's troops, there was more than 400kg (880lbs) of gold covering the chestnut-wood walls. The church authorities were so shocked at this blatant display of extravagance that they ordered the church

Statue of Henry the Navigator on Praça do Infante

A traditional grocers shopfront in Porto

to be deconsecrated. Notice the **Tree of Jesse**, in carved and gilded wood, adorning the north wall. The visit includes the **catacombs**, where there is an ossuary of human bones.

   Ribeira, the fishermen's district, is the most atmospheric quarter, with narrow streets and painted houses rising above riverside arcades. A morning market is held on weekdays, but the area comes alive at night, with quayside restaurants and bars in the shadow of **Ponte Dom Luís I**. This two-tier iron bridge links Porto to Vila Nova de Gaia (➤ 84–85).

TAKING A BREAK

Café Majestic (➤ 98) is belle époque with oak-framed mirrors and leather banquettes, serving cakes and scones.

✚ 198 A3

Tourist Information Office
✉ Rua Clube dos Fenianos 25 (top of Avenida dos Aliados) ☎ 223 393 470;
www.portoturismo.pt

Torre dos Clérigos
✉ Rua de São Felipe Néry ☎ 222 001 729 🕒 Apr–Oct daily 9:30–1, 2–7;
Aug 10–7; Mar–Nov 10–12, 2–5 💶 Inexpensive

Sé
✉ Terreiro da Sé ☎ 222 059 028
🕒 Mon–Sat 8:45–12:30, 2:30–6/7,
Sun 8:30–12:30, 2:30–6/7 💶 Church
free, cloisters inexpensive

Palácio da Bolsa
✉ Rua Ferreira Borges ☎ 223
399 000; www.palaciodabolsa.pt
🕒 Apr–Oct daily 9–7; Nov–Mar 9–1,
2–6 💶 Moderate

The ornate Baroque altar in the cathedral

Igreja de São Francisco
✉ Rua do Infante Dom Henrique
☎ 222 062 100 🕒 Daily
9–5:30/6/7/8 💶 Moderate

PORTO: INSIDE INFO

Top tips The best way to get around Porto is **on foot**, but you will need a good pair of shoes for all the steep hills and cobbled streets.

■ Take one of the **river cruises** that depart regularly in summer from the quayside at Cais da Ribeira or the waterfront at Vila Nova de Gaia. Just turn up and buy a ticket. For trips of 1 hour try **Doura Acima** (tel: 222 006 418; www.douroacima.pt) or **Rota do Douro** (tel: 223 759 042). For longer cruises try **Douro Azul** (tel: 223 402 500; www.douroazul.com).

■ For the **best views of Porto**, cross the upper level of the Dom Luís I bridge to reach the terrace of Nossa Senhora da Serra do Pilar on the south bank.

■ Visit the new **Port Wine Museum**, housed in an 18th-century building on Rua de Monchique, (tel: 222 076 300; www.cm-porto.pt).

2 Vila Nova de Gaia

The names of famous port shippers, Sandeman, Ferreira and Taylor, spelled out in neon letters on the hillside, draw you irresistibly across the water to Vila Nova de Gaia, the home of the port wine trade. Here, barrels of port mature in cool cellars and lodges, many of which can be visited for tastings and tours.

Although the grapes for port are grown in the Douro Valley, the ageing process takes place in Vila Nova de Gaia. It was British traders who first chose this spot at the mouth of the River Douro, whose north-facing position ensured a high level of humidity and a cool ocean breeze.

This area is changing however, the narrow, steep slopes are still full of port houses, but more and more of them are moving their storage and warehouse facilities to outside of the city, and converting their lodges into tourist centre, restaurants and hotels. The city council has even bigger ideas to transform this historic centre into a hot spot of leisure and tourism, with plans for a new pedestrian bridge across to Ribeira, cable-cars, a port wine cultural centre and a museum dedicated to Barcos Rabelos; the traditional flat bottomed boats that once transported the port wine downriver from the Duoro Valley. Currently, you can still see the Barcos Rabelos moored outside many port houses, or sailed once a year during the annual regatta on 24 June (➤ 177).

View of the famous port lodges

THE DOURO BY TRAIN
Take a train journey through the Douro Valley, from Porto to Pocinho by the Spanish border. It runs for 100km (62 miles) by the Douro River through seemingly endless stretches of beautiful scenery. There's a steam train on Saturdays from Regua to Tua (www.cp.pt).

The tasting terrace at Taylor's

The best way to approach Vila Nova de Gaia is to walk from Porto (► 80–83) across **Ponte Dom Luís I**. The new tram also goes across the bridge from Porto to Vila Nova de Gaia.

The tourist office on the waterfront will give you a map and a list of **port lodges** (a corruption of the Portuguese word *loja*, meaning "warehouse"). Most people start with **Sandeman** (Largo Miguel Bombarda 3, tel: 223 740 500, moderate), founded by Briton George Sandeman in 1790. The tour includes a museum, slide show and informative guides.

The tour is informative, but it is interesting to compare it with one of the smaller firms. **Ferreira** (tel: 223 746 107, inexpensive), also on the waterfront, was founded in 1751 and is still Portuguese owned. The tasting room is decorated with *azulejos* and there is an archive of historical exhibits.

Other lodges that can be visited include **Calem** (tel: 223 746 660; www.calem.pt) is Spanish owned and has an excellent visitor centre; **Ramos Pinto** (tel: 223 775 011); and **Real Companhia Velha** (tel: 223 775 100), founded by Dom José I in 1756 to challenge Britain's monopoly on port.

TAKING A BREAK

There are several restaurants and cafés down by the waterfront – try **Dom Luís** (► 98) for good-value Portuguese food.

✚ 198 A3

Tourist Information Office
✉ Avenida Diogo Leite   ☎ 223 703 735

VILA NOVA DE GAIA: INSIDE INFO

Top tip Let your tastebuds explore the many **different styles** of port: the aperitif, dry white, amber-coloured tawny, rich ruby and vintage (► 10–11).

Hidden gem It's worth making the steep climb to **Taylor's** (Rua do Choupelo 250, tel: 223 742 800), owned by the Fladgate partnership who also own Croft, Fonseca and Delaforce, founded in 1692 and the last surviving family-owned British port house. It is housed in an old-style lodge and offers a very friendly welcome, although this is due to be converted into an 84-room luxury hotel. The free tour is helpful, the tastings are generous and there are wonderful views from the terrace over the Douro and Ponte Dom Luís I.

③ Casa de Mateus

The building that graces the label of every bottle of Mateus Rosé is as perfect a Portuguese manor house as you can find. With fine furniture, paintings, formal gardens and family chapel, a visit to the Casa de Mateus offers a rare glimpse into the lives of the Portuguese aristocracy.

It was built in 1745 by the third *Morgado* de Mateus. His descendants, the counts of Vila Real, still live in a wing of the house. The architect is unknown, but it is attributed to Nicolau Nasoni, the Italian who designed the Clérigos tower in Porto (➤ 80) and who was a major influence on the development of Portuguese baroque.

The façade of the house is immediately impressive, a contrast of whitewash and granite reflected in a pool that was added when the gardens were extensively remodelled in the 1930s. The forecourt is dominated by an immense double stairway, whose balustrades lead the eye up towards the pediment, flanked by classical statues and crowned by a family escutcheon.

The house can only be visited on 30-minute guided tours, and the guides tend to rush you through. You begin in the entrance hall, with its carved chestnut ceiling, 18th-century

The landscaped gardens and elegant facade of the Casa de Mateus

CASA DE MATEUS: INSIDE INFO

Top tips Classical music concerts are held in the grounds on summer weekends.
- If you're looking for **Mateus Rosé**, don't look here – it is produced by the Sogrape company (www.sogrape.pt) from vineyards in the Beiras and has no connection with the Mateus estate, other than the label on the bottle. They do have their own wine on the estate also, called Alvarelhão, which you can buy in the shop.

In more depth The nearby town of **Vila Real** (Royal Town), dramatically perched above a gorge at the confluence of the Corgo and Cabril rivers, is the capital of the Upper Douro. The best sights are the Gothic cathedral and the house on the main street where the explorer Diogo Cão, who discovered the mouth of the Congo in 1482, was born.

sedan chairs and family coat of arms on the wall. This leads into the **Four Seasons Room**, which takes its name from the strange paintings of seasonal vegetables in human form. On the table in the centre stands a 16th-century Hispano-Arab plate, the oldest item on display.

The neighbouring **Blue Room** features Chinese porcelain in a 17th-century Chinese cabinet, while the **Dining Room** has a Brazilian jacaranda wood dresser containing stunning Portuguese china and silver.

The highlight of the **Four Corners Room**, where ladies gathered after dinner while the men smoked and drank port, is a fine, hand-carved Indo-Portuguese ivory and wood travelling desk.

The family **museum** has several rare treasures, including the original copperplates by Jean Fragonard for a limited edition of *Os Lusíadas* (*The Lusiads*) by Portuguese poet Luís de Camões, produced in 1817 and sent by the Morgado de Mateus to 250 libraries and noble families in Europe to promote Portuguese history and culture. Some of the letters of thanks are displayed, along with religious vestments and chalices, relics of saints and martyrs, a 17th-century ivory crucifix and a statue of the Virgin carved from a single piece of ivory.

Be sure to walk around the **gardens**, with their dark avenue of cedar trees, neatly clipped box hedges and peaceful views over the surrounding countryside.

TAKING A BREAK

There is a small **café** in the gardens for snacks and refreshments, which is open in summer.

🚩 198 C4   ✉ 4km (2.5 miles) east of Vila Real   ☎ 259 323 121; www.casademateus.com   🕐 Jun–Sep 9–7:30; Mar–May, Oct 9–1, 2–6; Nov–Feb 10–1, 2–5   🚌 Vila Real   💵 House expensive, gardens moderate

④ Braga and Bom Jesus

Braga likes to describe itself as the Portuguese Rome. The largest city in the Minho has a long history as a religious capital that has left it with churches, Renaissance mansions and Portugal's most spectacularly sited sanctuary, Bom Jesus.

Braga

An old saying has it that "while Coimbra studies and Lisbon plays, Porto works and Braga prays". The Roman bishop St Martin of Braga converted the local Swabian tribe to Christianity in the sixth century AD and established the custom, still used in Portugal, of naming the days of the week in numerical order rather than after pagan gods (Monday, *segunda-feira*, is "second day", Tuesday, *terça-feira*, "third day", etc). In the 12th century, following the Christian conquest, Braga became the seat of the Portuguese archbishops and has remained that way ever since.

Start your visit at **Praça da República**, an arcaded square at the end of a long public garden with fountains and children's playgrounds. Stallholders sell Minho artefacts such as clogs and wooden toys, and there are old-fashioned cafés beneath the arches close to the 14th-century town keep. From here, walk down Rua do Souto, a pedestrianised shopping street, passing the former bishop's palace on your way to the **sé** (cathedral).

Leisurely outdoor dining at the Cafe Vianna, Praca de Republica

The **cathedral** was begun in 1070 on the site of a mosque and is Portugal's oldest cathedral. Originally built in Romanesque style, the subsequent Gothic, Renaissance and baroque additions give it an eclectic feel. The main Romanesque doorway survives at the western end, though it is covered by a Gothic porch that was added in the late 15th century. Among the artists who worked on the cathedral are João de Castilho, one of the architects of the Mosteiro dos Jerónimos in Lisbon (➤ 48), and the French sculptor Nicolas Chanterene, whose statue of Nossa Senhora da Leite (Our Lady of the Milk) is sheltered beneath a Gothic canopy at the cathedral's eastern end.

The hilltop sanctuary of the Church of Bom Jesus

The cloister gives access to the **Museu de Arte Sacra**, whose junk-shop atmosphere is both fascinating and frustrating. There are amazing treasures here – gold, silver, ivory, diamonds, emeralds, pearls and jade – but it's all arranged haphazardly without labelling, and the guides do not allow you much time to linger. Among the items on display is a simple cross, used by Pedro Álvares Cabral in 1500 to celebrate the first ever Mass in Brazil.

The stairway is lined with statues of biblical figures

The tour of the museum also includes the **Capela dos Reis**, where Henry of Burgundy and Teresa of Castile, parents of Portugal's first king, are buried in 16th-century tombs.

Tickets also allow entry to the **Coro Alto** (upper choir), with gilded baroque organs and carved choir stalls.

Bom Jesus

At weekends, pilgrims and day trippers flock to Bom Jesus do Monte, a hilltop sanctuary 5km (3 miles) east of Braga. Although primarily a place for prayer, this is also a popular picnic spot, with gardens, woodland and a lake.

The centrepiece is the long **baroque stairway** with more than 1,000 steps. It was begun by the archbishop of Braga in 1722 and finished in the 19th century. True pilgrims ascend the stairway on their knees, but most people walk or take the old-fashioned **funicular** (daily 8–8, every 30 minutes). It's best to make the climb on foot to appreciate the architecture.

Via Sacra (Holy Way) begins with a winding path lined with chapels depicting the Stations of the Cross. Each of the chapels, dripping with wax from pilgrims' candles, is filled with life-size terracotta figures evoking scenes from Christ's Passion. As you near the summit, you reach a magnificent ornamental double stairway, whose grey granite is perfectly set off against whitewashed walls. Fountains depict the five human senses, with water gushing out of ears, eyes, nose and mouth, while further up, the **Staircase of the Three Virtues** features the allegorical figures of Faith, Hope and Charity.

The monumental stairway to Bom Jesus

TAKING A BREAK

Visit the old-world **Café Vianna** (➤ 99) on Praça da República for coffee or a light snack, but for if you want a more substantial, traditional Portuguese meal try **Arcoense** (➤ 98).

✚ 198 B4

Tourist Information Office
✉ off Praça da República
☎ 253 262 550

Sé/Museu de Arte Sacra
✉ Rua D. Paio Mendes ☎ 253 263 317; www.geira.pt/MSeBraga/
🕐 Sumer daily 9–6:30; winter 9–5:30 💲 Church free, museum inexpensive

---

BRAGA AND BOM JESUS: INSIDE INFO

Top tips Leave your car in the **underground car park** beneath Praça da República, from where everything of interest can be reached in a short walk.
■ There are **regular buses** from Braga to the foot of Bom Jesus do Monte, or you can drive your car right up to the summit.

In more depth The **Palácio dos Biscainhos** (near the Arco da Porta Nova gateway, Tue–Sun 10–12:30, 2–5:30, inexpensive; Sun 10–12, free) is a 17th-century mansion with stucco ceilings and *azulejo* tiles which has been turned into a decorative arts museum featuring Portuguese furniture, silverware and ornamental gardens.

5 Parque Nacional da Peneda-Gerês

Portugal's only national park, covering an area of 700sq km (270sq miles), is a wild and dramatic place of windswept peaks, granite crags, deep river valleys and pretty rural villages. These are the sort of villages where the shepherds still migrate to higher ground each spring in search of pasture for their flock. The park consists of two main *serras* (mountain ranges), Serra da Peneda and Serra do Gerês, which are divided by the River Lima.

With few clear entry points and villages scattered around, most of the time it doesn't seem as if you are in a national park at all. Despite the presence of wildlife, such as golden eagles, wild horses and wolves, and rare varieties of Gerês lilies and ferns, it is a way of life as much as anything that is preserved here.

Rio Cavado, with the hills stretching far into the distance

You can visit the park by car on a day trip from Braga or the Minho coast. The easiest approach is along the Lima Valley from Ponte da Barca. This brings you to **Soajo** and **Lindoso**, both of which have a some village houses for rent (Aldeias de Portugal, tel: 258 931 750, www.aldeiasdeportugal.pt).

Both villages are known for their *espigueiros*, communal stone granaries topped with a cross and raised above the ground as a precaution against pests. At Lindoso, a group of 60 *espigueiros* are huddled beneath the castle, resembling tombstones in a cemetery. The castle here, right next to the Spanish border, has been attacked many times. Nowadays it is a peaceful spot, with long-horned Minho cattle grazing beneath its walls.

A minor road runs north between the two villages, with views over the Lima Valley on the way to **Peneda**. This small village contains a remarkable sanctuary, **Nossa Senhora da Peneda**, modelled on Bom Jesus (➤ 90) and reached by a similarly long staircase. The chapel, which from below seems almost to be built into the cliff, is the focus for a huge pilgrimage each September.

The most direct route between the two sections of the park means crossing the Spanish border at Lindoso and re-entering Portugal at Portela do Homem. The road dips down through a delightful wooded glade to the spa resort of **Caldas do Gerês**, where wild herbs, wildflower honey and chunky woollen sweaters are for sale and the main street is lined with spa hotels. Just outside town, a *miradouro* (viewpoint) offers fabulous views over the reservoir of Caniçada.

Long-horned Minho cattle

TAKING A BREAK

There are **cafés and bars** in the villages of Soajo, Lindoso and Caldas do Gerês. Apart from that a good option would be to stock up on **picnic** provisions in any of the nearby towns.

➕ 198 B5

Park Office
✉ Avenida António Macedo, Braga ☎ 253 203 480; www.icn.pt 🕐 Mon–Fri 9–12:30, 2–5:30

PARQUE NACIONAL DA PENEDA-GERÊS: INSIDE INFO

Top tips Allow **plenty of time** for driving within the park – the roads are steep and narrow, and the distances are greater than they look on the map.
■ Arrive in **Soajo** on a Sunday morning and you will find market stalls set up on the main street selling sausages, leather boots and farming tools.
■ This is Portugal's wettest areas so don't forget to take **waterproofs**.

At Your Leisure

6 Guimarães

Considered to be a side attraction on many tourist itineraries, this may well change after Guimaraes has celebrated its year as European Capital of Culture in 2012. Guimarães is also a UNESCO World Heritage Site, with a gorgeous medieval old town centre, which is car-free and very atmospheric.

The first capital of Portugal and the birthplace of its first king, Afonso Henriques, has a special place in the heart of the Portuguese nation. Most of the sights are situated in the old town beneath the castle. Climb over the ramparts of the 10th-century fortress, and visit the Romanesque chapel of **São Miguel do Castelo**, where Afonso Henriques was baptised, and where the warriors who helped him to conquer Portugal are buried.

Near by, beside a statue of Afonso, is the **Paço dos Duques de Bragança**, built in the 15th century by the first Duke of Bragança and restored under the Salazar dictatorship as a presidential palace. It has Flemish tapestries, Persian carpets, Portuguese furniture and a gallery of paintings by local artist José de Guimarães.

A short walk along the cobbled **Rua de Santa Maria** is like stepping back to another time, as it has remained essentially unchanged for centuries. Leading from the castle into the old town, there are restored medieval houses lining the street, ending in a pair of delightful squares, the Praça de Santiago and Largo da Oliveira, where a lively market is held on Saturday mornings.

Praça de Santiago is surrounded by wooden-balconied houses, while **Largo da Oliveira** has a Gothic shrine outside Nossa Senhora da Oliveira (Our Lady of the Olive Tree), whose cloisters house a museum of sacred art. The remains of the old city walls are also worth exploring.

The commanding position of the Santa Luzia overlooking Viana do Castelo

🔢 198 B4
Paço dos Duques de Bragança
☎ 253 412 273; www.cm-guimaraes.pt
🕐 Jun–Sep daily 9:30–6:30; Oct–May Tue–Sun 9:30–12, 2–5 💰 Moderate (Sun 9:30–12:30 free)

7 Viana do Castelo

The capital of the Costa Verde enjoys a perfect setting on the north bank of the Lima estuary, overlooked by the pinewoods of Monte de Santa Luzia. Once a small fishing port, Viana supplied many of the seafarers who sailed during the Age of Discovery and returned to the town to build Manueline and Renaissance mansions. The main square, **Praça da República**, is the focus of daily life, with its 16th-century fountain and Renaissance palace.

In summer it is a busy resort. You can walk or take the funicular through the pinewoods to reach a basilica and the ruins of a Celto-

Iberian settlement, or take the ferry across the river to **Praia do Cabedelo**, the town's splendid beach.

➕ 198 A4
Tourist Information Office
✉ Rua do Hospital Velho ☎ 258 822 620

❽ Chaves

A drive from Braga on the N103 threads through the Gerês and Barroso mountains to Chaves, famous for its smoked hams and red wine.

Inscriptions on a column on the Roman bridge across the Tamega, Chaves

Founded by the Romans as the spa town of *Aquae Fluviae*, Chaves ("keys") was awarded by Dom João I to Nuno Álvares Pereira as a reward for his victory against the Spanish at the battle of Aljubarrota (➤ 113).

A statue of the first Duke of Bragança, who lived in the castle, stands on **Praça de Camões**, the main square of the old town. Also here are the **Misericórdia** church, with a gilded altarpiece, painted ceiling and *azulejo*-tiled walls, and the **Museu da Região Flaviense**, devoted to archaeology and local crafts.

➕ 199 D4
Tourist Information Office
✉ Terreiro de Cavaleria ☎ 276 340 661; www.rt-atb.pt

Museu da Região Flaviense/Museu Militar
✉ Praça de Camões ☎ 276 340 500 🕑 Daily 9–12:30, 2–5:30 💶 Inexpensive

❾ Bragança

The remote capital of Trás-os-Montes is closely identified with Portugal's last ruling dynasty, descendants of an illegitimate son of João I who became the first Duke of Bragança – though later dukes preferred to live in their palace at Vila Viçosa (➤ 136–137).

The city is built around a 12th-century **citadel**, a walled village and museum where ancient monuments sit side by side with whitewashed houses and cobbled streets. The

The Romanesque five-sided Domus
Municipalis in Bragança

castle contains a small military
museum, and there are great views
from the tower. Near here is a
medieval pillory, an ancient stone pig
on its pedestal, and the five-sided
Domus Municipalis, Portugal's only
surviving example of Romanesque
civic architecture, where public
meetings were held and the *homens
bons* (good men) would gather to
settle disputes.

Just beneath the citadel, on the
way to the cathedral, the **Igreja de
São Vicente** is where Dom Pedro is
believed to have secretly married Inês
de Castro (➤ 110).

Bragança is a good base for
excursions into the Montesinho
natural park (➤ 24).

✚ 199 E5
Tourist Information Office
✉ Avenida Cidade de Zamora ☎ 273 381 273

Castelo and Museu Militar
☎ 273 322 378 ⏰ Sep–Jun Tue–Sun daily
9–12, 2–5; Jul 9–6; Aug 9–6:30 💵 Inexpensive
(Sun 9–12 free)

🔟 Miranda do Douro
Set on a cliff overlooking a deep
gorge in the River Douro, Miranda
is a medieval border town whose
inhabitants speak their own particular
dialect, *mirandês*. The 16th-century

sé (cathedral) includes the **Menino
Jesus da Cartolinha**, a statue of the
child Jesus in 17th-century costume
and a top hat, who is said to have
appeared to rally the Portuguese
forces during a Spanish siege in 1711.

The excellent **Museu da Terra de
Miranda** features a reconstruction
of a farmhouse kitchen and folk
costumes such as those worn by the
pauliteiros (stick dancers) at festivals.
✚ 199 F4
Tourist Information Office
✉ Largo do Menino Jesus da Cartolinha
☎ 273 430 025

Museu da Terra de Miranda
✉ Largo Dom João III ☎ 273 431 164 ⏰ Tue
2–5:30, Wed–Sun 9–12:30, 2–5:30 (6:30 in
summer 💵 Inexpensive (free Sun)

WHAT TO DO WITH THE KIDS
■ Douro boat trips at Porto (➤ 83).
■ The climb to Bom Jesus either
on foot or by the funicular railway
(➤ 90).
■ Parque da Cidade, by Castelo
do Queijo, has duck ponds and
play areas.
■ Shopping for clay cockerels at
Barcelos market.
■ The spectacular beaches of the
Costa Verde around Viana do
Castelo (➤ 93–94).

Where to...
Stay

Prices
Expect to pay for a double room per night in high season
€ under €60   €€ €60–€120   €€€ €121–€180   €€€€ over €180

PORTO

Hotel da Bolsa €€
Well located between the Ribeira and the Baixa districts, this 3-star hotel sits alongside the Stock Exchange building and is 50m (55 yards) from the Port Wine Institute. Built on the site of the São Francisco monastery, its 19th-century façade conceals a modern interior and although the rooms are a little dated, this is a pleasant base from which to explore the city. There is a car park next to the hotel.
🖪 198 A3 ⊠ Rue Ferreira Borges 101 ☎ 222 026 768; www.hoteldabolsa.com

Pestana Porto Hotel €€–€€€
Located on the riverfront in Ribeira with views to Vila Nova de Gaia and the Dom Luís Bridge, this luxury boutique hotel interconnects six former townhouses (all UNESCO World Heritage Status) from the 16th, 17th and 18th centuries, that have been restored and converted to the highest standards. The rooms are well-appointed and comfortable. There is an excellent restaurant and bar, with the emphasis on regional food and wine. Ask for a room with river views.
🖪 198 A3 ⊠ Praça da Ribeira, No 1 ☎ 223 402 300; www.pestana.com

Residencial dos Aliados €–€€
The pleasantly appointed *en suite* rooms in this imposing stone building are soon snapped up, so it is wise to book ahead. The bedrooms overlooking the avenue are noisy, despite double-glazing, so you might ask for an interior room. Most of the hotel was renovated in the late 1990s so the bathrooms are modern. An excellent breakfast is included in the room price.
🖪 198 A3 ⊠ Rua Elísio de Melo 27 ☎ 222 004 853/4; www.residencialaliados.com

CASA DE MATEUS

Casa da Quinta de São Martinho €€
You will need to book ahead to stay at this tiny, popular guesthouse. It is a 200m (218 yards) hop across the main road from the Casa de Mateus (▶ 86–87), a short way east of Vila Real. A lovely swimming pool in the quiet grounds is the only luxury at this home-from-home country house. The two rooms inside the house and two self-contained flats are well decorated and the resident family is very welcoming. They also have a well-stocked cellar of port.
🖪 198 C4 ⊠ Mateus, Vila Real ☎ 933 202 326/933 437 291; www.quintasaomartinho.com

BRAGA

Albergaria Bracara Augusta €–€€
This is a cheerful, well decorated and perfectly located guesthouse in the pedestrianised centre of town – what more could you ask for? Some of the rooms have views over the attractive cathedral, all are cosily decorated in warm colours and thick carpets. The well regarded Centurium restaurant is elegantly decorated, with stone walls and columns, and crisp white tablecloths. There is also a terrace for eating outside when the weather is warm – make use of this, if possible, for afternoon tea in the garden.
🖪 198 B4 ⊠ Avenida Central 134 ☎ 253 206 260; www.bracaraaugusta.com

Hotel do Parque €€

Run by the same company as its sister hotel, the Hotel do Elevador, the Hotel do Parque assures a comfortable stay and situated at the top of the funicular, this renovated 19th-century hotel is located right alongside the Bom Jesus sanctuary (▶ 90), in well-manicured parkland. The plush, slightly old-fashioned rooms have all the modern comforts – TV, air-conditioning and mini-bar. The Restaurante Panorâmico lives up to its name and serves well-prepared regional dishes backed by an extensive cellar stocked with *vinho verde* and Dão red wines.

🚹 198 B4 ⊠ Monte do Bom Jesus, Braga ☎ 253 603 470; www.hoteisbomjesus.pt

Pousada Santa Marinha da Costa €€€

One of the most impressive pousadas in Portugal, this 12th-century former monastery is set on a hill overlooking the city of Guimarães, and has all kinds of balconies and terraces from which you can admire the magnificent views. The 49 bedrooms are large and stately, many with four poster beds and ornate bathrooms, and all the rooms are impeccably furnished. Guests can relax in the large gardens with fountains and a stream, underground caves, and a beautiful outdoor swimming pool. The restaurant is also excellent. This is a highly atmospheric and memorable place to stay.

🚹 198 B4 ⊠ Largo Domingos Leite Castro ☎ 253 511 249; www.pousadas.pt

Estalagem Casa Melo Alvim €€–€€€

Located next to Viana do Castelo's railway-station, this delightful Manueline *solar*, built in 1509 by the Conde da Carreira, was successfully extended in the 17th and 19th centuries. In the 1990s it was turned into a first-class inn, fully respecting the appearance of the imposing stone building. Furnishings and décor, including superb carpets and bedsteads, are a subtle blend of traditional styles with a modern preference for sobriety and sleek lines. Each of the 20 bedrooms is different. Alto Minho cuisine is the cuisine on offer at the exemplary Conde do Camarido restaurant.

🚹 198 A4 ⊠ Avenida Conde da Carreira 28, Viana do Castelo ☎ 258 808 200; www.meloalvimhouse.com

Estalagem do Caçador €€

The open fire at this cosy and comfortable inn is as welcome in winter as the swimming pool is in summer. Hunting motifs abound, and hare, rabbit and venison often end up on the excellent menu in the restaurant. Antlers, stuffed birds, prints and hunting scenes in the spacious rooms continue the theme, and the cabinets full of Toby jugs and other interesting knick-knacks lend the place the air of a rather eccentric, but homely, museum.

🚹 199 E4 ⊠ Largo Manuel Pinto de Azevedo, Macedo de Cavaleiros ☎ 278 426 354/61; www.estalagensdeportugal.com

Quinta Entre Rios €€€

Welcoming farm house accommodation about 3km (1.5 miles) outside of the town of Mirandela, with comfortable rooms and a lovely large drawing room for guests to use. The 18th century building was renovated in 1997, and has good sized bedrooms, attractively furnished although aiming at functionality rather than luxury. There are plenty of opportunities to relax here – a snooker room, cards, chess, a large terrace for reading, and a pool. Enjoy home cooked breakfasts of local cheeses and sausages.

🚹 199 D4 ⊠ Chelas, Mirandela ☎ 278 263 160; www.quintaentrerios.pt.vu

Where to...
Eat and Drink

Prices

Expect to pay per person for a three-course meal, excluding drinks and tips

€ under €12   €€ €12–€24   €€€ €25–€36   €€€€ over €36

PORTO

Café Majestic €

This is arguably the most beautiful café in Portugal. An intellectuals' haunt, which dates from the 1920s, this superb café has miraculously survived intact, complete with stucco cherubs and mouldings. Chandeliers, leather upholstery, marble-top tables and huge art deco mirrors complete the picture, along with a grand piano sometimes used for concerts. Ideal for coffee or tea and *pastéis*. Snacks and simple meals at lunchtime, too, served by liveried waiters.

➕ 198 A3 ✉ Rua de Santa Catarina 112
☎ 222 003 887; www.cafemajestic.com
🕐 Mon–Sat 9:30–12

Kool €€–€€€

This Italian-fusion restaurant is located on the 7th floor of the imposing Casa da Musica, and is one of the best – and most fashionable – places to eat in Porto. There's an airy terrace for hot days, and the menu includes locally caught fish cooked with seasonal ingredients. The wine list is extensive also, with a good selection of reds from the local Douro Valley, and further afield in Portugal.

➕ 198 A3 ✉ Avenue da Boavista
☎ 226 092 876; www.restaurantekool.com
🕐 Mon–Sat 12–3, Mon–Wed 7:30–11,
Thu–Sat 7.30–12

Filha de Mãe Preta €€

Try at least one of the restaurants along the atmospheric Cais da Ribeira, down at the riverside overlooking the port warehouses in Gaia. Grilled sardines and mackerel are the favourites on the seafood-dominated menu here, in perhaps the best of all the restaurants, with its gorgeous *azulejos* and arched windows. Despite its popularity with tourists and Porto locals alike, it maintains high standards.

➕ 198 A3 ✉ Cais da Ribeira 40 ☎ 222
086 066 🕐 Mon–Sat 12–3, 6:30–10

VILA NOVA DE GAIA

Bogani Cafe €€

There are many restaurants and bars to choose from along the newly spruced up waterfront in Gaia, but this is one of the most reliable, with wonderful views back over the river to Ribeira. Often live music, and comfortable low-slung armchairs on a wide terrace in which to nurse your drink for hours. This gets very lively in the early hours, but there are coffees and light snacks available during the day, and tapas-style food for early evening drinks.

➕ 198 A3 ✉ Cais de Gaia ☎ 223 747 070;
www.boganicafe.com 🕐 Mon–Thu 10–12,
Fri–Sat 10–1am

BRAGA

Arcoense €€

A seriously good local restaurant, serving up food that draws on Portuguese ingredients, such as wood-fired lamb or Barrosa beef from Tras-os-Montes, plenty of local cheeses and a large range of sweet custard-based desserts. The location is excellent, right next to the pretty River Este. Book ahead.

➕ 198 B4 ✉ Rua Engenheiro José Justino
Amorim 96 ☎ 253 278 952 🕐 Mon–Sat
12–2, 7:30–10:30

Where to...
Shop

PORTO

A triangle between the Estação São Bento, the University and the City Hall is the main shopping area, with stationers, grocers and clothes and shoe shops along **Rua de Santa Catarina**. **Via Catarina** is a shopping mall with nearly 100 shops in which to browse.

For a more authentic experience, head for the **Bolhão Market**, on Rua Sá da Bandeira, by Bolhão station. This covered market is held throughout the week and is a noisy, colourful sight where you can expect to haggle over everything from vegetables to lampshades.

For crafts go to the **Centro Regional de Artes Tradicionais** (Rua da Reboleira 33–37, tel: 223

Café Vianna €

Like its equally atmospheric neighbour, the Astória, this low-key and great value art nouveau coffee-house is a great place for people-watching over a drink and snack, either inside or on the *esplanada* (terrace) on warm days. The coffee, cakes and *pregos* (bread rolls filled with a sliver of sizzling steak) are excellent. Some of the delicious local pastries to sample are *rabanadas* (cinnamon-flavoured French toast) and *charutos de chila* (pumpkin-filled pastry rolls).

🏛 198 B4 ⊠ Praça da República ☎ 253 262 336 🕙 Daily 9–7

GUIMARÃES

Solar do Arco €€

Situated near a stone arch along Guimarães' prettiest street, this is not the usual tourist trap you might think, despite the multilingual menu (try the good-value *ementa turística* – tourist menu). Roast *bacalhau* and *tamboril* (monkfish)

are regular specials, but veal and pork dishes are also excellent.

🏛 198 B4 ⊠ Rua de Santa Maria 48–50 ☎ 253 513 072 🕙 Mon–Sat 12–3, 7–11, Sun 12–3

VIANA DO CASTELO

Os Três Potes €€

With its traditional granite walls and dark wooden furniture, this place can seem a little sombre, but the menu is varied with many Minho specialities on offer. Try the wood-oven-roasted kid (*cabrito*) or the chargrilled octopus (*polvo na brasa*). There are folkloric shows on Saturday evenings.

🏛 198 A4 ⊠ Beco dos Fornos 7/9 ☎ 258 829 928 🕙 Daily 12–3:30, 7–10:30

BRAGANÇA

Geadas €€

Good regional produce in attractive surroundings, with warm exposed stone walls, and a long wall of windows that open onto the pretty

view. This is just the kind of local restaurant that you hope to stumble across, and has consistently high standards of food and service. Expect plenty of freshly caught fish and local meats on the menu, and all served up in generous portions. Highly recommended.

🏛 199 E5 ⊠ 32 Rua do Loreto ☎ 273 326 002; www.geadas.net 🕙 Restaurant: Tue–Sun 12–2, 7–11; Pub: Tue–Sat 12–11

TRÁS-OS-MONTES

Bagoeira €€

A cavernous place to dine on the Campo da Feira (marketplace), this inn has been catering to merchants and visitors since the 19th century. *Minho* dishes and gargantuan roasts are served in traditional style, with jugs of vinho verde. *Bacalhau à minhota*, with onions and potatoes. *Bagoeira* is the house variation on *à minhota*, with onions and potatoes. It has a few ensuite rooms too (€).

🏛 198 A4 ⊠ Avenida Sidónio Pais 495, Barcelos ☎ 253 811 236 🕙 Daily 12–2:30, 7–10:30

320 076) and for design items head up to the **Casa de Ferrágens Carvalho e Baptista** (Rua Almada 79–83).

Garrafeira do Carmo (Rua do Carmo 17, tel: 222 003 285), a charming wine merchant, also sells *bacalhau*. For a spectacular display of the latter, there's **Casa Oriental** at Campo Mártires da Patria 111/112 (tel: 222 002 530).

Visiting the various lodges at **Vila Nova de Gaia** (▶ 84–85) is an experience in itself, but it's impossible to take them all in. If limited for time, go to **Sandeman's** (▶ 84) or **Taylor's** (▶ 85).

BARCELOS

Every Thursday the **Campo da Feira** in Barcelos has attractive stalls selling fresh sausages, cheese, breads and crafts.

The "Barcelos cock" (▶ 94) and distinctive Barcelos pottery – a rich brown with cream dots – originated here. Items are signed RR or JR.

Where to...
Be Entertained

FESTIVALS

São João (St John's Day), 23–24 June, is celebrated across the country. In Porto there is folk music, doll displays and general revelry. It ends with fireworks, and a *barcos rabelos* regatta (▶ 84).

Pálacio da Bolsa holds regular concerts throughout the year as part of its **Festival de Música**. And for there is **Ritual Rock** at the Palácio de Cristal in August.

The Igreja Matriz at Freixo de Espada à Cinta is the starting point for a famous Good Friday procession, the **Romaria de Sete Paços**.

Viana do Castelo is famous for its *romaria* (Nossa Sra da Agonia) a three-day carnival held around 20 August.

SPORT AND OUTDOOR PURSUITS

You can hire **surfing** gear at Viana do Castelo. The **Surf Club de Viana** (Rua José Espregueira 62, tel: 258 826 274)) teaches beginners. **Amigos do Mar** (tel: 258 829 028) does sailing and canoeing.

Hiking is a popular activity, especially in the national parks such as Peneda-Gerês (▶ 91–92) – watersports are also available on the Caniçada reservoir, hiring canoes, motorboats and windsurfing gear at AML (tel: 253 391 779; www.aguamontanha.com).

You might prefer a peaceful **river trip** on the Douro: contact Douro Acima (tel: 222 006 418) or Douro Azul (Rua de São Francisco 4, tel: 223 402 500) for one- or two-day cruises.

MUSIC AND NIGHTLIFE

For classical music, there's Porto's **Auditório Nacional Carlos Alberto** (Rua das Oliveiras 43, tel: 223 401 900) or **Casa da Música** at the Rotunda da Boavista (Avenida da Boavista 604-610, tel: 220 120 298). *Fado* is performed at **Mal Cozinhado** (Rua do Outeirinho 13, tel: 222 081 319).

Aniki-Bóbó (Rua da Fonte Taurina 36, Porto, closed Sun) is packed into the early hours.

For nightclubs there's **River Café** (Calçada João do Carmo 31, Mas-sarelos) or **Via Rápida** (R. Manuel Pinto Azevedo, 567, Armazem 5, www.viarapida.pt). **Swing** (Praceta Engeniero Amaro da Costa 766), is a disco with bars – one is gay, although Porto doesn't have a gay scene in the same way that Lisbon does. In Braga the clubs are around Praça da República – try **Sardinha Biba** (Lugar dos Galos, Carandá). Viana do Castelo's **Viana Sol** (Rua dos Manjovos), is open late.

Central Portugal

Getting Your Bearings

Central Portugal stretches almost from Lisbon to Porto and from the Spanish border to the Atlantic coast – yet apart from the charming university city of Coimbra and the fascinating pilgrimage town of Fátima it receives few visitors and is little known outside the country.

The heart of central Portugal is the Beira (border) region, a group of three provinces between the Douro and the Tagus rivers. This was the historic homeland of the *Lusitani* tribe, Celto-Iberians who resisted the Roman invasion of Portugal, whose leader Viriatus, killed in 139BC, remains a national hero. Coimbra, which takes its name from the Roman settlement at Conímbriga, was capital of Portugal for more than 100 years. These days it is the capital of Beira Litoral, a seaside province of sandy beaches, pine forests and dunes, which is popular with Portuguese holidaymakers in summer.

Further inland, Beira Alta is a region of solid towns and granite villages, where Dão wines and Serra cheese are made, the latter by the sheep farmers of the highlands of Serra da Estrela, while remote Beira Baixa is the setting for Monsanto, one of Portugal's most spectacular hilltop villages.

The twin provinces of Estremadura and Ribatejo are dotted with castles and monuments recalling the time when the Christian armies marched south through this region, reconquering land from the Moors. This is where you will find the holy trinity of great Portuguese churches, at Alcobaça, Batalha and Tomar, as well as the moving modern shrine at Fátima, attracting pilgrims from across the Catholic world.

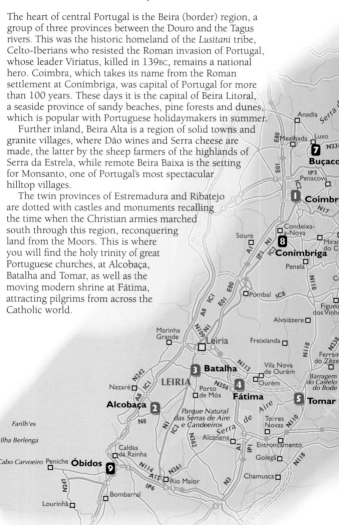

Church São Miguel in the castle ruins, Monsanto

Page 101: The basilica of Our Lady of Fátima

In Four Days

If you're not quite sure where to begin your travels, this itinerary
recommends a practical and enjoyable four days out in Central
Portugal, taking in some of the best places to see using the Getting
your Bearings map on the previous page. For more information see
the main entries.

Day 1

Morning
Start by exploring **❶ Coimbra** (➤ 106–109) on foot. Climb the hill to
visit one of the oldest university's in the world to visit the library, chapel
and graduation halls, then drop down through the old town, passing the
old cathedral on the way to the church of Santa Cruz. Have lunch in the
neighbouring Café Santa Cruz (➤ 124).

Afternoon and Evening
Cross the river and drive south on the N1 to see the Roman remains at
❽ Conímbriga (below; ➤ 121). Continue on this road as far as Leiria, then
pick up the A8/IC1 motorway to **❾ Óbidos** (➤ 122). Book ahead to stay in
the castle, a *pousada* (➤ 124) and enjoy a walk around the walls.

Day 2

Morning
Spend some time in Óbidos, admiring its whitewashed houses and views,
then go north on the A8/IC1 and take the exit to **❷ Alcobaça** (➤ 110–111)
to visit the monastery and wine museum before lunch.

Afternoon and Evening
From Alcobaça it is a short drive to the abbey of **❸ Batalha** (Capela do
Fundador ➤ 112–113). Afterwards, head east on the N356 to the
sanctuary at **❹ Fátima** (➤ 114–115). Stay at the *pousada* in the walled
town of Ourém. Climb the hill to the castle for views across the plain.

Day 3

Morning
Drive to **5 Tomar** (➤ 116–118) to visit the Templar church-fortress, then wander down to the town centre to see Portugal's oldest synagogue before enjoying lunch by the river. If you're feeling adventurous, try roast suckling pig, one of the specialities of Central Portugal.

Afternoon and Evening
Allow three hours for the drive to the **6 Serra da Estrela** (➤ 119–120). Go east on the IP6, then north on the IP2, bypassing Castelo Branco or taking a diversion to the hilltop village of **10 Monsanto** (➤ 122). If you are getting a taste for *pousadas*, stay at Pousada de São Lourenço (tel: 275 980 050), in a stone-built house above Manteigas with views over the Zêzere Valley (above). Alternatively, stay outside the national park at Solar de Alarcão in Guarda (➤ 123) and eat at one of the restaurants along Rua Francisco dos Passos, which specialise in mountain cuisine (➤ 125).

Day 4

Spend a full day exploring the mountains. Visit the information office in Manteigas for walking maps, then take a picnic to Poço do Inferno (➤ 119). If you don't want to walk, drive the circuit from Penhas da Saúde (➤ 119) to Torre (➤ 120) for spectacular views of the high sierra.

Coimbra

Portugal's oldest university sits on the crown of a hill overlooking the River Mondego. With historic buildings and churches, parks and gardens, and a lively student feel, Coimbra is one of the most enjoyable Portuguese cities in which to spend some of your time.

The first king of Portugal, Afonso Henriques, moved the capital here from Guimarães, but it was his successor, Dom Dinis, who founded the university that is today synonymous with Coimbra. Established in 1290 by papal decree to teach medicine, arts and law, the university moved back and forth between Lisbon and Coimbra before settling in João III's royal palace at Coimbra in 1537. Despite clinging to traditions, the students here are known for their liberal outlook. During the 20th century, Coimbra was a focus for radical opposition to the Salazar régime.

Visiting the University

The university is in the upper town, on the summit of Alcáçova hill. Despite the steep gradients, Coimbra is best explored on foot and it is easiest to start by climbing to the top of the hill and working your way back down.

From the river, head for the **Pátio das Escolas**. This handsome quadrangle, with buildings on three sides and a

Cross the water for the best views of Coimbra

ACROSS THE RIVER

Walk across Ponte de Santa Clara for the best view of the old town and the university. On the south bank, the Gothic convent of **Santa Clara-a-Velha**, where Inês de Castro (▶ 110–111) once lived, has been sinking into the sand for centuries but is being recovered and stands behind a new riverside park. The ruins of the convent reopened to the public in April 2009 with a new visitor centre and tours (Rua das Parreiras, tel: 239 801 161, Oct–May Tue–Sun 10–5:30; Jun–Sep Tue–Sun 10–7). Near here is **Portugal dos Pequenitos** (Rossio de Santa Clara, tel: 239 801 170, Mar–May, Sep 9–7; Jun–15 Sep 9–8; Feb, Oct–Dec 10–5; moderate). Aimed primarily at children, the park has miniature models of houses, monuments, historic buildings and a play area. Behind the park, the peaceful gardens of **Quinta das Lágrimas** (Villa of Tears) mark the spot where Inês de Castro was murdered. The palace at the centre of the gardens is now a luxury hotel (▶ 123).

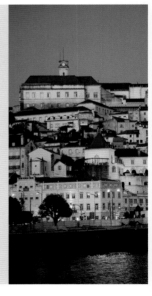

The venerable Coimbra university

terrace overlooking the Mondego, is at the heart of the old university. A statue of João III stands at the centre and in one corner is a baroque bell-tower.

You can visit most of the buildings, but you need a ticket to enter the **Biblioteca Joanina** (library), which has a collection of more than 30,000 books dating back to the 12th century, and **Sala dos Capelos** (ceremonial hall). The ticket office for both of these is in the main university building, at the left end of the colonnaded walkway on the north side of Pátio das Escolas. The baroque library, named after its benefactor, João V, is the main attraction, decorated in gilded wood and lacquered in green, red and gold. The Sala dos Capelos, where investitures and degree ceremonies take place, occupies the grand hall of the Manueline palace, with a panelled ceiling and portraits of Portuguese monarchs.

A corridor, offering fine views over the Coimbra rooftops, leads to the private examination hall, with a painted ceiling, tiled walls and portraits of former rectors.

On the east side of the square, the **Porta Férrea** (iron gate), built in 1634, contains carved figures representing the original faculties and statues of Dom Dinis and João III. This leads to the modern university buildings, including the faculties of medicine, science and technology. Most of these date from the 1960s, when the dictator António Salazar, a former economics professor at Coimbra, destroyed Manueline and Renaissance buildings in the name of modernisation.

The courtyard at the Museu Nacional Machado de Castro

Two Cathedrals

From the statue of Dom Dinis, steps lead down to **Praça da República**, with its student cafés. Behind the aqueduct, is the **Jardim Botânico** (tel: 239 855 233, Mon–Fri 9–5:30, Sat, Sun only if booked in advance, gardens: free, greenhouses: inexpensive), Portugal's largest botanical garden.

Go back up the steps and turn right to explore the rest of the upper town. The **Sé Nova** (New Cathedral) was actually built in 1598 and includes the choir stalls and font from the old cathedral. Just down the hill, the **Museu Nacional Machado de Castro** is housed in the 16th-century bishops' palace. It includes medieval painting and sculpture and the cryptoporticus in the basement, a series of underground galleries and part of the old Roman forum. Architect Gonçalo Byrne is currently expanding the museum.

Further downhill, the **Sé Velha** (Old Cathedral) is a Romanesque church-fortress on the site of the first cathedral in Portugal. Of interest here are the 13th-century cloisters and the Hispano-Arab tiles covering the walls.

Mosteiro de Santa Cruz

From here you can walk down to **Arco de Almedina**, the 12th-century gateway to the city. Go through the arch and turn right along a busy pedestrian street to the **Mosteiro de Santa Cruz**. Many of the leading artists of the Coimbra school, such as Jean de Rouen, worked on pieces for the monastery in the 16th century. The Renaissance porch is by Diogo de Castilho and Nicolas Chanterène, who also designed the pulpit and was responsible for the tombs of Portugal's first kings, Afonso Henriques and his son, Sancho I, behind the high altar. Buy a ticket to visit the **Sala do Capítulo** (chapter house) by Diogo de Boytac, with its Manueline ceiling, and the **Claustro do Silêncio** (Cloister of Silence), one of the purest examples of Manueline art.

Turn left on coming out of the church to return to the river at Largo da Portagem.

TAKING A BREAK

Try the **trendy student cafés** around Praça da República. **Trovador** (➤ 124), by the Sé Velha, is good for lunch.

---

198 B1

Tourist Information Office
Largo Dom Dinis 239 832 591

Universidade Velha (Biblioteca Joanina and Sala dos Capelos)
Paço das Escolas 239 482 001; http://mnmachadodecastro.imc-ip.pt Apr–Oct 8-30–7 (tickets), 9–7:30 (visits); Nov–Mar 9:30–5 (tickets), 10–5:30 (visits) Moderate

Sé Velha dates back to the reign of King Afonso Henriques

Museu Machado de Castro
Largo Dr José Rodrigues www.ipmuseus.pt
Oct–Mar Wed–Sun 10–12:30, 2–6; Apr–Sep Wed–Sun 10–6

Sé Velha
Largo da Sé Velha 239 825 273 Mon–Thu, Sat 10–1, 2–6, Fri 10–1, Sun only for services Church free, cloisters inexpensive

Mosteiro de Santa Cruz
Praça 8 de Maio 239 822 941 Daily 10–12, 2–6 Church free, cloisters inexpensive

COIMBRA: INSIDE INFO

Top tips Parking in central Coimbra is difficult – it is generally easier to park across the river and walk across Ponte de Santa Clara.

- To avoid the climb to the university, take **tram No 1** from Largo da Portagem.
- In summer there are river trips from a jetty in the park beside the Santa Clara bridge on the north bank.
- Look out for the chance to hear the **Coimbra version of *fado***, sung by men rather than women, with musicians and singers dressed in long black capes. It is less melancholy than its Lisbon counterpart. You are mostly likely to hear this in bars and restaurants and in the streets during student festivities. Or try to catch it at Trovador (➤ 125).

Hidden gem Following signs from Praça Dom Dinis, walk upstairs and ring the bell to be let into the **Museu Académico** (tel: 239 827 396, Mon–Fri 10–12:30, 2–5, inexpensive), with costumes, photos and artefacts describing university traditions such as *bedels* (beadles), *repúblicas* (communally run student houses) and the Queima das Fitas (Burning of the Ribbons) in May.

2 Alcobaça

The largest church in Portugal is a supreme example of Gothic architecture and would be worth a visit to Alcobaça for the building alone. What makes it even more special is that the church has become a shrine to one of the most tragic love stories in Portuguese history.

The **Mosteiro de Santa Maria** (more commonly known as the Mosteiro de Alcobaça) was founded by Afonso Henriques in 1153 to give thanks for victory over the Moors at Santarém. The baroque façade dates from the 18th century, but once you are inside everything is pure Gothic.

Clean lines and Soaring Columns

Unlike many Portuguese churches, which drip with ornamental detail, the simplicity of the central nave creates a harmonious feel. The only exception to the almost complete absence of decoration is the richly sculpted sacristy portal behind the high altar, designed by João de Castilho in 16th-century Manueline style and arrayed in floral motifs.

The tomb of Dom Pedro I and Inês de Castro

DOM PEDRO I AND INÊS DE CASTRO

Visitors crowd into the transept to see the tombs of Dom Pedro I and his lover, Inês de Castro. Inês was lady-in-waiting to Pedro's wife, Constanza of Castile, but Pedro's father, Afonso IV, had her banished from court to put an end to the affair. After Constanza died, Inês returned to live with Pedro at Coimbra, where she was murdered in 1355 on the orders of Afonso IV who feared Spanish influence over the Portuguese throne. Two years later, when Pedro assumed the throne, he wreaked revenge on the killers by having their hearts torn out and eating them himself. He also revealed that he and Inês had been secretly married at Bragança; her corpse was exhumed and he ordered the court to pay homage to their dead queen by kissing her decomposed hand.

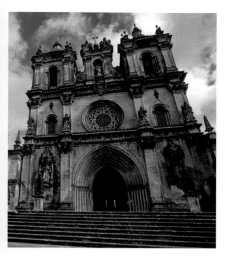

The baroque facade of the monastery at Alcobaça

Tombs and Cloisters

The **tombs of Dom Pedro I and Inês de Castro**, carved in limestone with scenes from the *Bible* (➤ box), face one another across the aisle. The reclining figure of Inês de Castro is supported by six angels, while her assassins, are thrown into hell at her feet. On Pedro's orders, the lovers were buried foot to foot, so that they could feast their eyes on one another when they rise on judgement day. The tombs are inscribed with *Até ao fim do mundo* ("Until the end of the world").

The entrance to the cloisters is through the **Sala dos Reis**, with statues of Portuguese kings carved by the monks and tiled walls telling the story of the monastery. The **Claustro de Silêncio**, added in the 14th century by Dom Dinis, has orange trees and a Renaissance *lavabo* where the monks would wash their hands before entering the refectory.

Alongside here are the **kitchens**, once famed for the extravagance of their banquets, with huge conical chimneys, and a stream that flowed straight from the River Alcôa, providing a plentiful supply of fish. A staircase from the cloister leads to the 13th-century dormitory.

TAKING A BREAK

Café Dom Pedro, across the square from the monastery, has a good range of snacks. There is also a smaller cafe in the gardens behind the cloister.

➕ 200 B4

Mosteiro de Santa Maria
☎ 262 505 120; www.ippar.pt 🕐 Oct–Mar daily 9–5; Apr–Nov 9–7
🎟 Church free, cloisters moderate

ALCOBAÇA: INSIDE INFO

Top tip Climb the hill to the ruined castle above the town for the **best views** of the monastery.

In more depth The **Museu Nacional de Vinho** (Rua de Leiria, Olival Fechado; tel: 262 582 222; Mon–Fri 9–12:30, 2–5:30; inexpensive) explains the history of wine making for which the region is famous and has a fascinating collection of old wine bottles, wine-making equipment and decorative posters.

3 Batalha

As you round a corner on the busy N1, a great church comes into view, with pinnacles, turrets and flying buttresses in honey-coloured limestone. This is Mosteiro da Batalha, a masterpiece of Gothic architecture that has become a symbol of Portuguese history and of independence from Spain.

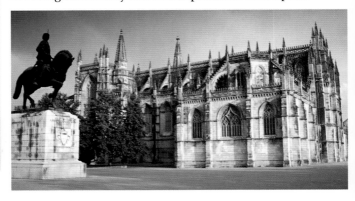

The **Mosteiro de Santa Maria da Vitória**, commonly known as the Mosteiro da Batalha (Abbey of the Battle), was built to celebrate the Portuguese victory over the Spanish at the Battle of Aljubarrota in 1385. Three years after King João I's victory work on the abbey began.

Batalha, built to celebrate victory in battle

Admire the worn exterior of the abbey and the **statue of Nuno Álvares Pereira** (► box opposite) on horseback on the square in front of the church. The main portal, beneath a Gothic window, features carved statues of Christ and the apostles, with angels, saints and João I's coat of arms. The long, tall nave is beautifully simple, with Gothic pillars and vaulting and stained glass.

The Founder's Chapel
Immediately to the right as you enter is the **Capela do Fundador** (Founder's Chapel), where João I and his wife, Philippa of Lancaster, are buried beneath an octagonal lantern, their tombs carved with effigies of the couple lying hand in hand. Also buried here are their four younger sons, including Henry the Navigator.

THE BATTLE OF ALJUBARROTA
King Fernando I of Portugal died in 1383 without leaving a male heir. King Juan I of Castile claimed the throne from his marriage to King Fernando's daugher, Beatriz, but was opposed by Fernando's illegitimate half-brother, João I. Heavily out-numbered by Spanish troops, João promised to build a magnificent church to the Virgin if he was suc-cessful, and with the help of his faithful lieutenant Nuno Álvares Pereira, and 500 English archers supplied by King Richard II, his supporters won the day. João's victory ushered in a new era for Portugal, with 200 years of independence under the rule of the House of Avis.

The church is full of space and light

The original **Claustro Real** (Royal Cloister) was embellished with rich Manueline tracery by Diogo de Boytac, architect of the monastery at Belém (➤ 48). All the main symbols of Manueline art are here, including armillary spheres, crosses of Christ, twisted branches and exotic foliage.

On one side of the cloister, the **Sala do Capítulo** (chapter house) contains Portugal's two Unknown Soldiers, one from World War I and the other from Portugal's wars in Africa. A museum dedicated to them is in the former refectory.

A second cloister leads to the **Capelas Imperfeitas** (Unfinished Chapels), begun by João I's eldest son Dom Duarte as a royal mausoleum and containing the tombs of Duarte and his queen, Leonor of Aragón. The chapels, which can also be reached from behind the main abbey, are perhaps the highlight of the entire complex, with an Indian-inspired Manueline portal and a magnificent roofless octagonal rotunda.

TAKING A BREAK

Behind the abbey the **Circunstancia Bar** (15 Estrada de Fatima, tel: 244 768 777; www.circunstancia.com.pt) is a good place for a glass of wine and a light snack.

➕ 200 B4

Mosteiro de Batalha
☎ 244 765 497 ⏰ Apr–Sep 9–6; Oct–Mar 9–5 💶 Church free, cloisters moderate

---

BATALHA: INSIDE INFO

Top tips The abbey is best seen on a **day trip** from Nazaré or Fátima, although there are express buses from Lisbon.
■ During the weekends of **13 May and 13 October**, Batalha is packed with people visiting from Fátima (➤ 114–115).

In more depth Visit the **battlefield of Aljubarrota**, 4km (2.5 miles) south of Batalha in the village of São Jorge. There is a small chapel, a military museum, a shop and café. (tel: 244 482 087; www.fundacao-aljubarrota.pt/index.htm; Tue–Sun 10–12, 2–5; inexpensive).

4 Fátima

The so-called "altar of Portugal", Fátima is Portugal's greatest Roman Catholic shrine. The story of what happened to three shepherd children in 1917 has moved millions, and made the town one of the biggest centres of pilgrimage in the Roman Catholic world.

The Vision

It was on 13 May, 1917 that the Virgin Mary appeared in an oak tree to 10-year-old Lúcia dos Santos and her cousins Jacinta and Francisco as they were tending their family's sheep in the village of Cova da Iria, near Fátima. The children spoke of a lady "brighter than the sun" who called them to return at the same time each month for six months. Although their story was greeted with much scepticism, the children returned and the visions continued.

On the final occasion, 13 October, a crowd of 70,000 people witnessed the sun dancing in the sky like a ball of fire and countless miracles occurred – the blind could see, the sick were cured and the lame walked.

On the same day, the Virgin revealed to Lúcia the "three secrets of Fátima", which are said to have foretold World War II, Russian communism and the assassination of a pope.

The Children

Jacinta and Francisco died of pneumonia in 1920, but Lúcia entered a Carmelite convent in Coimbra in 1928, where she died in 2005, age 97. Jacinta and Francisco, who are buried inside the basilica, were beatified in 1989 by Pope John Paul II, the first step on the path to sainthood.

The Basilica of Our Lady of Fátima towers over its steps and the tarmac esplanade

Pilgrims light candles for Our Lady of Fátima

The Basilica

A vast, neoclassical basilica was completed in 1953, and accommodates the millions of pilgrims who flock here. The esplanade in front of the basilica can hold a million people and is twice the size of St Peter's Square in Rome. In a corner of the square stands the **Capela das Aparicões** (Chapel of the Apparitions), on the site of the original visions, where pilgrims pray and light candles to a statue of the Virgin.

Pilgrimages to Fátima take place all year, and particularly on 13 May and 13 October, many of them making their way to the basilica on their knees.

TAKING A BREAK

The *pousada* at Ourém (➤ 123), built on a hilltop 10km (6 miles) northeast of Fátima, makes a good night's stop.

➕ 200 C4

Tourist Information Centre Office
✉ Avenida Dom José Alves Correia da Silva ☎ 249 531 139

Shrine of Our Lady of the Rosary of Fátima
✉ Apartado 31 ☎ 249 539 600; www.santuario-fatima.pt

FÁTIMA: INSIDE INFO

Top tips From Easter to October there are **candlelit processions** in front of the basilica at 9:30 each night. The procession is largest on 12th of the month.
■ You should be silent around the basilica and the Chapel of the Apparitions.

In more depth You can visit the village of **Aljustrel**, outside Fátima, to see the Casa Museu de Aljustrel where the three children grew up can be visited (further on in Valinhos, a statue marks the spot of the fourth vision), and the ethnographic museum next door (tel: 249 532 828, May–Oct Mon, Wed–Fri 10–1, 3–7, Sat–Sun 10–1, 2–7; Nov–Apr Mon, Wed–Fri 10–1, 2:30–7, Sat–Sun 9:30–1, 2:30–6; house free, museum inexpensive).

5 Tomar

The third in the trio of medieval churches, the Convento de Cristo stands in the grounds of a castle on a wooded slope overlooking Tomar. Once a powerful military and religious capital, Tomar is now a peaceful town on the banks of the River Nabão and makes a pleasant base for exploring the surrounding area.

The Monastery

The Knights Templar castle dominates the town. Within its walls stands the **Convento de Cristo**, one of Portugal's Unesco World Heritage Sites. It was begun in 1160 but has Gothic and Manueline additions.

The tour of the monastery begins in a pair of cloisters, **Claustro da Lavagem** and **Claustro do Cemitério**, both added by Henry the Navigator, whose ruined palace can be seen through the arches.

Next you come to the **Charola** (or Rotunda), the spiritual heart of the complex, a 12th-century round church that was modelled on the Holy Sepulchre of Jerusalem, with an octagonal chapel where the knights are reputed to have held services on horseback. The columns are richly painted with 16th-century frescoes. The Charola now forms the eastern end of a Manueline church, built under the reign of Manuel I.

From here you move into the **Claustro Principal** (Great Cloister), added in 1557 in neoclassical and Renaissance style. Climb onto the roof for the best views of the **great western window** by Diogo de Arruda and the **south portal** by João de Castilho, two of the most sumptuous examples of Manueline art

The Templar's 12th-century Convento de Cristo

A restored spiral staircase in the monastery

THE KNIGHTS AND TOMAR

Tomar was founded in 1157 by Gualdim Pais, the first Grand Master of the Knights Templar of Portugal, a military force with powerful religious overtones. The town was created on land donated by Afonso Henriques in return for the knights' help in the reconquest of Portugal from the Moors. Tomar subsequently became the knights' base. In 1314 the order was deemed too powerful and was suppressed by Pope Clement V, but it was reconstituted in Portugal by Dom Dinis under the name the Knights of Christ. Henry the Navigator became "governor" in the 15th century and tapped the order's wealth to fund his explorations, while the Knights of Christ were given spiritual control over all Portuguese conquests.

in Portugal. The window in particular contains all the familiar symbols of the Manueline era, including anchors, cables, twisted ropes, an armillary sphere and the Cross of the Knights of Christ. From here you can wander along corridors of monks' cells and step onto the rooftop terrace before finishing with the walkway around the castle walls.

The Town

The old town, to the west of the river, is centred around the elegant **Praça da República**, where a statue of Gualdim Pais stands in front of the town hall. On one side of the square, the church of **São João Baptista** has an elegant Manueline portal and a pulpit carved with the Templar cross and the royal coat of arms.

Just south is the oldest surviving **synagogue** in Portugal, lovingly maintained by one of two remaining Jewish families in Tomar. Built around 1430, and abandoned after the expulsion of the Jews in 1497, it has been used as a prison, chapel, hayloft and cellar, but is now a museum containing 13th- and 14th-century Jewish tombstones as well as sacred items donated by members of Jewish communities across the world.

Praça da República, with the statue of Gualdim Pais

Tomar's other museum, **Museu dos Fósforos**, is housed in a wing of a 17th-century convent. An eccentric display features more than 40,000 matchboxes, the largest collection in Europe, beginning with Queen Elizabeth II's coronation in 1953 and continuing with Portuguese politicians, Spanish bullfighters and Japanese topless models.

A warren of narrow streets leads down to the River Nabão, where the shady Parque do Mouchão, on an island in the middle of the river, has open-air cafés and a waterwheel, said to date from Roman times.

Manueline carving in Tomar

TAKING A BREAK

Chico Elias (tel: 249 311 067, daily 12–3pm, 7–10pm)is a traditional restaurant in a large old tavern. **Bela Vista** (► 125), by the old bridge, is another option.

🕂 200 C4

Tourist Information Office
✉ Avenida Dr Cândido Madureira
☎ 249 329 000;
www.rttemplarios.pt

Convento de Cristo
✉ 15-minute walk above the town ☎ 249 313 481 📷 ;
Oct–May Mon–Sat 9–5:30, Sun 9–2; Jun–Sep Mon–Sat 9–6:30, Sun 9–2 💰 Moderate

Sinagoga
✉ Rua Dr Joaquim Jacinto 73
☎ 249 322 427 🕐 Daily 10–1, 2–6. Closed Wed 💰 Free

Museu dos Fósforos
✉ Varzea Grande ☎ 249 329 829 🕐 Daily 10–5 💰 Free

TOMAR: INSIDE INFO

Top tip Come here on Friday when the riverbanks are taken over by a **large market**, with fresh food and flowers on the east bank, and clothes, shoes and household goods on the west bank.
■ Try a **Fatias de Tomar** (a slice of Tomar), a sweet treat made with a mixture of egg yolks, sugar and water, purchased in many shops and restaurants around the town.

Hidden gems Cross the Ponte Velha (Old Bridge) to the chapel of **Santa Iria** (Tue–Sun 10–6, free), Tomar's patron saint, a young nun who was murdered. The church, built in the 16th century, features a stone-carved calvary, a coffered painted ceiling and rich 17th-century *azulejos*.

A short drive away from Tomar is Constância, one of the most attractive villages in the area. The Festival of the Tabuleiros is held here once every four years. The next one will be held in June and July 2011.

6 Serra da Estrela

Rocky hillsides are carved up by glacial valleys in the Serra da Estrela, Portugal's highest mountain range. In summer you can walk across carpets of scented grasses and wild flowers, and in winter the peaks are covered in snow. Much of the area has been designated a natural park.

The Serra da Estrela forms a 60km by 30km (37 miles by 19 miles) range, with a summit of 1,993m (6,537 feet) and is Portugal's largest protected wildlife area. This is a land of shepherds, long-horned sheep, cheese-making and wool. The mainstays of the economy are farming and forestry, though outdoor tourism is becoming ever more important. In winter, there is skiing and hunting; in summer there is trout fishing in the rivers and walking in the hills.

Getting into the mountains

There is good access to the mountains from Covilha, a busy textile town with views over the mountains, where you can buy gloves, jackets and woollen goodies. From here, the N339 climbs through **Penhas da Saúde**, Portugal's only ski resort, on its way to the high sierra. In winter, you can try dog sledging and sleigh rides as well as skiing. This is a good starting point for a circular tour, allowing at least half a day. Soon after Penhas da Saúde, turn right on the N338 for a beautiful drive along the Zêzere Valley, a deep glacial gorge.

All along the valley, there are distant views of **Manteigas**, the small town at the centre of the park. Here you can pick up information on walking and hiking in the mountains, including the half-day circular walk from Manteigas to the **Poço do Inferno** ("Hell's Well") waterfall.

The glacial scenery of the Zêzere Gorge

Magnificent
views of the
High Sierra
near Torre

From Manteigas you can follow the twisting N232 towards
Gouveia. You pass a *pousada* and the source of the River
Mondego, which empties into the sea near Coimbra. The
scenery is stunning, with rock formations of wind-sculpted
granite such as the Cabeça do Velho (Old Man's Head).

A minor road leads to **Sabugueiro**, Portugal's highest
village, where cheese, ham, sausages and woollen blankets are
on sale. Turn left on the N339 for the slow climb to **Torre**.
The highest mountain in Portugal (1,993m/6,537 feet) takes
its name from the stone tower built here in the 19th century
so that the peak would top 2,000m (6,560 feet). On winter
weekends, families flock here to go sledging. On the way
down to Penhas da Saúde, look out for the statue of **Nossa
Senhora da Boa Estrela**, carved into a niche in the rock.

Two towns that make good bases for visiting the park
are **Guarda**, the highest town in Portugal (1,056m/3,464
feet), with a 14th-century Gothic cathedral, and **Belmonte**,
birthplace of Pedro Álvares Cabral, who discovered Brazil.
Belmonte was once home to a large population of *marranos*
(Jews who fled here after their expulsion from Portugal in
1497) and it still has a large Jewish community.

TAKING A BREAK

There are **cafés** in all the main villages offering *queijo da serra*,
sandwiches made with the local cheese.

✚ 198 C1/D1

Park Tourist Information Office
✉ Rua 1 de Maio, Manteigas ☎ 275 980 060; www.icn.pt

SERRA DA ESTRELA: INSIDE INFO

Top tips Try *queijo da serra*, a strong cheese made from sheep's milk and
curdled with thistle flowers. The runny, ripe cheese, usually scooped out with
a spoon, is at its best in winter.

■ The mountains need to be **treated with respect**. The weather can change
   quickly – it can be sunny in Manteigas while Torre is obscured in mist, or
   you might drive through the mist to emerge in sunshine above the clouds.
   Be prepared for anything, even in summer, and allow plenty of time.

At Your Leisure

Gardens at Palace Hotel do Bussaco

7 Buçaco

Buçaco is a place where you can still believe in fairies. The walled **Mata Nacional** (National Forest) is a magical landscape of sylvan glades and cedar-scented woods dotted with fountains, hermitages and shady walks, even its own vineyard. Once a monastic retreat from which women were banned by papal decree, the forest is dotted with fountains, hermitages and shady walks. At the centre is the bizarre neo-Manueline **Buçaco Palace**, designed as a royal hunting lodge and now one of Portugal's top hotels (➤ 124). The Carmelite convent next door has cork-lined cells and mosaic walls. Walk through the Buçaco forest up to Cruz Alta (High Cross), which offers impressive views over the ocean, and a museum, which tells of the Battle of Bucaco in 1812, in which the Duke of Wellington fought the French.

♦ 198 B1
Mosteiro dos Carmelitas
☎ 231 939 226 ◷ Tue–Sun 9–12:30, 2–5:30. Closed Oct–May Sun ◷ Inexpensive

8 Conímbriga

The best-preserved Roman remains in Portugal are situated 15km (9 miles) south of Coimbra. Some of the houses have detailed mosaics, with images of birds, fish, horses and dragons. Note the **Casa das Fontes**, a second-century villa with ornamental gardens and pools. The excavations here have uncovered evidence of a forum, aqueduct, shops,

BEST FOR KIDS
■ **Portugal dos Pequenitos**, Coimbra (➤ 106), a theme park of Portugal in miniature.
■ Visit a **sheep farm** in the hills of Serra da Estrela.
■ **Forest walks** in Buçaco (➤ above), which occupies a special place in the hearts of the Portuguese.
■ The beaches of the **Costa da Prata**, the coastline running along Central Portugal.

taverns and public baths. A museum contains archaeological finds, some of which date from a Celto-Iberian settlement before the arrival of the Romans in the first century BC.

➕ 200 C5 ✉ Condeixa-a-Nova ☎ 239 941 177; www.conimbriga.pt 🕐 Jun–Sep daily 9–8 (museum Tue–Sun 9–8); Oct–May daily 10–6 (museum Tue–Sun 10–6) 💷 Moderate (Sun 9–1 free)

❾ Óbidos

This walled town of whitewashed houses was traditionally given as a wedding gift by the Portuguese kings to their queens, a custom begun by Dom Dinis for Isabel of Aragón in 1282 and continued for 600 years. **Porta de Vila**, the gateway to the town, is lined with 18th-century tiles and leads to **Rua Direita**, the main street, with its souvenir shops and *ginja* (cherry brandy) bars. Halfway up the street, the church of **Santa Maria** has azulejo walls and there is a striking Manueline pillory in the church square. The **castle**, at the top of town, was converted into a royal palace in the 16th century and is now one of Portugal's finest *pousadas* the **Pousada do Castelo** (➤ 124). From here, climb onto the ramparts to make a circuit of the walls, which should take around 45 minutes.

➕ 200 B4

❿ Monsanto

One of the oldest settlements in Portugal, inhabited in pre-Roman times, Monsanto is perched on the side of Monte Santo (Sacred Mountain), with houses built into the mountainside between huge granite boulders. This village has the odd claim to fame of having been once voted 'Most Portuguese village in Portugal'. Climb to the **ruined castle**, built in the 12th century, for magnificent views stretching as far as the Serra da Estrela. On 3 May during the Festa das Cruzes, the younger village women throw flowers from the ramparts in memory of a famous siege when the starving inhabitants threw their last calf from the castle walls in a successful attempt to fool

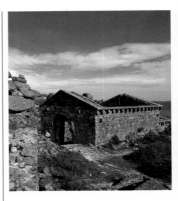

The roofless Church Sao Miguel in the ruins of the castle in Monsanto

their attackers into thinking that they were able to last out for a long time. There are a few signs of tourist development – a small *estalagem*, a couple of restaurants and craft shops – but mostly life goes on as it always has in this remote, quintessential hilltop village.

➕ 201 F5

⓫ Viseu

The capital of the Beira Alta and the Dão wine region, Viseu is an attractive town. At the heart of the old town is **Largo da Sé**, with two churches facing one another across the square. The larger and more imposing façade is that of the baroque church of Misericórdia; the Sé (cathedral) has Renaissance cloisters and a Manueline ceiling.

The main attraction is the **Museu de Grão Vasco**, named after Vasco Fernandes (1480–1543), a leading figure in the 16th-century Viseu school of painting. It includes his painting, *St Peter Enthroned*.

➕ 198 C2

Tourist Information Office
✉ Avenida Calouste Gulbenkian
☎ 232 420 950; www.cm-viseu.pt

Museu de Grão Vasco
✉ Paço dos Três Escalões ☎ 232 422 049; www.ipmuseus.pt 🕐 Tue 2–6, Wed–Sun 10–6 💷 Moderate (Sun 9:30–12:30 free)

Where to...
Stay

Prices
Expect to pay for a double room per night in high season

€ under €60   €€ €60–€120   €€€ €121–€180   €€€€ over €180

COIMBRA

Casa Pombal €

By the university and commanding views across the rooftops to the river, this guesthouse is a delightful place to stay. You feel as though you are staying at one of the famous *repúblicas* or student houses. A steep staircase leads to a number of antiquated but comfortable rooms, some with bathrooms. A hearty breakfast is served in the dining room where delicious meals can be prepared to order.
🏠 198 B1 ⊠ Rua das Flores 18 ☎ 239 835 175; www.casapombal.com

Quinta das Lágrimas €€€–€€€€

Famous for having received the Duke of Wellington in 1808, this luxurious hotel is set in wooded parkland. In addition to a pool, spa and tennis courts there's a golf academy with a 9-hole pitch-and-putt and driving range. Inside the main house the décor is elegant and the bedrooms are huge, in the modern spa wing rooms are minimalist-chic. Meals are served in the restaurant, and the cellar offers more than 200 vintages.
🏠 198 B1 ⊠ Rua António Augusto Gonçalves, Santa Clara ☎ 239 802 380; www.quintadaslagrimas.pt

OURÉM

Pousada Conde de Ourém €€–€€€

This charming renovated *pousada*, converted from medieval houses, is a good base from which to visit Fátima and Tomar. Climb to the castle for distant views of Fátima. Rooms are spacious and comfortable, and there is a pool open in summer. Spend the evening in the *pousada's* restaurant enjoying local specialities like fried rabbit with cabbage "Conde de Ourém" and a buffet of cheeses and desserts.
🏠 200 C4 ⊠ Largo João Manso ☎ 249 540 920; www.pousadas.pt

TOMAR

Estalagem de Santa Iria €–€€

As Tomar's *pousada* is a long way out of town, this is the best choice, especially if charm and tranquillity are your criteria. Even the early 20th-century writer Somerset Maugham has signed the visitors'

book. This unpretentious inn, with 14 bright, spacious rooms, is idyllically located on a wooded island in the middle of the town. The dining room serves delicious, well-cooked dishes. Recommended.
🏠 200 C4 ⊠ Parque do Mouchão ☎ 249 313 326; www.estalagemsantairia.com

BUÇACO

Hotel Palace do Bussaco €€€€

The Buçaco Forest (➤ 121), where Napoleon suffered a major defeat in the Peninsular Wars, benefits from a microclimate and is a holy place, under papal protection since the 17th century. The hotel was built as a royal hunting lodge just before the monarchy was abolished in 1910, but it's still fit for a sovereign. The mock-Manueline palace houses 34 luxurious rooms, a fabulous dining room and some impressive *azulejos*. There are also tennis courts. The cellar is one of the best in Portugal.
🏠 198 B1 ⊠ Mata do Buçaco, Luso ☎ 231 937 970; www.palacehoteldobussaco.com

Where to...
Eat and Drink

ÓBIDOS

Casa das Senhoras Rainhas €€€

The whitewashed walls make this hotel feel like a haven of peace and relaxation even before you step inside. The building itself has been perfectly renovated and preserved, but inside there is a luxurious space with good sized, well-appointed bedrooms, a large terrace for outside eating in warm weather and a cosy drawing room with fireplace for colder evenings. Even better, it is located directly next to the old city walls, so it is perfectly located for exploring.

🕂 **200 B4** ⊠ **6 Rua Padre Nunes Tavares** ☎ **262 955 360; www.senhorasrainhas.com**

Pousada do Castelo €€€–€€€€

The magnificent site – commanding fantastic views – alone justifies splashing out to stay here. It's one of the most prestigious *pousadas* in Portugal, if only because there are only nine rooms, a couple of them in the eyrie-like tower. Exuberant tapestries enhance the romantic atmosphere in the impeccably restored medieval interior. Rooms are comfortable and well-appointed. Traditional meals are served in the charming refectory – or you could drop by for afternoon tea.

🕂 **200 B4** ⊠ **Rua do Castelo** ☎ **262 955 080; www.pousadas.ot**

MONSANTO

Hotel Estalagem de Monsanto €€

Monsanto's *estalagem* is set in a modern building that perfectly blends in with the fine houses in this hilltop town. With only ten rooms this hotel quickly gets booked up in summer, but if possible get the corner room upstairs, which has fantastic views in two directions across the verdant Beira-Baixa landscapes. The food is hearty and the service friendly. Recommended.

🕂 **201 F5** ⊠ **Rua da Capela 3** ☎ **277 314 471; http://monsanto.homestead.com**

COIMBRA AND ENVIRONS

Café Santa Cruz €

University students keep this wonderfully atmospheric café-bar alive and buzzing, especially in the evening. It is housed in the former sacristy of the 16th-century Igreja Santa Cruz. Coffee, wine and beer are served with inexpensive snacks in a fabulous vaulted room – stone walls and leather benches. The superb *esplanada* (terrace) is packed out in summer.

🕂 **198 B1** ⊠ **Praça 8 de Maio** ☎ **239 833 617** 🕐 **Mon–Sat 7–11:30 (1:30 in summer)**

A Cozinha €

Rua das Azeiteiras is located in a quiet narrow alleyway in the Baixa, lined with interesting traditional eateries that it's hard to choose between them. This place, with its mock *azulejos* jostling for space with an almost clinical décor, is a favourite with locals. *Chanfana* (goat in a wine sauce) and *carne de porco à alentejana* (pork simmered with clams and fresh coriander), are typical dishes, served in huge helpings (this is definitely a place to ask for *meia dose* – half portions), along with decent house wine, dished up by no-nonsense staff and with the inevitable TV for atmosphere. It's certainly an authentic experience.

⊞ 198 B1 ☒ Rua das Azeiteiras 65–67 ☎ 239 827 115 ☺ Mon–Sat 12–3, 7–10:30

Arcadas da Capela €€€

Easily one of the best restaurants in the region, award-winning chef Albano Lourenço has come from Lisbon and made this a must destination for foodies in Portugal. Seasonal, local ingredients are the key here, and the elegant restaurant looks out over the gardens of this attractive hotel. There are two tasting menus on offer, where the chef will suggest an array of fresh ingredients, and can match each one with local wines. There are over 300 Portuguese and international wines on the list here. Wild rabbit, duck and free-range chicken feature on the slightly unusual menu, while *ensopado de enguias* (eel stew) draws customers from a wide radius. This goldmine of a restaurant (30km/19 miles west of Coimbra), with its rustic décor and charming *patio*, is renowned for its locally grown or caught produce and expert Bairrada cooking. It gets packed on market day (every other Wednesday). Recommended.

⊞ 198 B1 ☒ Rua Antonio Augusto Gonçalves ☎ 239 802 380; www. arcadasdacapela.gastronomias.com ☺ Jul–Sep 7pm–10pm, Oct–Jun 12–2, 7–10

Trovador €€–€€€

Not only is the food good here, but this is one of the rare places in Coimbra where you can be sure to hear the local version of *fado*, sung by men instead of women, and more important for the lyrics than the tune. All kinds of regional specialities can be tasted, with *chanfana* (goat in a wine sauce) leading the way. The wine list is top notch, including local Bairradas, but also vintages from all over Portugal. The delightful décor, with wood panelling and crisp white linen, plus charming service and great food, make this restaurant, near the old cathedral, the best in the old town. Recommended.

⊞ 198 B1 ☒ Largo da Sé Velha 17 ☎ 239 825 475 ☺ Mon–Sat 12–3, 7:30–10. Closed 15–31 Dec

ALCOBAÇA

O Cantinho €€–€€€

A favoured local, with friendly owners and a good range of hearty meals based on traditional, regional ingredients. Try the chicken casserole, a speciality of the house. There are some lighter snacks and tapas-style meals available also.

⊞ 200 B4 ☒ Rua Engenheiro Bernardo Vila Nova ☎ 262 583 471 ☺ 9–12

TOMAR

Bela Vista €€

The fantastic location by Tomar's Old Bridge, with pleasant views overlooking the ducks (cooked with *arroz de pato*, a kind of rice, which are a house special) on the River Nabão, is only part of the reason why this is the locals' favourite haunt. A reliable but expertly executed menu of family-style dishes, deft service and a homelike interior keep hungry locals and visitors alike coming back. In good weather try and get a table on the shady front terrace under the vines. The *ementa turística* (tourist menu) is unbeatable value.

⊞ 200 C4 ☒ Rua Marquês de Pombal 68 ☎ 249 312 870 ☺ Wed–Sun 12–3, 7–9:30; Mon 12–3. Closed 1–15 Nov

FÁTIMA

Tia Alice €€

The simple interior of this restaurant and traditional food cooked to the highest quality means this restaurant is a real find. Among the many renowned dishes is *morcela com arroz* – a type of black pudding of pork mixed with red wine, rice, herbs and spices.

⊞ 200 C4 ☒ 152 Rua do Adro ☎ 249 531 737 ☺ Tue–Sat 12–2:30, 7:30–10:30, Sun 12–2:30

Where to... Shop

MARKETS

Every Tuesday **Viseu** has a market at **Largo Castanheiro dos Amores**. A cheese market is held in **Celorico da Beira** every other Friday. In the **Serra da Estrela**, **Gouveia's** Thursday markets are worth seeing, as is the **Montemor-o-Velho**, 30km (18.5 miles) west of Coimbra, every other Wednesday. The daily market in **Coimbra** is in a hangar behind the City Hall.

CRAFTS

Óbidos has ceramic and craft shops along Rua Direita – try the **Centro de Artesanato**. In **Alcobaça**, quality glazed earthenware is on sale at **Raul da Bernarda** (Ponte Dom Elias). In **Coimbra** you can pick up earthenware goods along **Rua Quebra** Costas. **Ruas Ferreira Borges** and **Visconde da Luz** are Coimbra's main shopping arteries, lined with boutiques, grocers, bookshops and tobacconists. Just outside, at Condeixa-a-Nova, factories sell hand-painted ceramics.

FOOD AND DRINK

In Coimbra, **A Camponesa** (Rua da Louça) has an excellent range of wines and spirits or try **Dom Vinho** on rua Armando Sousa. Buy bottles of Dão wine in Viseu's grocers.
Buy *queijos da serra* (mountain cheeses) in the covered market in **Guarda** on Rua D Nuno Álvares Pereira on Saturday mornings. In **Viseu**, **Pastelaria Horta** (Rua Formosa) has pies and cakes.

Where to... Be Entertained

SPORT AND OUTDOOR PURSUITS

Surfing is first class at **Buarcos**, near Figueira da Foz. At **Aveiro**, rent **bikes** to explore the lagoon from **Agência de Viagens Culturália** (Rua João Mendonça 31, tel: 23 442 3142) or of BUGA, free Aveiro's bicycle service.
Hiking in the **Serra da Estrela** is great, and trails are well marked (▶ 119–120).
Several **spas** are located in this region – **Termas de Monfortinho**, enjoys a stunning location and you can play tennis and hire mountain bikes (www.monfortur.pt).

FESTIVALS

The **Queima das Fitas** ("ribbon burning") enlivens **Coimbra** in May.
Don't miss **Aveiro's Festa da Ria**, in the second half of August, when the distinctive *moliceiro* boats are decorated. "Holy Bathing" can be witnessed at **Figueira da Foz**, along with other partying, on and around **St John's Day** (24 June).

MUSIC AND NIGHTLIFE

Nightlife is focused on **Coimbra** and **Figueira da Foz**, where there's also a **film festival** in September. A good nightclub is **Bergantim** (Rua Dr Lopes Guimarães 28, Figueira da Foz). In Coimbra, **Diligência** (Rua Nova 30) is the best place for local *fado*, while **Boémia** (Rua do Cabido 6) is a beautiful venue for jazz.
Scotch Club (Quinta da Ínsua) and **Via Latina** (Rua Almeida Garrett 1) are Coimbra's liveliest discos.

The Alentejo

Getting Your Bearings

The Alentejo ("Beyond the Tagus") is a sun-baked plain that stretches across southern Portugal, occupying land between the River Tagus and the Algarve. This is both the largest and the most sparsely inhabited region of Portugal, where just 12 per cent of the population are scattered across a third of the country in isolated hamlets and small market towns. It is a proud region whose people share a strong sense of identity, expressed through their music, rural traditions and hearty peasant cuisine.

The landscape of the Alentejo is almost entirely man-made and agricultural. The Romans established vast feudal estates (*latifúndios*) to grow olives, vines and wheat, many of which survived right up to the 1974 revolution. Even today, when many of these estates have become co-operatives, the whitewashed *monte* (farmhouse) surrounded by vineyards is still a familiar sight. Wine and wheat are still important products, but the region is best known for its cork oaks, which provide more than half of the world's cork, used in everything from aircraft insulation to bottle stops.

Alongside the wide open spaces and strong elemental colours of the landscape the region has also made some important gourmet contributions to Portugal. The most famous of these is the Alentejo black pig.

Upper Alentejo in particular has several interesting sights, from the Renaissance city of Évora to the marble towns of Estremoz and Vila Viçosa, and the hilltop villages of Monsaraz and Marvão. The Moorish history of the region is more evident in Lower Alentejo, in towns like Mértola and Serpa, with their low, whitewashed, blue-trimmed houses.

Looking down on the walled hilltop village of Monsaraz

Page 127: Whitewashed houses and cobbled streets in Marvão

0 _____ 30 km
0 _____ 20 miles

Castelo de Vide
Alpalhão
Marvão 3
N244
N245
IP2 E802
N246
N359
Ponte de Sor
Crato
Portalegre
1025
N119
Seda
N369
Alter do Chão
Parque Natural de Serra de São Mamede
N2
IC13
PORTALEGRE
N245
Cabeço de Vide
Arronches
Barragem do Maranhão
Avis
Fronteira
Monforte
N246
Barragem do Caia
Campo Maior
Sousel
IP7
E802
Santa Eulália
Veiros
Pavia
N251
Estremoz 4
IP7 E90 A6
Elvas 5
Badajoz
Vimieiro
Borba
N4
Vila Viçosa 2
N2
N370
Évoramonte
Arraiolos
E802
Alandroal
N114
Barragem do Divor
ÉVORA
Azaruja
A6
N18
Redondo
Montemor-o-Novo
Cromeleque do Almendres
São Miguel de Machede
N254
Guadiana
Santiago do Escoural
Casa Branca
Évora 1
Pias
Barragem Pego do Altar
N380
Xarrama
IP7
E802
Montoito
Monsaraz 6
Alcáçovas
São Manços
N256
Viana do Alentejo
Reguengos de Monsaraz
Mourão
Torrão
N1
Portel
Degebe
N5
Alvito
Barragem do Alvito
Barragem do Alqueva
Barragem de Vale de Gaio
Vidigueira
Alqueva
Odivelas
Cuba
IP2
E802
Amareleja
IP8
Barragem de Odivelas
Moura
Ardila
N255
Ferreira do Alentejo
Beringel
N121
Beja 7
N260
Pias
Ervidel
N18
Serpa
N2
Aljustre
Barragem do Roxo
Santa Iria
A2
Albernoa
IP2
E802
N265
Guadiana
IP1
BEJA
Vale de Açor
Vale do Poço
N122
Parque Natural do Vale do Guadiana
Castro Verde
Mértola 8
E01
N2
N267
Chança
Semblana
Vascão
N124

In Two Days

If you're not quite sure where to begin your travels, this itinerary recommends a practical and enjoyable two days out and about in The Alentejo, taking in some of the best places to see using the Getting your Bearings map on the previous page. For more information see the main entries.

Day 1

Morning

Walk around the walled city of **1 Évora** (right; ➤ 132–135). Climb to the Roman temple, then visit the cathedral, museum and Capela dos Ossos (Chapel of Bones) before lunch at one of the cafés on Praça do Giraldo.

Afternoon

Leave Évora on the N18 in the direction of **7 Beja** (➤ 142). When the road to Beja turns right, keep ahead on the N256 to Reguengos de Monsaraz. Turn left here, following signs to Monsaraz across a landscape of vineyards and olive groves. Just beyond the pottery-producing village of São Pedro de Corval, look out for Rocha dos Namorados (Lovers' Rock), a prehistoric *menhir* beside the road. Continue to **6 Monsaraz** (➤ 141), visible on its hill across the plain.

Evening

Spend the night in the sleepy village of Monsaraz and wake to superb views from its 13th-century castle walls over the plains and the new Alqueva Dam (➤ 141). Book ahead for a room at Dom Nuno (➤ 144).

Day 2

Morning

Retrace your route to Reguengos de Monsaraz and follow signs north to Alandroal and Vila Viçosa on the N255. Arriving in **2 Vila Viçosa** (right; ➤ 136–137), leave your car outside the old royal palace and take a guided tour of the palace before wandering up to the castle and down to the town centre for lunch beside the orange trees and marble fountain on Praça da República.

Afternoon

The road from Vila Viçosa (right) to Borba leads past the quarries that are the source of the local marble. Turn right in Borba to reach the N4, passing more quarries on your way to **4 Estremoz** (➤ 140). Drive up to the castle at the top of the town for a drink at the Pousada da Rainha Santa Isabel (➤ 144) and visit the municipal museum to admire the pottery (left). Leave Estremoz on the IP2, go north to Portalegre, bypass Portalegre and turn right to **3 Marvão** (below; ➤ 138–139), whose hilltop castle dominates the view as you approach. Leave your car outside the village and walk up to the castle in time to enjoy the sunset walk around its walls.

Evening

Ask at the tourist office (➤ 139) about rooms in private houses in Marvão (below), or stay the night at the Pousada Santa Maria (➤ 143) and celebrate your arrival with a hearty Alentejan meal of roast lamb or goat.

❶ Évora

With its Moorish alleys, shady squares, fountains and Renaissance mansions, the largest city in the Alentejo makes a good place for a stroll. Founded by the Romans, strengthened by the Moors and recovered from them for Afonso Henriques by Geraldo Sempavor (Gerald the Fearless), Évora rose to prominence in the 15th and 16th centuries as a centre of arts and learning – a reputation that survives to this day.

The Romans built their walled city of *Ebora Cerealis* high on a hill above the Alentejo plain. At the summit of the town, they erected the temple of Diana, now the **Templo Romano** and the best-preserved Roman monument in Portugal.

Used as a slaughterhouse during the 19th century, the granite columns and marble capitals of this second-century AD temple have only recently been restored. Floodlit at night, it makes a spectacular sight.

Templo Romano illuminated at night

Carved apostles on the door of the cathedral

Convento dos Lóios

All the main sights are within the walled town, made a World Heritage Site by UNESCO in 1986. Directly behind the temple, the **Convento dos Lóios** is a 15th-century monastery that has been converted into an appealing *pousada* (➤ 143), where you dine in the cloisters and sleep in the monks' cells. Even if you're not staying here, it's worth going in to admire the Gothic cloisters and the Manueline chapter-house door.

The attached church, **Igreja dos Lóios**, was the private chapel of the dukes of Cadaval, who are buried beneath marble tombstones. The nave is lined with floor-to-ceiling *azulejos* depicting the life of a former patriarch of Venice. You can peek through a pair of grilles in the floor to see a medieval cistern and an ossuary of human bones.

The Cathedral

The **sé** (cathedral), completed in 1250, has a fortress-like Romanesque appearance similar to that at Coimbra (➤ 108). A Gothic portal, carved with figures of the apostles, stands between two strangely unmatched towers. Inside, there is marble everywhere, in the lectern, pulpit and high altar. The entry to the **Museu de Arte Sacra** also gives access to the Coro Alto, where the carved oak choir stalls feature scenes of rural life such as grape-picking and pig-sticking (hunting wild boars with spears), and the **Gothic cloister**, where you can climb onto the roof for views over Évora and a close-up look at the cathedral lantern and towers. In the museum there is an extraordinary 13th-century figure of the Virgin, whose innards open up to reveal biblical scenes.

Museu de Évora

The **Museu de Évora** is housed in the former archbishop's palace. It contains Roman tombstones and funerary inscriptions, medieval and Renaissance sculpture and 17th-century *azulejos* from Lisbon.

Among the paintings on the first floor, look for *Holy Virgin with Child* by Alvaro Pires de Évora, painted around 1410. Pires is the earliest identified Portuguese artist, and although a number of his paintings are on show in Pisa and Florence, this is the first to be permanently exhibited in Portugal.

The Capela dos Ossos – not for the squeamish

Also here is a 16th-century Flemish polyptych of 13 panels depicting the *Life of the Virgin*, which was previously the cathedral altarpiece. The museum reopened in June 2009, with enlargements carried out to the space for permanent exhibitions, as well as work on the building itself.

The Town

A staircase beside the cathedral leads down towards **Largo da Porta de Moura**, one of Évora's most attractive squares, with a Renaissance fountain and 16th-century houses which have Manueline-Moorish arcades. Alternatively, take Rua 5 de Outubro (lined with souvenir and craft shops), opposite the cathedral, to reach **Praça do Giraldo**, a handsome square with arches, a marble fountain and café terraces. During the Inquisition this was an execution ground, but today it is a lively square that is often the scene of book fairs, music concerts or open-air theatre.

A short distance away, the **Igreja de São Francisco** is home to one of Portugal's most macabre sights. To the right of the façade, with its unusual portico of pointed, rounded and horseshoe arches, a separate entrance leads to the cloister and the **Capela dos Ossos** (Chapel of Bones), whose walls and columns are covered with the skulls, femurs, tibias and other bones of 5,000 monks. Grinning skulls stare down from the ceiling and a grisly corpse hangs on one wall.

For a change, walk across the square to the **Jardim Público**, and the remains of a 16th-century Moorish-style palace.

About ten minutes drive from Évora is the **Alimendres Megalithic Site**, which has some of the oldest prehistoric remains in Europe.

TAKING A BREAK

There are **outdoor cafés** on Praça do Giraldo, in the Jardim Público and the gardens by the Templo Romano. If you want a more substantial meal, there's the excellent **Taberna Tipica Quarta Feira** (➤ 145), popular with tourists, or **O Fialho** (➤ 144), famous across Portugal for its traditional dishes.

✚ 201 D2

Tourist Information Office
✉ Praça do Giraldo ☎ 266 777 071; www2.cm-evora.pt/guiaturistico

Igreja dos Lóios
✉ Largo do Conde de Vila Flor ☎ 266 704 714 🕐 Tue–Sun 9–12, 2–5
💵 Moderate

Museu de Évora
✉ Largo do Conde de Vila Flor ☎ 266 702 604; http://museudevora.imc-ip.pt
🕐 Tue 2:30–6, Wed–Sun 10–6.

Sé
✉ Largo Marquês de Marialva ☎ 266 769 800 🕐 Jul to mid-Sep Tue–Sun 9–5; mid-Sep–May 9–12:30, 2–5 💵 Museum inexpensive

Igreja da São Francisco/Capela dos Ossos
✉ Praça 1 de Maio ☎ 266 704 521 🕐 Daily 9–12:30, 2:30–5:30
💵 Inexpensive

ÉVORA: INSIDE INFO

Top tips Évora's medieval appearance does not lend itself to modern transport. If you are driving, it is best to **park on the outskirts** and walk in.
■ There are a number of well signposted Ruta dos Vinhos starting from Evora. These are co-ordinated by a central office (Praça Joaquim António de Aguiar 20–21; Mon–Sat 9–1, 2–6; Tel: 266 746 609).

Hidden gem A steep hill behind the cathedral and Museu de Évora leads to the **old Jesuit university**, founded by Cardinal Henrique, the future king, in 1559. The university was closed down in 1759 by the Marquês de Pombal, but is now open, so you can wander around its beautiful tiled courtyard.

In more depth Take a walk through the old Moorish quarter, **Mouraria**, with its whitewashed houses and lamplit, cobbled streets. From beneath the gardens in front of the Roman temple, Rua dos Fontes drops steeply through Mouraria to Largo do Avis, beside the only remaining medieval gateway to the walled town. From the square of Largo do Chão das Covas, Rua do Cano follows the course of the old aqueduct, parts of which can still be seen outside the walls.

② Vila Viçosa

The power and wealth of the Portuguese kings is on display in Vila Viçosa, the seat of Portugal's last ruling dynasty, the dukes of Bragança. Built of marble, this is a prosperous town whose shining "white gold" can be seen everywhere.

Begin at **Terreiro do Paço**, the vast square in front of the Paço Ducal. A statue of João IV on horseback stands at the centre. The palace, fronted with marble, dominates the square. To one side is the royal chapel; to the other, Convento das Chagas, the mausoleum of the duchesses of Bragança, now a *pousada*. Across the square is the Mosterio dos Agostinhos, where the dukes are buried.

The **Paço Ducal** can only be visited on a guided tour, with additional charges to see the armoury, treasury, Chinese porcelain and Museu dos Coches. Most interesting are the private apartments of Dom Carlos (Portugal's penultimate king) and Dona Amelia, abandoned on the day of Carlos' assassination in 1908, with the table still set for dinner, family portraits and Dona Amelia's sketches on the walls. A large park outside the palace is home to deer and wild boar.

The **Museu dos Coches** (Coach Museum), in the Royal Stables, contains beautifully maintained coaches, landaus and state carriages. This is an annex to the popular coach museum in Lisbon, and exhibitions are sometimes exchanged between the two sites.

From the Terreiro do Paço, the **Avenida dos Duques de Bragança** leads towards the old walled town, dominated by a 13th-century *castelo* (castle). This was the original residence

A statue of Dom João IV, the first of Bragança's kings, stands before the Paço Ducal

THE DUKES OF BRAGANÇA

Although the town was given a royal charter as early as 1270, it was the dukes of Bragança who made Vila Viçosa. The title of Bragança was created in 1442 for an illegitimate son of João I of Avis; the second duke, Dom Fernando, moved his court to Vila Viçosa, and the fourth duke, Dom Jaime, began the building of the Paço Ducal (Ducal Palace) in 1501. Vila Viçosa became the finest address in Portugal, with banquets, balls and bullfights held in the palace for the leading families of the day. All that changed in 1640 when the eighth duke, João IV, reluctantly accepted the throne, ending 60 years of Spanish rule. The Braganças ruled Portugal until the fall of the monarchy in 1910 and continued to live in the palace, though many of its treasures were taken to Lisbon and the royal palaces at Mafra (► 66) and Sintra (► 60–61).

of the dukes of Bragança and has a small archaeological museum.

TAKING A BREAK

Café Restauração, Praça da República, serves snacks.

➕ 201 E2

Tourist Information Office
✉ Praça da República ☎ 268 881 101; www.cm-vilavicosa.pt

Paço Ducal
✉ Terreiro do Paço ☎ 268 980 659; www.museudoscoches-ipmuseus.pt/en/museu_vicosa.htm ⏰ Tue–Fri 9–1, 3–5:30, Sat–Sun 9–1, 3–6 (5 in winter). Last admission one hour before closing. 💶 Moderate (expensive with additional charges)

The main street is overlooked by the 13th-century castle

VILA VIÇOSA: INSIDE INFO

Top tip Accommodation in Vila Viçosa is not plentiful, although the tourist office should be able to help you find somewhere.

Hidden gem What looks like a pair of red garage doors at the end of a row of houses on Avenida dos Duques de Bragança opens up to reveal a **Passo**, one of a series of 16th-century Stations of the Cross remodelled in the 18th century with a marble portal and *azulejo* tiles depicting scenes from the life of Christ.

❸ Marvão

The most spectacular of all Portugal's hilltop villages perches like an eagle's nest on a rocky ridge 862m (2,827 feet) up in the Serra de São Mamede. The castle and medieval walls seem to grow out of the rock, and it is clear that this must have been a near-impregnable fortress. During the 16th century, Marvão had a population of more than 1,400, but today fewer than 200 people live here.

The Romans came here, and so did the Moors – the village takes its name from Ibn Maruán, the 9th-century Islamic Lord of Coimbra (Marvão comes from Maruán). After the Christian conquest, it was Dom Dinis who fortified the castle here at the end of the 13th century. It was to become one of a long chain of defensive outposts protecting the border with Spain.

View from the castle of the typical white dwellings of the medieval village

Unless you are staying the night, it is best to park outside the village and enter on foot through the main gate, **Porta de Rodão**. From Praça do Pelourinho, with its 16th-century pillory, Rua do Espírito Santo, known for its whitewashed houses with wrought-iron balconies, leads into Rua do Castelo, which leads to the castle.

Rua do Castelo – a living museum

The Gothic and Renaissance architecture of Rua do Castelo has been preserved untouched during the centuries of Marvão's decline and only now being rediscovered and restored. You can climb onto the walls, with their battlements, turrets and towers, and make a complete circuit, but it is easier to walk up to the castle along the village streets. The **castle**, rebuilt in the 17th century, is magnificent. Two fortified gates lead to a courtyard where you can climb onto

Marvão was one of a chain of fortified towns and villages along the Portuguese border with Spain

the parapet for views over the village. Breaching a second line of defence, you come to another courtyard, which contains the armoury (a military museum) and the castle keep. The views from here are impressive. To the north are the snow-capped peaks of the Serra da Estrela (➤ 119–120); to the south, the mountains of the Serra de São Mamede; to the west, the Alentejo countryside; to the east, Spain.

Just outside the castle walls, the **Museu Municipal**, in the 13th-century church of Santa Maria, displays folk costumes, baptismal outfits, religious art and archaeological finds.

TAKING A BREAK

Casa do Povo , in Rua de Cima, offers well-prepared, filling Alentejan cuisine (tel: 245 993 160).

➕ 201 E4

Tourist Information Office
✉ Largo de Santa Maria ☎ 245 909 131; www.cm-marvao.pt

Museu Municipal
✉ Largo de Santa Maria ☎ 245 909 132 ◷ Daily 9:30 –12:30, 2–5:30
▧ Inexpensive

MARVÃO: INSIDE INFO

Top tips Try to stay overnight to watch the **sunset** from the castle walls and enjoy the evening peace of the village.
- As well as the **Pousada Santa Maria** (➤ 143), there are several **private houses** with rooms to let – ask at the tourist office.
- **Chestnut trees** thrive in this area, and a festival is held in November that sees the village come alive with music, wine and chestnut roasting.

Hidden gem Walk down the steps inside the castle entrance to see a **monumental cistern** and capable of storing six months' water.

In more depth The surrounding **Serra de São Mamede** is a natural park with Roman and neolithic remains and wildlife including griffon vultures, red deer and Europe's largest colony of bats. Also here, is the spa town of Castelo de Vide, with an attractive old Jewish quarter, a golf course and its own spring.

At Your Leisure

◩ Estremoz

The largest of the Alentejo "marble" towns seems to have an extra sheen of white as marble from the local quarries is used as an everyday building material. Life here centres on the **Rossio Marquês de Pombal**, a huge square where one of Portugal's biggest markets is held on Saturdays.

Other sights of interest are in the upper town, around the 13th-century **castle** built by Dom Dinis for his future wife, Isabel of Aragón (and now one of the most famous *pousadas* in Portugal – ➤ 144). As queen, Isabel became known for her devotion to the poor and she was sainted after her death. Her story is told in *azulejos* in the **Capela da Rainha Santa Isabel**, including that of the Miracle of the Roses. Her

THREE OF THE BEST... ALENTEJAN CUISINE

- *Ensopado de borrego* – lamb stew served on slices of bread
- *Porco à alentejana* – Alentejo pork stewed with clams
- *Sopa alentejana* – soup with bread, garlic, coriander and poached egg

The whitewashed, red-roofed buildings of Elvas within its star-shaped fortifications

husband disapproved of her giving alms to the poor, so she hid the bread in the folds of her skirt where he would not see it. When he became suspicious and challenged her she opened her skirt and the bread had miraculously turned into roses. A marble statue of the saint stands on the castle terrace, from where there are views to Évoramonte.

The **Museu Municipal** features folk art in cork, oak and marble, and *bonecos* (terracotta figurines for which Estremoz is famous).

✚ 201 E2
Tourist Information Office
✉ Praça da República ☎ 268 339 200

Museu Municipal
✉ Largo Dom Dinis ☎ 268 333 608
🕐 Tue–Sun 9–12:30, 2–5:30 (May–Sep to 6:30)
💶 Inexpensive

◪ Elvas

Besides being famous for its Ameixa da Elvas greengage plums, Elvas is a heavily fortified frontier town, which sits just 12km (7.4 miles) from Portugal's border with Spain and 15km (9.3 miles) from the Spanish citadel at Badajoz. Captured by Afonso Henriques in 1166, retaken by the Moors, and finally seized by Christian forces in 1226, Elvas has been besieged many times but only once been taken by Spanish troops.

The star-shaped fortifications that surround the town, built according to the designs of the French military engineer, Vauban, date largely from the 17th century. They are supplemented by two fortresses, one of which, **Forte de Santa Luzia**, can sometimes be visited (check at the tourist information office).

The streets of the old town radiate from Praça da República. At one end stands the **Igreja de Nossa Senhora da Assunção**, which had cathedral status until 1882, when the town lost its bishopric.

Behind the church, **Largo de Santa Clara** is an attractive triangular "square" with a Manueline marble pillory, still with its original iron hooks to which prisoners were tied.

On one side of the square, the **Igreja de Nossa Senhora da Consolação** looks plain from the outside but the interior is extraordinary, an octagonal chapel with painted marble columns and blue-and-yellow *azulejos* lining the walls.

Just outside of the town, there is a large reservoir, Barragem da Caia, where you can enjoy fishing and swimming in attractive surroundings.

BEST FOR KIDS
- **Capela dos Ossos**, Évora (for older children, ➤ 134): Grisly corpses and grinning skulls.
- **The castle at Marvão** (➤ 139): Fabulous views across the Serra da Estrela and magnificent fortifications.
- Europe's largest manmade reservoir at Alqueva has created a beach culture in lower Alentejo. From Estrela, you can organise boat trips, fishing, sailing and swimming (www.alqueva.com).

🔁 201 F2
Tourist Information Office
✉ Praça da República ☎ 268 622 236

Igreja de Nossa Senhora da Consolação
✉ Largo de Santa Clara ⏰ Tue–Sun 9–12:30, 2–5:30

🟦 Monsaraz

Monsaraz would be just another attractive hilltop village were it not for the famously fantastic views enjoyed by hordes of day trippers, and the plaques on the Porta de Vila recalling visits by Portuguese presidents Soares and Sampaio.

The peaceful countryside around the attractive village of Monsaraz

You can climb the 40m (131-foot) high walls of the castle keep at Beja

There are two parallel streets – **Rua Direita**, with a tourist office, the parish church, Igreja Matriz and 16th-century houses, and **Rua de Santiago**, which has a more lived-in feel, with shops, restaurants and crafts. Rua Direita leads to the 13th-century **castle**, once a Knights Templar fortress. The ramparts have unparalleled views over the village and the Alentejo countryside. The courtyard is sometimes the bullring.

🚩 201 E2
Tourist Information Office
✉ Largo Dom Nuno Alvares Pereira
☎ 266 557 136

🄻 Beja

The capital of Lower Alentejo is a pleasing town of whitewashed houses, founded by Julius Caesar as *Pax Julia* to commemorate a peace (*pax*) treaty between the Romans and the Lusitani tribe. A new airport at Beja is due to open the lower Alentejo to international visitors, but for now this still remains a sleepy, if attractive, town. The most striking monument is the 13th-century castelo (castle); you can climb the keep for views over the Alentejo wheatlands.

Beja is best known as the home of Mariana Alcoforado, the nun whose (possibly fictional) love letters to a French cavalry officer were published in France in 1669 as *Lettres Portugaises*. The convent where she lived, Nossa Senhora da Conceicão, is now the **Museu Regional**, with many interesting prehistoric and Roman finds.

Of more interest are the convent buildings, especially the baroque chapel, tiled cloisters and 16th-century Hispano-Arab *azulejos* in the chapter house.

Another convent is now the **Pousada de São Francisco** (➤ 144).

🚩 201 D1
Tourist Information Office
✉ Rua Capitão João Francisco de Sousa
☎ 284 311 913

Castelo
✉ Largo do Lidador ☎ 284 311 912
🕐 Summer Tue–Sun 10–1, 2–6; winter, Tue–Sun 9–12, 1–4 💶 Inexpensive (Sun free)

Museu Regional
✉ Largo da Conceicão ☎ 284 323 351; www.museuregionaldebeja.net 🕐 Tue–Sun 9:30–12:30, 2–5:15 💶 Inexpensive

🄼 Mértola

This pretty little walled town at the confluence of the Guadiana and Oeiras rivers has a long history as a trading port at the highest navigable point on the Guadiana.

These days, Mértola promotes itself as a *vila museu* (museum town), with small museums s around the town devoted to its Roman, Islamic and Portuguese history. You can visit all of them on one ticket, including the castle keep for views over the rooftops. Don't miss the parish church, converted from a mosque at the end of the 12th century, whose *mihrab*, niche facing east to Mecca, is visible behind the altar and the arches and columns retain a strong Islamic feel.

🚩 202 D2
Tourist Information Office
✉ Rua da Igreja 1 ☎ 286 610 109; www.cm-mertola.pt 🕐 Daily 9–12:30, 2–5:30 💶 Museums moderate

Where to... Stay

Prices

Expect to pay for a double room per night in high season:
€ under €60 €€ €60–€120 €€€ €121–€180 €€€€ over €180

ÉVORA

Residencial Riviera €€

Well located in the centre of town, near to the cathedral square, this modern and well-priced hotel is a good base for exploring the town. The interior and public areas are functional rather than luxurious, but the 21 bedrooms are all a good size and well appointed to ensure a comfortable stay. There is an attractive dining room where a large Alentejo breakfast is served by the friendly staff.

🕂 201 D2 ⊠ Rua 5 do Outubro, 47–49
☎ 266 737 210; www.riviera-evora.com

Pousada dos Lóios €€€–€€€€

The fabulous 15th-century monastery of the Lóios has an excellent restaurant in the ornate cloisters, and is one of the country's leading pousadas. The majestic rooms are furnished and decorated with valuable antiques, in particular the "presidential" suite, which has Indo-Portuguese furniture. There is also a good-sized swimming pool. This is the perfect choice if you want to experience staying in an authentic pousada while enjoying plenty of modern comforts.

🕂 201 D2 ⊠ Largo Conde de Vila-Flor
☎ 266 730 070; www.pousadas.pt

Convento do Espinheiro €€–€€€

Housed in a former convent, this atmospheric hotel has an excellent restaurant (open to non-residents also), and wonderful gardens with a large heated swimming pool and tennis court. The hotel itself is spacious and luxurious, with white washed walls and good-sized, attractively furnished rooms, particularly in the new wing. The restoration work has been done with great care, and has retained enough calm nooks and crannies to remind you of the former purpose of the building.

🕂 201 D2 ⊠ Quinta Convento Espinheiro
☎ 266 788 200; www.conventodoespinheiro.com

VILA VIÇOSA

Aldeamento de Peixinhos €€

This attractive self-catering apartment complex has outdoor swimming pools, and a large restaurant. There is a choice of accommodation with one, two- and three-bedroomed apartments and villas, all with their own kitchens that are stocked with basic cooking equipment. Well located, just on the outskirts of town, this is a good value option that is popular with families.

🕂 201 E2 ⊠ 7160–285 Vila Viçosa ☎ 268 980 472; www.casadospeixinhos.pa-net.pt

MARVÃO

Pousada Santa Maria €€–€€€

Perfectly cool in summer and warm in the winter, like the other whitewashed houses in this picturesque hilltop village, this well-appointed pousada is a delight inside and out. The large spacious rooms and simple dining room look across the beautiful olive trees and cork-oaks of the Alentejo. Enjoy the beautiful views while sampling local specialities, including excellent cheeses and well-chosen wines. Recommended.

🕂 201 E4 ⊠ Rua 24 de Janeiro 7
☎ 245 993 201; www.pousadas.pt

Where to...
Eat and Drink

Prices
Expect to pay per person for a three-course meal, excluding drinks and tips
€ under €12   €€ €12–€24   €€€ €25–€36   €€€€ over €36

ÉVORA

Cozinha de Santo Humberto €€€

Évora probably has more reliably excellent restaurants than any other city outside Lisbon and this is one of them. When you go down into the pristine white cellar (used to store wine), you'll notice a sideboard loaded with delicious starters and desserts. Another trademark of the restaurant is the row of blackened kettles hanging from the ceiling. In season go for the game – the wild boar ragout is exceptional – or try *chispe assado* (roast pork).

🔒 201 D1 ⊠ Largo Dom Nuno Álvares Pereira, 7801-901 Beja 🕿 284 313 580; www.pousadas.pt

O Fialho €€€–€€€€

🔒 201 D2 ⊠ Rua da Moeda 39 🕿 266 704 251 🕒 Fri–Wed 12–3, 7–10. Closed third week in Nov

Justly famous – gourmets even come especially from Lisbon to eat here – O Fialho is surprisingly simple to look at and calls itself a *cervejaria* (beer house). A few hunting trophies and simple *azulejos* are the only ornaments. This is not a place to turn down the *acepipes* (▶ 38), even though the starters are fabulous. What sets the food apart is the use of herbs and spices, for example in the *bacalhau*

ESTREMOZ

Pousada da Rainha Santa Isabel €€€

Generally regarded as the most prestigious *pousada* of all, this one is contained in an austere-looking medieval castle. Details such as four-poster beds, tapestries fit for a museum, entire walls of *azulejos* and the long vaulted refectory earn the whole ensemble the epithet of "grandiose". When you are not exploring the local sights, you can relax by the swimming pool and dine on Alentejo specialities, sampling fine wines from the extensive cellar.

🔒 201 E2 ⊠ Castelo de Estremoz, Largo Dom Diniz 🕿 268 332 075; www.pousadas.pt

MONSARAZ

Casa Dom Nuno €

Along the main street near the church, this popular guesthouse has charming small rooms and serves a very good breakfast. The main

attraction, apart from the prime location, is the terrace, which offers guests stunning views for miles across the Alentejo. This guesthouse is often closed in winter, and is popular in summer so you need to book well ahead to stay here.

🔒 201 E2 ⊠ Rua do Castelo 66 🕿 266 557 146 🕒 Closed part of Dec

BEJA

Pousada de São Francisco €€€

The cells of this ancient Franciscan monastery have become comfortable rooms. Don't be put off by the impersonality of the huge entrance hall and mammoth staircase – the guest areas are intimate and cheery. A cool 13th-century chapel in the complex has been carefully restored, and a pool installed in the grounds – much needed in a city where summer temperatures can top 40°C.

carpaccio, sprinkled liberally with capers. *Lombos de javali* (medallions of wild boar) are set off with a hint of rosemary. Attentive service, outstanding wines and home-made liqueurs complete the experience. Recommended.

➕ **201 D2** ✉ Travessa das Mascarenhas 16, near Praça Joaquim António de Aguiar ☎ 266 703 079; www.restaurantefialho.com ⏰ Tue–Sun 12–12. Closed 1–21 Sep

Taberna Típica Quarta Feira €€

Well located in the centre of town, this attractive restaurant is accustomed to serving hungry tourists, but manages to do so while still managing to keep the emphasis on good fresh food and friendly service. The menu offers traditional Portuguese dishes but includes a minimal choice each day, so be prepared to be led by whatever was available in the market that morning. Recommended.

➕ **201 D2** ✉ Rua do Inverno ☎ 266 707 530 ⏰ Daily 11–11

VILA VIÇOSA

Taverna dos Conjurados €€–€€€

Classic interior with exposed stone wall and white-washed walls, this is a deceptively simple restaurant, which serves well-cooked, authentic cuisine. All the food is very fresh, very local, and well regarded by local residents. Expect to sit at the classic wooden tables and enjoy excellent food and hearty portions.

➕ **201 E2** ✉ Largo 25 de Abril ☎ 268 989 530 ⏰ 12–2:30, 7:30–11

ESTREMOZ

Adega Típica do Isaías €€

Huge, age-old amphorae tell you this has long been a wine cellar, and jugs of red are plonked onto every table. This wonderfully down-to-earth place attracts locals from every walk of life interested only in the delicious food, from *pimentos assados* (roast red peppers) to *bolo de mel* (honey cake), via *borrego no forno* (roast lamb) or *estufado de lebre* (hare stew). Meat and fish are barbecued out on the street.

➕ **201 E2** ✉ Rua do Almeida 21 ☎ 268 322 318 ⏰ Mon–Sat 12–2, 7–10:30. Closed 2nd and 3rd weeks in Aug

ELVAS

A Coluna €–€€

This is a discreet but popular restaurant with a whitewashed interior and white table linen. The menu is simple, and everyone swears by the *cabrito* (goat), the *bacalhau* dishes and the *cataplana* (fish stew). It's slightly hidden away from the central square, but soon fills up with locals.

➕ **201 F2** ✉ Rua do Cabrito 11 ☎ 268 623 728 ⏰ Wed–Mon 12–3, 7–10

MONSARAZ

O Alcaide €€

Breathtaking views across the open plains from the picture window are a wonderful backdrop for simple home cooking. *Migas de pao con carne de porco* (pork with croutons) and *borrego* (roast lamb) are just two of the regional specialities on offer here. Recommended for an authentic dining experience.

➕ **201 E2** ✉ Rua de Santiago 18 ☎ 266 557 168; www.ciberevora.pt/alcaide ⏰ Fri–Wed 12–3, 7–9. Closed 1–15 Jul and Oct

BEJA

Café Luís da Rocha €–€€

This bustling café-bar is not a particularly beautiful place, but if you linger long enough over your coffee, you'll see an interesting cross section of the city as people pop in for a coffee or beer or a chat. Apart from the fascinating people-watching, the *queijadas* (cheese-filled cakes) are excellent.

➕ **201 D1** ✉ Rua Capitão João Francisco de Sousa 63 ☎ 284 323 179; www. luizdarocha.com ⏰ Dining room daily 12–3:30, 7–10. Café daily 8–11. Closed Sun Jul–Sep

Where to...
Shop

MARKETS

Visit the market in **Évora**, every second Tuesday morning. Every week, Tuesday to Friday you can bargain for ceramics on **Praça Primeiro de Maio**.

Estremoz has a market every Saturday on the Rossio – the cheeses are superb. Earthenware is a speciality, especially the oddly shaped *moringues* (water jars).

CRAFTS

For carpets visit **Arraiolos**, 20km (12.5 miles) north of Évora. The fine Arraiolos hand-knotted rugs are sold at workshops just outside the town, at Ilhas; or at several shops on Rua 5 Outubro, where prices are far lower than in Lisbon.

Flôr da Rosa, west of Portalegre, is renowned for its pottery, sold at traditional *olarias* near the convent.

Fine crafts are sold at **Millfores** (Rua Dr Matos Magalhães 1, Marvão). Unusual goods in wood, wicker and cork are crafted by **Joaquim Canoas Vieira** (Largo de Nossa Senhora do Passo, Barbacena, near Elvas, tel: 268 662 151).

FOOD AND DRINK

The cornfields are the first hint that this is bread country – often used as a key ingredient in soups. Try also to buy some Alentejo charcuterie. Look for charcuterie with the Denominacão de Orignm Protegida DOP status to be sure of quality.

Picnic provisions can be bought at Évora's covered market.

Where to...
Be Entertained

FESTIVALS

The last third of June is Évora's **Feira de São João**, which combines music and crafts with food. There is also a film festival in November.

May is festival month for **Beja** when a number of bullfights are held. In the last week of September it's the turn of **Elvas** – the Festa de São Mateus, which features a large procession through the town.

Monsaraz holds a *vacada* (bloodless bullfight) in the castle on the second weekend of September. During the second week of July there's a crafts and folk festival.

SPORT AND OUTDOOR PURSUITS

The Atlantic beaches on the west coast are some of the most natural dramatic in the country – head for **Zambujeira** and **Odeceixe**.

One of the best places for **horse-riding** is run by **Miguel Palha** at Rua da República, Chança, near Alter do Chão.

The 18-hole **golf** course at Marvão, in the lee of the castle, has a spectacular location – **Ammaia**, Quinta do Prado, San Salvador da Aramenha 7330-330 (tel: 245 993 755; www.portugalgolf.pt).

NIGHTLIFE

Évora is about the only town in the region with any nightlife. *Titeres* (puppet shows) at the theatre on Praça Aguiar are worth seeing. Or check out the **Bar Casa do Vinho** (Praça 1 de Maio) or **Desassossego Bar** (Travessa do Janeiro).

The Algarve

Getting Your Bearings

Sandy beaches and sunny skies. Whitewashed villas with geraniums around the door. Fishing boats and the scent of freshly grilled sardines. These are the classic images of Portugal, and they are also the images of the Algarve.

For many people, the Algarve *is* Portugal, yet this small region at the southwest corner of Europe is in fact the least typical of all. The climate is more Mediterranean than Atlantic, the landscape more north African than Portuguese. This was *al-gharb*, the western outpost of Moorish Spain, which held out against the Christian Reconquest for a century after the fall of Lisbon. Reminders of the Arab presence are everywhere, from latticed chimneys to the almond trees that carpet the ground with a "snowfall" of white blossom in January.

The Algarve shoreline is neatly divided in two by the provincial capital, Faro. East of here is the *sotavento* (leeward) coast, sheltered by the barrier islands and lagoons of the Ria Formosa. To the west, the *barlavento* (windward) coast is battered by the Atlantic, producing the typical rock formations of sandstacks, grottoes, cliffs and coves of the Algarve. Henry the Navigator had his school at Sagres, and towns like Tavira and Lagos played a key role in the *descobrimentos* (discoveries, ► 13).

Later, the region was levelled by the 1755 earthquake, which had its epicentre near Lagos. But the greatest influence on the Algarve has been mass tourism, bringing eight million visitors a year. High-rise resorts, golf courses and waterparks have mushroomed from Faro to Lagos, and the development shows no sign of ending. To escape it, head inland to the villages of the Barrocal and the mountains of Monchique, or spend some time in the charming town of Tavira.

Odeceixe

Praia de
Monte Clérigo   Aljezur

Arrifana   Ma

Alfambras

Beaches 4

Carrapateira   Bordeira

Bensafrim

Castelejo   **Lagos**

Cabo de   Vila do
São Vicente 3   Bispo   Burgau

3   **Beach**
Ponta de
Sagres   **Sagres**

Page 147: The beach at Praia de Marinha

Right: Armação de Pera
Left: Praia de Rocha

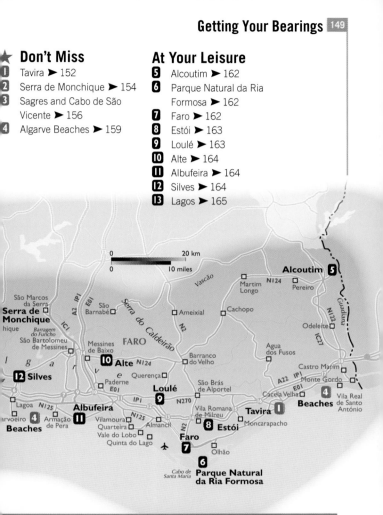

In Three Days

If you're not quite sure where to begin your travels, this itinerary recommends a practical and enjoyable three days out in the Algarve, taking in some of the best places to see using the Getting your Bearings map on the previous page. For more information see the main entries.

Day 1

Morning
Explore the old town of ❶ Tavira (➤ 152–153). Climb to the castle ruins for the excellent views, then wander down to the riverside for a picnic in the gardens or lunch at Bica, a no-frills café (➤ 167).

Afternoon and Evening
Walk, drive or take the bus to Quatro Águas, 2km (1.2 miles) east of Tavira, and catch the ferry to Ilha de Tavira for a lazy afternoon sunbathing on the beach, sunbathing and swimming. The Portas do Mar seafood restaurant, on Quatro Águas beside the jetty, is a good place for dinner.

Day 2

Morning
Leave Tavira on the N125 towards Faro. Stop in Luz da Tavira to admire its 16th-century parish church and platibanda houses, with windows and doorways framed in floral and geometric motifs. Continue to Quinta de Marim for a walk around the ❻ Parque Natural da Ria Formosa (➤ 162). Try to arrive in ❼ Faro (➤ 162) to visit the archaeological museum before lunch by the harbour.

Afternoon and Evening
Continue west on the N125. Just before Almansil, pull off the road to see the astonishing church of São Lourenço, whose interior is completely covered in blue-and-white *azulejos*. Arrive at ⓫ Albufeira (left; ➤ 164) in time for a quick dip in the sea or a bracing walk along the beach (left). Albufeira has restaurants to suit every taste and budget, but the traditional food here is salt-baked fish. If you want to splash out, try **Vila Joya** (➤ 168)

Day 3

Morning

Make an early start and head inland towards Paderne and Portela in the foothills of the Barrocal region. You can take a brief diversion east on the N124 to see the pretty village of **10 Alte** (➤ 164) before returning on the same road to **12 Silves** (above; ➤ 164). Drive up to the castle and visit the cathedral before a seafood lunch at Rui Marisqueira (➤ 169).

Afternoon and Evening

Continue west on the N124 and right on the N266 to climb to the **2 Serra de Monchique** (➤ 154–155). Drive up to the summit of Fóia for great views, then explore the spa village of Caldas de Monchique. Next take a scenic drive through eucalyptus and pinewoods to Aljezur, and follow the N268 south along the wild west coast. You should arrive in **3 Sagres** (below; ➤ 156–158) in time to visit the fortress before watching the sun set from **3 Cabo de São Vicente** (➤ 157–158).

◻ Tavira

This elegant riverside town has somehow managed to escape the tourist tide sweeping the Algarve. It straddles the River Gilão and is close to some of the area's best beaches. A seven-arched bridge, dating from Roman times, joins one side of the town to the other, and its noble houses are adorned with wrought-iron balconies and latticework doors.

Tavira is the most beautiful town of the Algarve's *sotavento* (leeward) coast. It has palm-lined gardens, handsome 18th-century mansions overlooking the river and more than 35 churches. One of the most enjoyable ways to sample the many churches in Tavira is through the Música Nas Igrejas (music in the churches) – a series of concerts held throughout the year.

During the Islamic era this was one of the three biggest towns in *al-gharb*, and it continued to flourish up to the 16th century as a port. Tuna fishing became a major industry until it was ended by the 1755 earthquake, which silted up the harbour. Today the town thrives as a low-key, low-rise resort.

The best place to start is **Praça da República**, the arcaded square on the west bank of the River Gilão. Climb the steps to **Igreja da Misericórdia**, with its 16th-century portal featuring carvings of Our Lady of Mercy flanked by saints Peter and Paul and the coats of arms of Tavira and Portugal.

A short climb to the left ends at **Castelo dos Mouros**, a ruined Moorish castle fortified by Dom Dinis, where you can walk around the walls for great views over Tavira and its distinctive *telhadas de tesouro* (treasure roofs), hip-gabled, pyramid shaped rooftops, which each cover a single room.

The waterfront is lined with grand houses and balconies

Behind the castle, the **Igreja de Santa Maria do Castelo**, built on the site of an old mosque, contains the tombs of Dom Paio Peres Correia, who captured the city in 1242.

An interactive science and technology museum offers a more modern diversion, with rotating exhibits on everything from the solar system to the Internet.

From Praça da República, shady **waterfront gardens**, with an iron bandstand at the centre, lead to the **old fish market**, reopened in 2000 with craft shops and cafés clustered around a central courtyard.

Ilha de Tavira

From the jetty at Quatro Águas, 2km (1.2 miles) east of town, ferries depart (regularly in summer and occasionally in winter) for Ilha de Tavira, an offshore island that forms part of the **Parque Natural da Ria Formosa** (➤ 162).

Walk across the mudflats to reach the magnificent 11km (6.8-mile) **beach**, backed by sand dunes and lapped by the warmest waters in the Algarve. With beach bars and a

Ilha de Tavira's superb sandy beach

campsite, this is a world away from the big resorts to the west. You can also reach the island by boat from Santa Luzia, or by walking across the causeway and taking the miniature train from the nearby holiday village of Pedras d'el Rei.

TAKING A BREAK

Veneza, on Praça da República, is a popular café and pastry shop. **Portas do Mar** (➤ 167), a fish restaurant by the jetty at Quatro Águas, has an excellent reputation too.

✚ **202 D1**

Tourist Information Office
✉ Rua da Galeria 9 ☎ 281 322 511; www.tavira.com.pt

Interactive Science Museum
✉ Convento do Carmo 9 ☎ 281 326 231; www.tavira.cienciaviva.pt
🕐 Sat–Sun 2–6, Tue–Fri 10–6, closed Mon 💲 Moderate

TAVIRA: INSIDE INFO

Top tip Try the local speciality, *bife de atum cebolada* (tuna steak with onions) at one of the riverside restaurants.
■ Try **tuna** straight off the boat, head to the nearby fishing village of Cabanas.

Hidden gem Cacela Velha, 10km (6 miles) east of Tavira, is a tiny village with a fort, church and houses perched on a cliff overlooking a sandy beach on the edge of the Ria Formosa. It is one of the few unspoiled Algarve coastal spots.

2 Serra de Monchique

The green hills of the volcanic Monchique mountain range provide a welcome respite from the summer heat of the Algarve coast. A trip into the mountains offers the chance to experience a different Algarve, far removed from the overcrowded beaches and busy resorts of the south.

The mountains provide a natural barrier between the Alentejo and the Algarve, sheltering the coastal region, helping to ensure its famous mild climate. Cork oaks, chestnut and eucalyptus trees grow on wooded hillsides, and the meadows are alive with wild flowers in spring.

A Spa Village and a Monastery

The easiest approach to the mountains is to drive north from **Portimão**, one of the Algarve's largest towns. After 20km (12.5 miles) you reach **Caldas de Monchique**, a spa village since Roman times. Climb up to the vantage point for views of the spa nestling in the valley. This is a delightful spot, made more attractive by the recent renovation of the 19th-century spa buildings and neo-Moorish casino.

You can taste the water at **Fonte dos Amores** (Lovers' Spring), then walk up through the woods to a picnic area by a stream. Bear in mind that the most famous visitor to the spa,

The scattered buildings of Caldas de Monchique

The restored spa buildings at Caldas de Monchique

João II, died soon after taking the waters in 1495.

The road continues for 6km (3.7 miles) to **Monchique**, the main town of the region. Climb the steps in the old town to reach the 16th-century parish church, Igreja Matriz, with Manueline portal columns carved into knotted ropes.

Keep going to eventually reach the ruins of a Franciscan monastery, Nossa Senhora do Desterro, destroyed in the 1771 earthquake, with gardens of lemon and magnolia trees and views across the town to the peak of Picota (773m/2,535 feet).

A short drive from Monchique is the highest summit in the Algarve, **Pico da Fóia** (902m/2,960 feet). The peak is often shrouded in mist, but on clear days the views stretch to Portimão, Lagos (➤ 165) and Cabo de São Vicente (➤ 157).

Return to Portimão the same way you came, or follow the N267 on a scenic mountain road to Aljezur and the **beaches of the west coast** (➤ 159–161).

TAKING A BREAK

There are several **inns** on the road to Fóia offering rustic mountain cuisine or order a plate of tapas and a bottle of Monchique mineral water at **Charrete** (Rua Dr Samora Gil 30–34, Tel: 282 912 142) in the centre of the old town.

✚ 202 B2

Tourist Information Office
✉ Largo de São Sebastião, Monchique ☎ 282 911 189

Monchique Thermal Spas
✉ Caldas de Monchique ☎ 282 910 910; www.monchiquetermas.com

SERRA DE MONCHIQUE: INSIDE INFO

Top tips Look out for *medronho*, a local firewater spirit made from the fruit of the arbutus (wild strawberry) tree.
■ Skirting Monchique on the road back down to the coast, stop to look at the handmade **folding wooden chairs**, a design brought to Monchique by the Romans and kept alive by the "Chair Man of Monchique" at a workshop halfway down the hill. Each chair is individually signed.

In more depth Ask at the tourist information office in Monchique for information about **walking in the mountains**. A popular walk is the climb to the summit of Picota, the second highest in the range, which takes around 1.5 hours from Monchique.

3 Sagres and Cabo de São Vicente

This wild and windswept cape at the southwest tip of Europe was once known as *O Fim do Mundo* (The End of the World). Standing on the headland and gazing out into the ocean as the waves crash against the cliffs, it is difficult not to feel the excitement of the medieval explorers who set off from Sagres into the great unknown, wondering what perils lay ahead and whether they would ever return.

School of Navigation

It was here in the 15th century that Prince Henry the Navigator founded his School of Navigation, gathering together the greatest cartographers, astronomers, mariners and shipbuilders in Europe. Great advances were made, including the design for a new type of ship, the caravel, a lateen-rigged sailing vessel that was later used by Christopher Columbus for his Atlantic crossings. It was the invention of the caravel that paved the way for Portugal's era of maritime discovery (► 12–14). Among the explorers who studied at Sagres were Vasco da Gama, Pedro Álvares Cabral and Ferdinand Magellan.

Henry's school was pillaged in 1587 by the British buccaneer Sir Francis Drake, and his precious library was burned to the ground. It probably stood on the site of the **Fortaleza de Sagres**, a 17th-century fortress on a windy promontory on the edge of town. All that remains from an earlier age are the simple chapel of **Nossa Senhora da Graça** and the huge **Rosa dos Ventos** (Wind Compass), 43m (47 yards) in diameter, possibly dating from Henry's time. Today there is a visitor centre, shop and café.

View across water to Fortaleza

The Town

Sagres is an end-of-the-road sort of town, attracting surfers and backpackers in summer, with a wide range of accomodation.

The real attraction of the town lies in its **beaches**, which are some of the best in the Algarve – as long as you don't mind freezing water and strong ocean winds. To the east of the fortress are more sheltered beaches.

Praia da Mareta is the most accessible, just below the main square. From **Praia da Baleeira**, by the harbour, it is a short walk to the windsurfing beach of **Praia da Martinhal**.

The rugged cliffs on the peninsula of Sagres

Cabo de São Vicente

From the *fortaleza*, the road continues for 6km (3.7 miles) across the headland to Cabo de São Vicente, named *Promontorium Sacrum* (Sacred Promontory) by the Romans, who thought the sun sank into the water here every night. Later it became a Christian shrine, based on the legend that the body of St Vincent had been washed ashore here in the fourth century AD. Later still, in the 12th century, the relics were said to have been transferred to Lisbon in a boat piloted by ravens, and St Vincent is now the patron saint of the capital.

Henry the Navigator is thought to have built his palace on the headland, roughly where the lighthouse now stands. This is one of the most powerful lighthouses in Europe, its 3,000-watt bulb visible up to 100km (62 miles) out at sea. The waters around the cape have been the site of numerous naval battles, but these days there is not much to disturb the peace, although it is still one of the world's busiest shipping routes.. The gusts up on the 60m (197 feet) cliffs can be fierce, and fishermen risk their lives by dangling oversize rods into the sea from the edge of the rock face. Come up here at sunset for magical views.

The best places to eat are at the **Pousada do Infante** (tel: 282 620 240), where you can also stay or head into Sagres town to one of the several eateries on the Praça da República. Try **Cochina** (€) with its extensive menu, or head a little out of town to **Mar a Vista** for its superb views (tel: 282 624 247).

The huge wind compass at Sagres is thought to date from the 15th century

➕ 202 B1

Tourist Information Office
✉ Rua Comandante Matoso, Sagres ☎ 282 624 873

Fortaleza de Sagres
✉ Ponta de Sagres ☎ 282 620 140 🕐 Oct–Apr daily 9:30–5:30; May–Sep daily 9:30–8 💰 Moderate

---

SAGRES AND CABO DE SÃO VICENTE: INSIDE INFO

Top tips Take a **sweater** to the cape even in summer. If you forget, stalls by the lighthouse sell chunky cardigans and rugs.
■ You can walk from Sagres to Cabo de São Vicente along a **clifftop path**. It's a good way of admiring the wild flowers that burst into life on the rocky cape in spring.

Hidden gem Praia do Beliche is a secluded, sheltered cove beneath the cliffs on the way from Sagres to Cabo de São Vicente.

In more depth If Sagres has given you a taste for wild Atlantic beaches, continue up the west coast on the **Costa Vicentina** (➤ 161).

4 Algarve Beaches

You could spend your entire holiday searching for the perfect beach. Everyone has their favourite, from long stretches of golden sand to tiny coves hidden beneath grottoes and ochre cliffs. There are beaches for families, watersports or for a sheltered, away-from-it-all feeling – just take your pick.

The beach at Albufeira is popular with fishermen

Family beaches

Praia Verde is a "green beach" and is reached by crossing a valley of pine trees and walking down through the dunes. The sea here is calm and warm – perfect for small children. This is one of a chain of beaches that stretch from Cacela Velha to Monte Gordo, 2km (1.2 miles) east.

In Tavira take the ferry to reach **Ilha de Tavira**, a popular island beach (➤ 153). The main beach is suitable for families, but be warned that there are some nudist sections further along. Praia do Barril, 4km (2.5 miles) away at the island's western end, is usually less crowded

Albufeira is another classic Algarve beach. Walk through the rock tunnel to reach the beach, with sandstacks beneath the cliffs. West of Albufeira is a series of attractive cove beaches, such as Praia de São Rafael and Praia da Galé.

The biggest and possibly most famous beach in the Algarve is **Armação de Pêra.** This superb beach has sandstacks at one end and flat sands stretching towards Albufeira. The resort is popular with Portuguese families.

Praia da Rocha was the first tourist town in the Algarve, giving it a certain time-worn appeal, although a new paved beachside walk has smartened up the resort. From the old fortress there are views over the wide beach of sand, with eroded rocks sheltering beneath 70m (230-foot) cliffs.

Sheltered Coves

Praia da Marinha is the largest of the cove beaches around the fishing village of Carvoeiro, now a growing resort. In summer, you can take boat trips from Carvoeiro to other nearby cove beaches, including Praia do Benagil and Praia Senhora da Rocha. Another perfect cove beach is **Praia de Dona Ana,** located just outside Lagos, which means it gets crowded on summer weekends. You can take a boat trip to see the grottoes and caves of Ponte da Piedade (➤ 185).

Perfect for watersports

Many of the Algarve beaches are popular with watersports enthusiasts. One of the best is **Meia Praia**, on the east side of Lagos, which has a long crescent-shaped beach stretching for 4km (2.5 miles). Popular with windsurfers, children like this beach too, as there are lots of shells washed up on the sand. Watch the strong currents.

The largest resort as you head west is **Praia da Luz**. This beach has windsurfing and diving schools and a splendid beach backed by cliffs at its eastern end. A clifftop path leads past Ponte da Piedade to Lagos (➤ 185). Alternatively head for the sheltered, dark sandy cove of **Praia de Odeceixe** on the borders of the Alentejo and the Algarve. This beach sits at the mouth of the Seixe estuary 4km (2.5 miles) from a village of white houses. The beach is especially popular with surfers.

Off-The-Beaten-Track

If you have your own transport, then it is worthwhile heading to some of the more remote beaches, such as **Boca do Rio**, located halfway between Burgau and Salema on the edge of the Budens wetland reserve. This small beach is situated at a river mouth inside the Costa Vicentina natural park. You can walk along the cliffs to the beach at Cabanas Velhas.

Alternatively, boats depart from the fishing port of Olhão for the attractive holiday island of **Ilha da Armona**. There are sand dunes on the sheltered, landward side, or you can escape the crowds by walking across to the other side of the island to a magnificent ocean beach. You can also camp on the island.

The sheltered cove beach at Praia de Marinha

The superb beach at Boca do Rio is located on the edge of a wetland reserve

Another remote beach is **Praia da Cordoama**, which is reached by following a dirt track beneath grey slate cliffs. The nearby beach of **Praia do Castelejo** is slightly more accessible and surrounded by black schist rocks with white sand. Alternatively, head for the huge, curving beach of **Praia da Bordeira**, backed by sand dunes, and situated around a lagoon at the mouth of the Bordeira River near Carrapateira. **Praia do Amado**, 4km (2.5 miles) south on the other side of the headland, is just as impressive.

Praia da Arrifana is another beautiful crescent of sand, which shelters between cliffs about 10km (6 miles) outside Aljezur. There are good views along the coastline from the ruined fortress above the beach. **Praia de Monte Clérigo**, 8km (5 miles) from Aljezur, which is good for families.

TAKING A BREAK

Most of these beaches have **summer restaurants and bars**. If you are visiting remote beaches like Cordoama and Odeceixe out of season, take a **picnic**.

Praia Verde ✚ 202 D1	Praia de Odeceixe ✚ 202 B2
Ilha de Tavira ✚ 202 D1	Boca do Rio ✚ 202 B1
Albufeira ✚ 202 C1	Ilha de Armona ✚ 202 D1
Armação de Pêra ✚ 202 C1	Praia da Cordoama ✚ 202 A1
Praia da Rocha ✚ 202 B1	Praia do Castelejo ✚ 202 B1
Praia da Marinha ✚ 202 C1	Praia da Bordeira ✚ 202 B1
Praia de Dona Ana ✚ 202 B1	Praia do Amado ✚ 202 B1
Meia Praia ✚ 202 B1	Praia da Arrifana ✚ 202 B1
Praia da Luz ✚ 202 B1	Praia de Monte Clérigo ✚ 202 B1

ALGARVE BEACHES: INSIDE INFO

Top tips Beware of **dangerous currents** on the west coast beaches (Arrifana, do Amado, Bordeira, Castelejo, Cordoama and Odeceixa). On calm days the sea can seem almost benevolent, but only experienced swimmers should go in.
■ The easiest **access** to the west coast beaches is from Lagos to Arrifana or Sagres to Bordeira.

At Your Leisure

5 Alcoutim

A giant casuarina tree stands by
the harbour in the sleepy village of
Alcoutim, looking across the River
Guadiana to the Spanish village of
Sanlúcar de Guadiana. Here you are
close enough to Spain to hear dogs
barking, children playing and the
church clock chiming the hour on the
far bank. Local fishermen will ferry
you across, and in summer you can
take river trips as far south as Vila
Real. Climb to the 14th-century castle
at the top of the village for the best
views. Take the time to explore the
little archaeological museum in the
castle, and then follow the beautiful
drive along the valley on a twisting
road to Foz de Odeleite.

🕂 202 D2
Tourist Information Office
✉ Rua 1º de Maio ☎ 281 546 179

6 Parque Natural da Ria Formosa

The Ria Formosa nature reserve
covers 60km (37 miles) of coastline,
sheltered from the ocean by partly
submerged sand dunes and a network
of salt marshes and lagoons.

The best introduction to the
ecology and human history of the
park is to follow the 3km (2-mile)
self-guided trail at the Quinta de

*The impressive remains of the castle
walls at Alcoutim*

Marim Environmental Education
Centre near Olhão. The centre also
has a good café and shop. The trail
leads through pinewoods and along
the shore, passing a working tide
mill on the way to a freshwater lake
where you might spot herons, storks
and purple gallinule (a relative of the
moorhen). Also here is a bird hospital
for injured wild birds and a kennel
where you can see web-footed Portuguese water dogs. You can pick up a
map at the reception gate.

🕂 202 C1
✉ 3km (2 miles) east of Olhão, signposted off
the N125 ☎ 289 700 210; www.icn.pt ⏰ Daily
9–12:30, 2–5:30 (office); 10:30–6 (park)
💶 Inexpensive

7 Faro

The capital of the Algarve is one
of the most underrated cities in
Portugal, known mainly for its airport
through which millions pass on their
way to the south coast beaches.

Starting at the marina, you enter
the old town through **Arco da Vila**,
a handsome gateway – just inside the
gateway, an 11th-century horseshoe
arch is all that remains of the Moorish
walls. Climb to the cathedral square,

cobbled and lined with orange trees, then make your way to the **Museu Municipal**, housed in a former convent. Besides the Renaissance cloisters, the chief attraction here is a third-century Roman mosaic depicting the head of Neptune surrounded by the four winds.

It's worth making the short stroll through the new town to the Igreja do Carmo, best known for its chilling **Capela dos Ossos** (Chapel of Bones), whose walls are covered with more than 1,200 skulls and body parts – though this is not as impressive as the similar chapel in Évora (➤ 134).

🚩 202 C1

Tourist Information Office
✉ Rua da Misericórdia 8–12 ☎ 289 803 604; www.cm-faro.pt

Museu Municipal
✉ Praça Dom Afonso III ☎ 289 897 400
🕐 Oct–May Tue–Fri 10–6, Sat–Sun 10:30–5; Jun–Sep Tue–Fri 10–7, Sat–Sun 11:30–6. Last entry 30 mins before closing ✋ Inexpensive; Sun free entry until 2

Capela dos Ossos
✉ Largo do Carmo ☎ 289 824 490 🕐 Apr–Oct Mon–Fri 10–1, 3–5, Sat 10–1; Nov–Mar Mon–Fri 10–1, 3–6, Sat 10–1 ✋ Inexpensive

The handsome Arco da Villa, which marks the entrance to the old town at Faro

A statue in the palace grounds of Estói

🎱 Estói

The pink rococo palace that dominates the village of Estói was begun in 1840 for the Conde de Cavalhal. The palace has been restored and opened as a glamorous pousada with a very good restaurant. Just down the hill from the village are the Roman ruins at **Milreu**.

🚩 202 D1

Milreu
☎ 289 997 823 🕐 Apr–Sep Tue–Sun 9:30–12:30, 2–6; Oct–Mar Tue–Sun 9:30–12:30, 2–5 ✋ Inexpensive

🎱 Loulé

The Algarve's second city is also a thriving crafts centre and market town. The best time to come is for the busy Saturday market, when local produce and pottery is sold in and around a neo-Moorish market hall. In the streets beneath the castle, you can watch craftspeople at work, carving wood, weaving baskets and making lace in tiny workshops. Loulé is known across Portugal for its Carnival celebrations, the biggest in the country, which take place each February before Lent. Look out for two contrasting churches – the parish church of **São Clemente**, its bell tower housed in a 12th-century minaret, and the space-age **Nossa Senhora da Piedade**, beside an 18th-century chapel on a hill overlooking the town.

🚩 202 C1

Tourist Information Office
✉ Avenida 25 de Abril 9 ☎ 289 463 900

⑩ Alte

This charming village of whitewashed houses is found in the foothills of the Barrocal, a fertile region north of Loulé, which produces almonds, oranges and figs. You could easily spend an hour or two pottering around the village, admiring the parish church with its Manueline portal and 16th-century *azulejos*, then walk up to the Fonte Pequena and Fonte Grande to drink water from the springs at this well-known beauty spot by the River Alte. While you're there, don't miss the stunning Queda do Vigario waterfall.

➕ 202 C1

⑪ Albufeira

What was once a quiet fishing village has been transformed over the last 50 years into Portugal's biggest seaside resort. Yet the old town has also survived. Here is a maze of medieval alleyways on a cliff overlooking the beach, its Moorish archway and whitewashed houses lit by old-fashioned lanterns at night. A tunnel carved through the cliff face leads to the main beach, with its curious sandstacks; a second beach, Praia dos Barcos, has fishing boats on the sand. Beyond here is the nightlife area known as "the Strip", which has good restaurants and lively bars.

➕ 202 C1
Tourist Information Office
✉ Rua 5 de Outubro ☎ 289 585 279

⑫ Silves

The Moorish capital of *al-gharb* was once a magnificent city, a place of poets, princes and splendid bazaars described in Islamic chronicles as ten times greater than Lisbon. The modern town is dominated by the impressive red sandstone walls of its **castle**, which you can walk around. Near here is the 13th-century **cathedral**, the pink granite columns of its Gothic nave uncluttered by the baroque decoration that affects so many Portuguese churches. The tombstones are those of medieval crusaders who helped capture the town in 1242.

Walk downhill to reach the **Fábrica do Inglês**, an interesting museum and leisure complex inside an old cork factory.

➕ 202 B1
Castelo
☎ 282 445 624 ⏰ Mid-Jul to mid-Sep daily 9–6:30; mid-Sep to mid-Jul 9–5:30
💷 Inexpensive

Fábrica do Inglês
✉ Rua Gregório Mascarenhas ☎ 282 440 480; www.fabrica–do–ingles.pt ⏰ Museum daily 9:30–12:45, 2–6:15 (May–Sep to 8:45). Closed Sun Oct–Jun). Fábrica daily 9am–midnight. Closed Sun Oct–Jun and first 2 weeks Jan 💷 Museum inexpensive, Fábrica free

Silves makes a good day out from the Algarve beaches

The detailed gilded woodwork in the tiny chapel of São Antonio in Lagos

🔳 Lagos

The port at the mouth of the Bensafrim River played an important role during the Age of Discovery, when ships departing for Africa sailed from here. A **statue of Henry the Navigator** stands on Praça da República, facing the harbour. On a corner of the same square is a darker reminder of those seafaring days, the site of the first European *mercado de esclavo*s (slave market, now an art gallery). In the backstreets, the **Museu Municipal** has an eclectic collection of Bronze Age *menhirs*, Roman mosaics, African artefacts, Algarve fishing nets, pickled animals, weapons, coins and a gilded chapel.

➕ 202 B1

Tourist Information Office

✉ Rua Belchoir Moreira de Barbudo   ☎ 282 763 031

Museu Municipal

✉ Rua General Alberto da Silveira   ☎ 282 762 301   🕐 Tue–Sun 9:30–12:30, 2–5
📖 Inexpensive

BEST FOR KIDS

If your children are bored with the beaches, here are some suggestions to keep them busy:

- Karting Algarve, try karting in Almancil (www.kartingalgarve. com), with junior carts, and other activities.
- Museu Municipal, Lagos, with a collection of oddities from mosaics to pickled animals.
- Zoomarine (on N125 near Guia; closed Mon; www.zoomarine.com), an aquarium with dolphin and parrot shows.
- Slide and Splash (on N125 near Lagoa; open Easter–Oct; www. slidesplash.com), the Algarve's biggest waterpark.
- The Big One (on N125 near Porches; open Easter–Oct), a waterpark that is good for younger children.
- Lagos Zoo (in the village of Barão de São João; May–Sep daily 10–7; Oct–Apr 10–5), features birds, primates and a children's farm.

Where to...
Stay

Prices
Expect to pay for a double room per night in high season
€ under €60   €€ €60–€120   €€€ €121–€180   €€€€ over €180

TAVIRA

Convento de Santo António
€€–€€€€

This gem of a hotel was converted from a 17th-century Capuchin convent, and has been in the same family for the past 200 years. From the exterior you wouldn't know it was a hotel – the large white portal of the chapel hides the garden and the 17th-century cloisters. The atmosphere and peace of the former convent have been preserved, and most of the rooms are converted monks' cells. Breakfast is served in the arched courtyard and guests are free to linger here or relax by the pool. Booking in advance is essential and minimum stays are two to four nights, depending on the season.

✚ 202 D1 🖂 Rua de Santo António 56
☎ 281 321 573 🕒 Closed Jan

FARO

Hotel Quinta do Lago €€€€

Thirty minutes by car from Faro, the Quinta do Lago sits in verdant luxury, overlooking the lagoon and the sea. Arguably justified in calling itself "the finest hotel in the Algarve", it provides abundant facilities and luxurious accommodation for discerning guests. Sports enthusiasts are spoiled for choice, and it is particularly popular with golfers who can choose from three different championship courses (▶ 170). Guests can dine on Portuguese gourmet fare while watching the sun set in the Brisa do Mar, or feast on Venetian cuisine in the intimate Ca D'Oro restaurant. Stylish and comfortable rooms come with spacious terraces, and little luxuries such as praline chocolates, a carafe of port and flowers.

✚ 202 C1 🖂 Quinta do Lago, Almancil
☎ 289 350 350; www.quintadolagohotel.com

Hotel Eva €€€

Attractively positioned on the edge of the Marina, you can enjoy superb views from the rooftop pool over the Ria Formosa, and the boats in the harbour – the hotel can even arrange boat trips out to sea. Some of the more expensive rooms also share this stunning view. Sleek and contemporary in feel throughout, the main areas are light and airy. The service is excellent and all rooms have WiFi.

✚ 202 C1 🖂 F1 Avenida de Republica
☎ 2289 803 354; www.tdhotels.pt

ESTÓI

Estalagem Monte do Casal
€€€–€€€€

This small and exclusive English-run hotel is tucked away in the gentle hills above Faro, with fine views down to the sea. Surrounded by peaceful gardens and terraces, it has its own swimming pool, bar and a first-class restaurant. The rooms are attractive and comfortable, and have a private terrace where breakfast is served. The restaurant is a converted coach house that specialises in sophisticated French cuisine. In summer, guests can dine on the terrace under the palms; in cooler months, open log fires and candlelit tables provide guests with a warm welcome.

+ 202 D1 ⊠ Cerro do Lobo ☎ 289 990 140; montedocasal@mail.telepac.pt; www.montedocasal.pt ☻ Closed late-Nov–early-Feb

ALBUFEIRA

Casa Bela Moura €€–€€€

A modern house decorated in Moorish style, the Casa Bela Moura is a family-run guesthouse with rooms divided between the main house and a nearby annexe. The bar, breakfast room and reception are welcoming, and the 13 rooms are very clean. It has its own pool and is only 1.5km (1 mile) from the pretty cove of Nossa Senhora da Rocha.

+ 202 C1 ⊠ Estrada de Porches 530, Alporchinhos ☎ 282 313 422; www.casabelamoura.com ☻ Closed Nov and Dec

SILVES

Casa das Oliveiras €€

Peace and quiet reigns at this comfortable guest house, which is not far outside of Silves and surrounded by orange groves and olive trees. There is no restaurant, but breakfast is substantial and the friendly owners will point you in the direction of a number of good local places to eat. This makes a very good base for exploring both the beautiful inland towns and villages, and heading off to the nearby coast. Recommended.

+ 202 C1 ⊠ Montes da Vala ☎ 282 342 115; www.casa-das-oliveiras.com

LAGOS

Casa Grande €–€€

The Casa Grande is a delightful, rambling guest house furnished with antiques and curiosities. The house is a short walk from the beach. The attractively furnished rooms are large, comfortable and good value for money. Upstairs rooms have their own balconies.

There's also a restaurant.

+ 202 B1 ⊠ Burgau, Lagos ☎ 282 697 416; www.nexus-pt.com/casagrande

Where to...
Eat and Drink

Prices

Expect to pay per person for a three-course meal, excluding drinks and tips

€ under €12   €€ €12–24   €€€ €25–36   €€€€ over €36

TAVIRA

Grelha Peixe €€

You will know what to expect as soon as you walk into this attractive and nautical-themed restaurant, and you're not likely to be disappointed – plenty of delicious, fresh seafood. Good choice of grilled meats also. Expect cheerful service, closely set tables and a lively atmosphere. Popular, in the evenings particularly, so you will need to book ahead.

+ 202 D1 ⊠ Rua Comandante Henrique Tenreiro ☎ 281 370 491 ☻ Fri–Wed 12:30–3, 7:30–10:30. Closed Nov

Portas do Mar €€

Located on the waterfront where the River Gilão meets the Rio Formosa estuary. The Portas do Mar is one of a cluster of fish restaurants downstream from Tavira. It's a modern building with a pretty blue-and-white interior and a terrace for views of the estuary. The choice of fish, the freshest of which is hauled ashore at the nearby port, ranges from lobster and crayfish to monkfish or shellfish *cataplana*.

+ 202 D1 ⊠ Sítio das Quatro Águas ☎ 281 321 255 ☻ Jul–Sep Wed–Mon 12:30–3, 7–midnight; Oct–Jun 12:30–3, 6:30–10:30

MONCHIQUE

Albergaria Bica-Boa €€

Located on a scenic mountainside surrounded by beautiful flower-filled gardens, the Bica-Boa is a delightful guesthouse and restaurant. The restaurant provides a warm welcome and some of the best-value food in the region. The menu features well-cooked and presented Monchique dishes such as chicken *piri-piri* (with a chilli pepper sauce) and *cabrito estufado* (goat stew) as well as fish and a good choice of vegetarian dishes. Recommended.

➕ 202 B1 ⊠ Estrada de Lisboa 266 (1km/0.6 miles north of Monchique on the Lisbon road) ☎ 282 912 271 ⊛ Daily 12–2, 7–10

FARO

Dois Irmaos €€–€€€

Hungry visitors can expect reliably excellent food at this fish restaurant, one of the oldest and best known in

Faro. Well located close to the main downtown shopping street, Dois Irmãos has been in this location since 1925. Enjoy dining in the traditional tiled interior or there's a sunny terrace and garden outside for enjoying the (almost inevitable) sunshine.

➕ 202 C1 ⊠ Largo Terreiro do bispo, 14 ☎ 289 823 337 ⊛ Daily 12–11

LOULÉ

Casa Paixanito €€

This friendly and relaxed restaurant serves food tapas-style – perfect for sampling the best of the region (there are nearly 50 different small dishes to choose from), and a selection of wines by the glass. The decoration is attractive – walls cluttered with photos and pictures, but the crisp white tablecloths keep it feeling spacious and modern. There's a very good wine list, with a detailed and well-chosen selection of Portuguese wines from around the country.

➕ 202 C1 ⊠ 11 Olho de Agua, Estrada Loule-Querenca ☎ 289 412 775 ⊛ Sep–Jun 11–11, Jul–Aug 7–11

ALBUFEIRA

O Cabaz da Praia €€€

For many years "The Beach Basket" has been considered to be the best restaurant in Albufeira, and the location is superb. Built on the cliffs, it overlooks the beach and has great views from the rooftop terrace. The service is excellent, the atmosphere friendly and the dishes well presented. The menu features French and international cuisine, and might include monkfish flambéed with mango sauce, duck breast with quinces and honey or home-made tagliatelle with prawns.

➕ 202 C1 ⊠ Praça Miguel Bombarda 7 ☎ 289 512 137 ⊛ Fri–Wed 12–2:30, 6:30–11

Vila Joya €€€€

One of the Algarve's best restaurant, and worth seeking out for an

extra special dinner, with local ingredients given a imaginative twist by the very talented chef, Dieter Koschina. The food not only uses freshly sourced Portuguese ingredients, but also the best ingredients from international cuisine, from Wagyu beef to Italian white truffles. There are rooms here also if you can't bear the thought of driving home. Book well ahead.

➕ 202 C1 ⊠ Praia da Gale ☎ 289 591 795; www.vilajoya.com ⊛ Daily 12–2.30, 7–11

LAGOS

Dom Sebastião €€

The central location on the main pedestrian street and warm welcome here ensures a steady stream of visitors. It's not the cheapest place in town, but there are fine appetisers, the fish and seafood excellent and there are home-made desserts. Choose from prawns, crayfish or lobster or the fish risotto. Extensive wine list.

Where to... Shop

MARKETS

Olhão has the best fish market in the Algarve, held daily, except on Sunday, alongside the fruit and vegetable market.

Loulé is at its liveliest on Saturday mornings when the market is busy and all the surrounding streets are packed with stalls selling olives and sausages, poultry and pottery.

The covered fruit market in **Lagos** (Rua das Portas de Portugal, Mon–Sat 8–1) has a splendid display of fresh fish, fruit and vegetables, and there's a very colourful "gipsy market" in town on the first Saturday of every month.

The market in **Monchique** is held on the second Friday of each month and an excellent market takes place daily in **Tavira**.

CLOTHING AND CRAFTS

Many of Tavira's shops specialise in crafts. Visit the **Casa do Artesanato** (Calçada da Galeria II) or the **Artesanato Regional Bazar** (Rua José Pires Padinha) for woven goods, and **Alart** (Rua do Galeria) for pottery. The main shopping street in Faro is **Rua de Santo António**. The **Casa Verde** (Rua Dr. Francisco Gomes, tel: 289 825 153) in Faro has excellent lace, pottery and leather. Loulé is one of the best towns to see Algarvio craft workers in action: old liquor stills and copper *cataplana* pots are sold at several shops along Rue de Barbacá. The **Centro de Artesanato** (Rua de Barbacá) offers a wide range of ceramics and homemade rugs. Chunky woollen cardigans and jumpers are sold at **Cabo de São Vicente** stalls.

In Silves, **Peter Liescgon** (Largo Jerónimo Osório) is an antiques and art shop specialising in ceramics.

FOOD AND DRINK

For a great choice of port try the **Supermercado Garrafeira** (Praça de Almeida 28, Faro). The shop also stocks wines, cheeses and pastries.

The **Adega Cooperativa** between Portimão and Lagoa holds daily guided tours including tastings (tel: 282 342 181 to book). **Quinta da Figueirinha** in Silve is an organic farm shop selling fruit, vegetables and home-made liqueurs. (282 440 700; www.qdf.pt).

For almond cakes try Pastelaria Taquelim Conçalvesa (Rua Portas de Portugal, Lagos).

Caldas de Monchique, 7km (4.3 miles) south of Monchique, is famous for *medronho*, a firewater made from local arbutus berries – taste it at the craft centre.

---

202 B1   Rua 25 de Abril 20   282 762 795; domsebastiao@ip.pt   Daily 12–11

SILVES

Rui Marisqueira €€–€€€

This is one of the Algarve's best-known fish restaurants, with a great choice of shellfish on the menu and it is understandably popular with locals and tourists. The décor is nothing very special, it is fairly noisy inside and the service can be offhand, but all is forgiven when the generous-sized seafood platters arrive at your table overflowing with fresh lobster and juicy crab, prawns and oysters. Main courses range from grilled fresh fish to clams *cataplana* and fish risotto. Fish dishes are priced by the kilo, so ask the price before you order that fat bass or bream. Recommended.

202 C1   Rua Commendador Vilarinho 27   282 442 682   Wed–Mon 12–3:30, 6:30–10:30

Where to...
Be Entertained

WATERSPORTS

Algarve is one of Europe's main centres for watersports. On the coast try the **Watersports Centre** near Albufeira (tel: 289 394 929) for surfing, windsurfing, parasailing, diving and boat trips.

WATERPARKS

There are plenty of waterparks in the Algarve. In Lagoa, try **Slide & Splash** (along the N125, Vale de Deus, Estômbar; tel: 282 340 800) is a huge complex of water chutes, slides and swimming pools.

GOLF

Golf (www.portugalgolf.pt) leads the way for land sports – there are 24 excellent courses in the region. The luxury resorts of **Quinta do Lago** and **Vale do Lobo** have six scenic courses between them, the most famous being the Quinta do Lago (tel: 289 351 900). One of the latest, in Vilamoura, is the **Millennium** (tel: 289 310 188), opened in 2000. **Penina** (5km/3 miles west of Portimão on the N125, tel: 282 420 223) is an 18-hole course designed by Henry Cotton, who also came up with **Alto Golf** between Alvor and Portimão (tel: 282 460 870).

TENNIS

Portugal's leading academies are **Vale do Lobo** (tel: 289 357 850), with 14 courts, pool and gym, and **Barrington's** (tel: 289 351 940).

MUSIC AND NIGHTLIFE

Albufeira is the social hotspot. The best discos are out of town, such as top-rate **Libertos** on the main strip (Praia da Oura). Just don't expect a quiet night out.

For something more intimate there's the **St James' Club** in Almancil, an exclusive bar-disco enforcing a dress code and offering a drive-you-home service.

In Vilamoura **Vilamoura Jazz Club**, which has live jazz at least three nights a week (918 779 213) while folk dancing takes place at local hotels. Other popular venues for live music are **Harry's Bar** and **Central Station** on Largo Duarte Pacheco, Albufeira.

Faro's nightlife is concentrated on **Rua do Prior**, where you'll find **Faro with Dux** (No 38). July is the best month for classical and jazz.

In Lagos there is the **Centro Cultural** (tel: 282 770 450) and in Almancil is the **Centro Cultural de São Lourenço** (tel: 289 395 475). Both host music festivals, concerts and recitals featuring international musicians. In July there is an open-air festival of European Films in Tavira (www. cineclube-tavira.com). Fado nights are Saturday at **Adega do Papagaio** (Espiche, tel: 282 789 423), a converted wine cellar.

BOAT TRIPS AND FISHING

To see some of the least spoiled scenery in the Algarve, take a boat trip along the River Guadiana. These depart three times a week from Vila Real de Santo António; contact **Riosul** (Rua Tristão Vaz Teixeira, Monte Gordo, tel: 281 510 200). For trips to Alcoutim try **Turismar** (tel: 281 513 504).

Several companies offer half-day cruises from Portimão (not in winter), visiting caves, grottoes and beaches. These include **Portitours** (tel: 282 470 063; www.portitours. pt) – they will arrange transport from hotels.

Walks and Tours

1 LISBON

Walk

This walk introduces you to three very different districts – **Alfama, Baixa** and **Bairro Alto** – which together make up the rich and diverse historic core of Lisbon. The journey includes a tram ride and a climb on a funicular, which are not only enjoyable in themselves, but also a convenient way of getting up the hills. Although the walk can be done in as little as two hours, it is best to allow at least half a day, allowing some time for window shopping, cafés and visits to churches and museums along the way.

DISTANCE 4km (2.5 miles) walking plus tram and funicular rides **TIME** 2–2.5 hours
START/END POINT Praça do Comércio ✚ 196 C1

1–2

Start in **Praça do Comércio**, the large open square on the waterfront, with your back to the river. The square is still known as Terreiro do Paço, after the royal palace which once

stood on this site. At the centre is a statue of Dom José I, king of Portugal at the time of the 1755 earthquake and the subsequent rebuilding of Lisbon. Walk straight ahead through the triumphal arch, the symbolic gateway to the city from the river. This brings you into Rua Augusta, the principal shopping street of the Baixa (lower town). On sunny days the promenade comes alive with buskers, street traders, busy news stands and café terraces. The shops along here are an eclectic mix of high street fashion chains and quirky local stores such as **Casa Macário** (No 272–274), an old-fashioned coffee shop

Page 171: People walking through the beautiful Praça do Comércio in Baixa

Right: The grand Arco da Rua Augusta, Praça do Comércio, in the Baixa area

TOP TIP

A **one-day bus pass,** valid on buses, trams and funiculars and the Elevador de Santa Justa, is available at the ticket booth in Praça da Figueira (near Rossio).

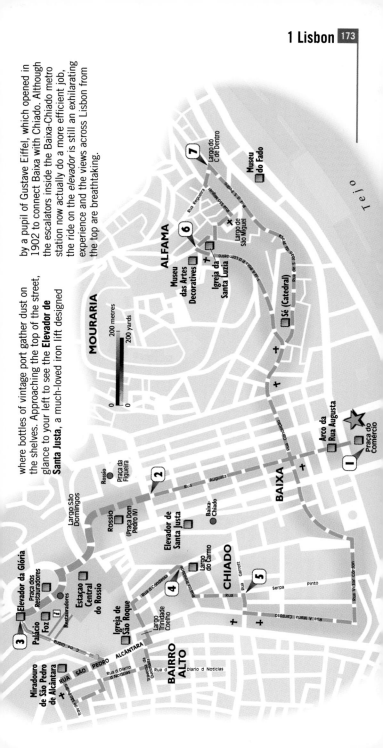

where bottles of vintage port gather dust on the shelves. Approaching the top of the street, glance to your left to see the **Elevador de Santa Justa**, a much-loved iron lift designed by a pupil of Gustave Eiffel, which opened in 1902 to connect Baixa with Chiado. Although the escalators inside the Baixa-Chiado metro station now actually do a more efficient job, the ride on the *elevador* is still an exhilarating experience and the views across Lisbon from the top are breathtaking.

2–3

Rua Augusta ends in the **Rossio**, the nearest thing in Lisbon to a central square, with its fountains, flower stalls and a wavy mosaic pavement. The square is officially named Praça Dom Pedro IV after the statue of the king at its centre – though the statue was initially designed as a likeness of Emperor Maximilian of Mexico, who was executed before it could be completed. Café Nicola and Pastelaria Suiça, facing each other across the Rossio, offer a choice of terraces for people watching, and there are good views of the ruined **Igreja do Carmo** (▶ 175), high on the hill above the western side of the square.

Leave the square by the far left corner and you find yourself in front of Rossio station, with its imposing neo-Manueline façade. Built as Lisbon's central station in 1892, it was the departure point for trains to Sintra (now Sete Rios Station).

Continue onwards into **Praça dos Restauradores**, a large square with an obelisk at the centre commemorating Portugal's independence from Spain. On your left is **Palácio Foz**, a former nightclub and Ministry of Propaganda building now housing the city tourist office.

3–4

Just beyond the palace, the **Elevador da Glória** funicular trundles up to the Bairro Alto on what must be one of the world's steepest, and most enjoyable, public transport rides, emerging opposite the **Solar do Vinho do Porto** (▶ 71–72). Turn right at the upper terminus to reach the garden and *miradouro* of São Pedro de Alcântara, with magnificent views of the cathedral, castle and Tagus estuary. Now you can head into the intriguing warren of medieval streets that make up the **Bairro Alto** (▶ 63–64).

Dom Pedro IV statue and Teatro Nacional de Dona Maria, Dona Maria National Theatre in Rossio Square

This area rewards random exploration, but one possible route is to take Travessa de São Pedro from opposite the fountain, take the second left along Rua dos Mouros (Street of the Moors), then turn left and immediately right along Rua do Diário de Notícias. As you reach Travessa da Queimada, turn left, passing Café Luso, one of Lisbon's famous *fado* houses, which has *fado* and folk dancing on most nights.

district. The ruined convent here, an empty shell following the 1755 earthquake, is now an interesting archaeological museum.

4–5

Leave the square by Rua da Trinidade. When you see a house with a *azulejo*-tiled façade on your right, turn left along Rua Serpa Pinto. This brings you out onto Rua Garrett, Chiado's most fashionable shopping street, restored after a disastrous fire in 1988. Treat yourself to a coffee and pastry at one of two venerable institutions, Pastelaria Bernard or A Brasileira (▶ 70). The poet Fernando Pessoa used to meet his friends at A Brasileira and his statue on the pavement acts as a magnet for tourists.

5–6

Cross Rua Garrett to reach Rua António Maria Cardoso where you can hop on to tram 28, dropping back down to Baixa and passing the cathedral on the way up to Largo das Portas do Sol. Get off the tram opposite the **Museu de Artes Decorativas** (▶ 55).

From the *miradouro* (viewpoint) there are views over the Alfama rooftops to the churches of São Vicente de Fora and Santa Engrácia. From here you can plunge down to explore **Alfama** (▶ 54–57).

6–7

Take the staircase beside **Santa Luzia church** to enter a secret world of cobbled lanes, washing hanging from balconies, fountains, patios and hidden courtyards of orange trees. Turn left down more steps to reach Largo de São Miguel, where a tall palm tree stands guard in front of the church. Turn left here along Rua de São Miguel. At the end of this street, turn right and right again to reach Largo do Chafariz de Dentro, an open square facing the **Museu do Fado** (▶ 56–57).

7–8

Leave this square by the far corner along Rua de São Pedro, where women sell sardines from their doorways on weekday mornings. Look out in particular for **Beco de Azinhal**, a pretty courtyard with restaurant tables, immediately on your right at the start of the street.

Continue along Rua de São Pedro, passing a rare surviving section of Moorish wall. The road widens and becomes Rua de São João da Praça, where several of the apartment blocks and shopfronts are decorated with *azulejo* tiles. Continue on this street, passing the *sé* (cathedral), then follow the tramlines down to Rua da Conceição and turn left along Rua Augusta to return to Praça do Comércio.

TAKING A BREAK

Café Nicola €
🏠 196 C4 ☒ Praça Dom Pedro IV (Rossio) 24–25 ⓦ Mon–Fri 8–10, Sat 9–10, Sun 10–7

Pastelaria Suiça €
🏠 196 C4 ☒ Praça Dom Pedro IV (Rossio) 96–104 ☎ 213 214 090
ⓦ Daily 7–10 (9 in winter)

Pastelaria Bernard €
🏠 196 B3 ☒ Rua Garrett 104
ⓦ Mon–Sat 8–11

Lautasco €€
🏠 197 F3 ☒ Beco de Azinhal 7
☎ 218 860 173 ⓦ Mon–Sat lunch and dinner

This brings you out opposite Largo Trinidade Coelho, known as Largo da Misericórdia and dominated by the Jesuit **Igreja de São Roque.** This is the headquarters of the Misericórdia charity, beneficiaries of Portugal's national lottery – hence the bronze statue of a ticket seller on the square in front of the church. Leave this square by the Calçada do Duque steps and take the second right along Rua da Condessa to reach **Largo do Carmo**, a pretty square located at the heart of the Chiado

2 PORT COUNTRY
Drive

DISTANCE 130km (80.5 miles) **TIME** 4 hours
START/END POINT Vila Real ✚ 198 C3

This spectacular drive takes you through the steeply terraced vineyards of the Douro Valley, where the grapes in port wine are grown. The scenery is magnificent at any time of year but at its best in summer when the grapes are ripening on the vines, or in September and October when the harvest is taking place. Some of the roads are twisting and narrow, so allow plenty of time.

1–2
Start in **Vila Real** and follow signs for the IP4 in the direction of Porto and Amarante. Take care as this motorway climbs steeply and it is a notorious spot for accidents. After 24km (15 miles), turn off at the sign for "pousada" and cross the bridge to reach the **Pousada de São Gonçalo**. Turn right, follow the minor N15 for around 12km (7.4 miles) as it snakes down through the pine forests of the Ovelha Valley in the foothills of the Serra de Marão.

The fountain at Nossa Senhora dos Remédios, Lamego

LAMEGO
A short detour south from Peso da Régua on the new IP3 motorway leads to Lamego, an attractive town of Renaissance and baroque mansions overlooked by two hills. On one hill stands a ruined 12th-century castle; on the other is the sanctuary of Nossa Senhora dos Remédios, reached by a magnificent baroque stairway similar to that at Bom Jesus near Braga (➤ 90). The chapel is the focus for a major pilgrimage, which takes place on 8 September each year. Lamego was the setting for the first Cortes (National Assembly), a meeting of the nobility, clergy and townspeople which proclaimed Afonso Henriques first king of Portugal in 1143. These days it is better known as the centre of production for Raposeira, Portuguese sparkling wine. For a tour visit Quinta da Pacheca to see the process of port and still wine making (tel: 254 313 228; tours daily. For sparkling wine, try Caves da Raposeira (tel: 254 655 003; http://cavesdaraposeira.com).

and their strange granite boulders, then reaches a plateau and drops down through the vineyards to **Mesão Frio**. Cross the stone bridge across the River Teixeira to enter the town and soon you have your first view of the great sweep of the River Douro down below.

3–4

Now you are in the heart of port wine country, surrounded by the steep slopes of the vineyards, painstakingly carved into fertile terraces by generations of farmers. As a local saying has it: "God created Earth, but man created the Douro." The road narrows, twisting and turning as it drops down to the river, passing the Pousada Solar da Rede, one of the finest of the *pousadas*, set on an 18th-century wine estate with great river views. Follow the river along its north bank (N108) through the spa town of Caldas de Moledo as far as **Peso da Régua**. This busy town, usually known as Régua, was built to serve the port trade and acts as a centre for transporting wine to Porto. *Barcos rabelos* boats, which these days serve a decorative purpose only, are moored

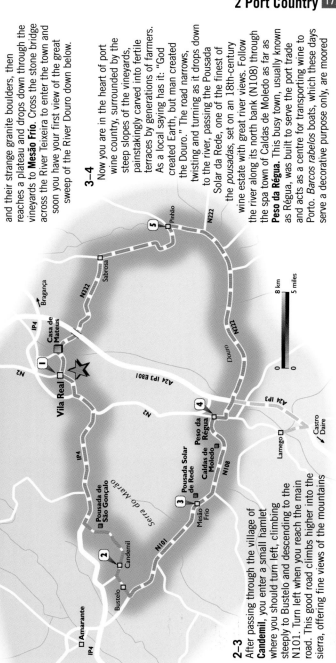

2–3

After passing through the village of **Candemil**, you enter a small hamlet where you should turn left, climbing steeply to Bustelo and descending to the N101. Turn left when you reach the main road. This good road climbs higher into the sierra, offering fine views of the mountains

on the riverbank and in summer you can take a cruise along the river to the nearby *quintas* (wine estates). **Quinta de São Domingos** (Peso da Régua, tel: 254 320 260; Mon–Fri 9–12:30, 2–5; Sat–Sun 9–6; tours take about 20 minutes, free), in the town centre, offers tours and tastings throughout the year. There are plenty of restaurants and cafés along the waterfront at Peso da Régua or try O Malheiro, set just back from the river on the main street. (For a detour to **Lamego ▶ 176**.)

4–5

Take the lower of the two bridges across the River Douro and keep right to swing back under the bridge and emerge beside the river. Now follow the N222 along the south bank of the Douro to Pinhão. This is a lovely drive, clinging close to the river with views of vineyards, olive groves, dry-stone walls and white-painted *quintas* with the names of the famous port houses emblazoned on the hillsides. Several of the *quintas* are open to visitors – **Quinta do Panascal** (on the slopes above the River Tãvora, tel: 254 732 321; Mon–Fri 10–5:30, also weekends Apr–Oct) has audio tours, vineyard walks and a stone *lagar* where the grapes are crushed by foot

TAKING A BREAK

O Malheiro €
🅘 198 C4 🖂 Rua dos Camilos, Régua
☎ 254 313 684 🍴 Daily lunch and dinner

About 23km (14 miles) from Régua, turn left to enter **Pinhão**, crossing an iron bridge over the Douro to return to the north bank. Drive along the main street; don't miss the station building with its *azulejo* tiles depicting vineyards and rural scenes. This small town is one of the main centres of quality port production, and several of the leading houses have *quintas* here. For a glass of port, drop into the **Vintage House Hotel** (Lugar da Ponte, Pinhão, tel: 254 730 230), in a beautiful setting on the riverbank.

5–6

Leaving Pinhão, fork left where the road divides, following signs for Sabrosa and Vila Real. The road climbs through terraced vineyards. At **Sabrosa**, birthplace of the great navigator Ferdinand Magellan, turn left towards Vila Real. You pass the Roman site of **Panóias** on your way to **Casa de Mateus**

The town of Lamego, set in hilly, fertile countryside

LEAVING THE CAR BEHIND

The dramatic landscapes of the Douro Valley can also be explored on scenic train and boat journeys from Porto. River trips run from Porto and Vila Nova de Gaia between March and October, typically travelling upstream as far as Peso da Régua and returning to Porto by train. Several trains a day leave Porto's São Bento station on the Douro Valley train line, which joins the river about 60km (37 miles) from Porto and follows its banks as far as Peso da Régua (2.5 hours), Pinhão (3 hours), Tua and Pocinho. Tickets are inexpensive and can be bought in advance or at the time of travel from São Bento station in Porto, or from the stations at Peso da Régua or Pinhão. There are also two scenic narrow-gauge branch lines along tributaries of the River Douro – the Corgo line running from Régua to Vila Real, and the Tua Valley line from Tua to Mirandela.

(▶ 86–87), the impressive Portuguese manor house which you can see from a bend in the road as you approach. Turn right immediately after Mateus to return to Vila Real.

There are several quintas (wine estates) in Pinhão

3 LOWER ALENTEJO

Drive

DISTANCE 222km (138 miles) TIME 4 hours
START/END POINT Beja ✚ 201 D1

This enjoyable drive takes you into Lower Alentejo, a region ignored by most visitors in the dash from Lisbon to the Algarve. Few people live here and there are few must-see sights – the pleasures of this region are to be found driving along empty roads and pottering around small towns. Despite, or perhaps because of, the absence of other visitors, it is in places like Serpa and Moura that you can really feel the soul of southern Portugal and the influence of its Moorish past.

1–2

Start in **Beja** (▶ 142) and leave the city by following the IP2 in the direction of Faro. The road crosses a wide open landscape of wheat fields and cork oak trees, many with numbers painted on the stripped bark to indicate the date of the harvest. After 15km (9.3 miles), turn left on the N122 towards **Mértola**, on

The convent at Beja, where the love letters of a Portuguese nun are said to have been written

a quiet road with more cork oaks and the occasional isolated farmhouse or roadside hamlet. Turn right at the roundabout to enter **Mértola** (▶ 142) and park beneath the castle in the centre of town.

2–3

Once you have explored Mértola, leave by the same way you entered and take the bridge across the River Guadiana, following signs to Serpa – be sure to glance back as you cross the bridge for a lovely view of the town. The road climbs steeply at first, then levels out, with avenues of eucalyptus trees to either side. After 17km (10.5 miles) you reach **Mina de São Domingos**, an old copper-mining town first discovered by the Romans and still mined until the 1960s. The mines are now being turned into a tourist attraction with people visiting to see the effects of 2,000 years of mining on the landscape (free access at any time). There is also a large reservoir here, with a picnic area and a small beach

3–4

Continue driving across typical Alentejo countryside, with its cork oaks, wheat fields and sheep. The road is long and straight and the absence of traffic is remarkable – this is one of the most sparsely populated regions in Portugal. Shortly after passing through the olive and orange-growing village of **Santa Iria**, you reach a main road where you turn left and immediately left again to **Serpa**. Before entering the town, follow the signs to your left to climb the hill to the *pousada*, where

Nossa Senhora de Guadalupe, Serpa

THE STORY OF SALÚQUIA

Look at the coat of arms on the town hall in Moura and you will see a young girl lying dead at the foot of a tower. This is Salúquia, a Moorish princess, who lived in Moura at the time of the Christian conquest of the town in 1233. The story goes that on her wedding day her fiancé and his entourage were murdered by Christian knights on their way to the wedding ceremony. The Christians put on their victims' clothes and masqueraded as the wedding party in order to gain access to the castle, and Salúquia threw herself from the tower in despair. There are many similar folk legends in Portugal, but this one is unusual as it casts Christians in the role of villains and Moors as their unfortunate victims.

square sell the strong local sheep's cheese, *queijão de Serpa*. For a fuller meal of hearty Alentejano specialities, walk up the street to Molho Bico, beside the old town walls. From here it is a short stroll to the castle, where you can walk around the ramparts for views over the town and its surroundings.

The castle walls, which incorporate an earlier aqueduct, were built by Dom Dinis following the expulsion of the Moors in the 13th century, but were heavily damaged 500 years later during a raid by Spanish troops. Notice the boulder which forms a porch above the castle entrance, precariously balancing in the very spot where it was left hanging after the attack.

Return to the N265 main road (signposted "Espanha" – Spain) and turn left, then take the next right towards Moura. Soon you reach the village of

there is a small whitewashed Moorish-looking chapel, **Nossa Senhora da Guadalupe**, and sweeping views over the plain.

4–5
Serpa is known as *vila branca* (white town) because of the typically Portuguese whitewashed houses lining its narrow cobbled streets. Like the other towns on this route, it makes a pleasant place to while away a couple of hours. It has a watch museum, a folk museum, a botanical garden and a small archaeological museum housed within the castle walls. From the town's square, Praça da Republica, you can climb the steps past the tourist office to reach the parish church, with its separate bell-tower standing opposite. Cafés on the main

Drive out of Moura with the castle on your right-hand side and stay close to the town walls, following signs to Amareleja as the road swings round to the right beneath the gardens.

After crossing over the picturesque River Ardila, the road forks – keep left for Portel. Soon you come to **Barragem de Alqueva**, where a dam crosses the River Guadiana (creating the largest artificial lake in Europe).

Continue on this road, crossing through rolling countryside on the way to **Portel**, whose castle is visible from afar. Follow signs to Beja and return on the IP2.

PULO DO LOBO

The Pulo do Lobo (Wolf's Leap) waterfall is a place of rapids and weird rock formations in a deep gorge carved out by the River Guadiana between Mértola and Serpa. Although it is signposted from the Mértola to Serpa road, the easier approach is from a minor road 3km (2 miles) out of Mértola on the way to Beja.

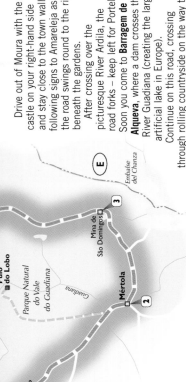

Pias, known for its strong red wines and the frescoes in the Santa Luzia church. Turn left to pass through the centre of the village then continue on this road through the vineyards and olive groves to the spa town of **Moura**.

5–6

Moura means "Moorish Maiden" and the town takes its name from the legend of the Princess Salúquia (➤ 181). This is another town with a ruined castle, cobbled streets and a long history. The Moorish quarter of Mouraria has whitewashed houses, ornamental chimneys and is particularly atmospheric.

Follow signs to the castle and park your car near the parish church of São João Baptista, with its rich Manueline portal. There are also some fine Sevillian *azulejos* adorning the high altar, the side chapels and the niche in the façade of the bell-tower. Across the street, storks can sometimes be seen nesting in the castle tower. Near here are the peaceful public gardens of the old spa, where people come for an evening stroll and to enjoy sunset views over the hills.

The thermal spa town of Moura has its own castle, grand mansions and pretty houses

4 LAGOS TO PRAIA DA LUZ
Walk

DISTANCE 6km (3.7 miles) **TIME** 3.5–4 hours
START POINT Lagos A202 B1 **END POINT** Praia da Luz ✚ 202 B1

The cliffs of western Algarve offer some superb walking, with sweeping views over the Atlantic and the bizarre rock formations that characterise this stretch of coast. Although you are hardly likely to find yourself alone, walking on the cliffs can be a good way of escaping the crowded beaches in summer. This walk is best done in the late afternoon or early evening, when the heat of the day has relented and the sunlight casts a softer glow of ever-changing colours on the ocean. If you are lucky you might catch one of the famous Atlantic sunsets from the cliffs above Praia da Luz.

1–2

Begin on the riverfront at **Lagos** (➤ 165), opposite the fishing harbour, and follow Avenida dos Descobrimentos towards the sea. Across the road is the municipal market, which opened in 1924. Fresh fish is sold downstairs, and there is a produce market upstairs selling fruit, flowers and jars of honey and piri-piri (hot pepper sauce).

Beside the market, **Praça Gil Eanes** contains an extraordinary statue of the boy-king Sebastião, a national hero who died in 1578 during a disastrous naval expedition from Lagos to Morocco. Take the opportunity for a coffee and snack at one of the pavement cafés here, as there will be few other opportunities for refreshment on this walk.

Continue walking along the riverside promenade, lined with palm trees. This place has a powerful feel of the great Age of Discovery, when Henry the Navigator's caravels sailed from here. There is a statue of Prince Henry across the road in Praça da República and a statue of the explorer Gil Eanes outside the nearby castle. To your left, beyond the harbour walls, ocean waves wash the shore of Meia Praia, Lagos' long and windswept town beach. Walk past the Ponte da Bandeira fortress, which contains a small museum devoted to the discoveries. Alongside the fort is the pretty cove beach of Praia da Batata. Now climb the main road out of town, passing

a *miradouro* with a monument to São Gonçalo, a local fisherman's son who became a monk and is now the patron saint of Lagos.

Praça Gil Eanes, with the Statue of King Sebastian in the centre of Lagos

2–3

Reaching the top of the hill, leave the road by taking the path to the left, signposted to Praia do Pinhão. Continue on this path as it leads along the cliffs to **Praia de Dona Ana**, one of the most attractive of the Algarve's beaches, with its typical rock formations and sandstacks. Cross the car park above the beach and climb back on to the cliffs, taking care on the partly eroded track. There is a choice of routes from here, but you really can't go wrong – just keep the sea to your left as you continue across the cliffs towards

Ponte da Piedade (Bridge of Piety), a well-known beauty spot where the red rock has been sculpted by the wind and sea into a series of dramatic boulders, arches and caves. Walk out past the lighthouse on to a spit for the best views along the coast. In summer, fishermen offer

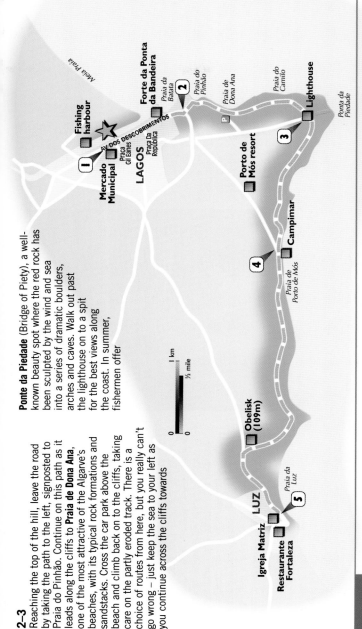

and offers spectacular views over the Atlantic, as far as **Cabo de São Vicente** (▶ 157–158) on a clear day.

After about 45 minutes you reach an obelisk marking the summit (109m/358 feet). Just beyond the obelisk, look for a gap in the bushes to your left and scramble down towards **Praia da Luz**, emerging on a cobbled path that leads to the beach. Praia da Luz is a low-key but growing resort of whitewashed apartments and villas climbing above a splendid beach. Stroll along the beachfront promenade, with its mosaic pavement, to reach the balcony at the end. Near here is the restaurant **Fortaleza da Luz**, inside an old fortress, facing the parish church (▶ below). Regular buses to Lagos stop beside the church.

Stop to admire the stunning views over the coves and grottoes of Ponte da Piedade

boat trips into the grottoes from a small landing stage at the foot of the cliffs.

3–4

Leaving the lighthouse, head west along the clifftop path. You need to stay close to the sea to avoid being forced into the resort development at Porto de Mós. Instead, drop straight down to the **beach** (watch your step here, although as building work is completed, this descent will get easier) where there are a couple of decent restaurants. If you feel you've done enough walking by now, there are occasional buses from here back to Lagos.

4–5

The next stretch of the walk is the hardest as it involves a long (but steady) climb to the highest point of the cliffs. The path is clear

ESCAPE ROUTE

The coastal footpath between Praia de Dona Ana and Ponte da Piedade also gives access to Praia do Camilo, a classic cove beach that is usually quieter than the others on this walk.

TAKING A BREAK

Campimar €€€
🔢 202 B1 ☒ Praia do Porto de Mós ⏲ Daily lunch and dinner

Fortaleza da Luz €€€
🔢 202 B1 ☒ Rua da Igreja 3, Praia da Luz ⏲ 282 789 926 ⏲ Daily lunch and dinner (closed mid-Nov to mid-Dec)

DADE DE SUBURBANOS
GRANDE LISBOA

Practicalities

BEFORE YOU GO

WHAT YOU NEED

		UK	Germany	USA	Canada	Australia	Ireland	Netherlands	Spain
● Required	Some countries require a passport to								
○ Suggested	remain valid for a minimum period								
▲ Not required	(usually at least six months) beyond								
△ Not applicable	the date of entry – check beforehand.								
Passport/National Identity Card		●	●	●	●	●	●	●	●
Visa (regulations can change – check before booking)		▲	▲	▲	▲	▲	▲	▲	▲
Onward or Return Ticket		○	○	○	○	○	○	○	○
Health Inoculations (tetanus and polio)		▲	▲	▲	▲	▲	▲	▲	▲
Health Documentation		▲	▲	▲	▲	▲	▲	▲	▲
Travel Insurance (▶ 192, Health)		○	○	○	○	○	○	○	○
Driver's Licence (national)		●	●	●	●	●	●	●	●
Car Insurance Certificate		●	●	●	●	●	●	●	●
Car Registration Document		●	●	●	●	●	●	●	●

WHEN TO GO

High season   Low season

JAN	FEB	MAR	APR	MAY	JUN	JUL	AUG	SEP	OCT	NOV	DEC
15°C	16°C	18°C	21°C	24°C	30°C	35°C	37°C	33°C	28°C	19°C	17°C
59°F	61°F	64°F	70°F	75°F	86°F	95°F	99°F	91°F	82°F	66°F	63°F

Sun

Sunshine and showers

Temperatures are the **average daily maximum** for each month. Spring (April to June) and autumn (September to October) are the best times to visit Portugal as the summer months can be unbearably hot and crowded. Added attractions are wild flowers in spring and the Douro Valley grape harvest in autumn. Summer is hot and dry inland, and mild on the coast where sea temperatures vary from 16°C (61°F) on the west coast to 23°C (73°F) in the Algarve. Winters are cool and wet in the north, but pleasantly mild in the Algarve, where walking and golf are year-round activities and swimming is possible from March to November, although you will probably need a wetsuit – the sea temperature can be quite chilly. Hotel rates tend to be much lower in January and February, making this a good time to visit Lisbon and the Algarve.

GETTING ADVANCE INFORMATION
Websites
- Welcome to Portugal: www.portugal.org
- Portugal National Tourist Office: www.visitportugal.com
- Algarve Net: www.visitalgarve.pt
- Pousadas de Portugal: www.pousadas.pt
- Solares de Portugal: www.solaresdeportugal.pt

In the UK
Portuguese National Tourist Office
11 Belgrave Square
London SW1X 8PP
☎ 0845 355 1212

GETTING THERE

By Air There are international airports at Lisbon, Porto and Faro. **British Airways** and the Portuguese national airline **TAP-Air Portugal** operate scheduled flights from London to all three cities, with a flight time of around two and a half hours. There is also a wide selection of charter flights, especially to Faro in summer, from British, Irish and European airports. Most seats on charter flights are sold by tour operators as part of a package holiday, but it is usually possible to buy a flight-only deal through travel agents or on the internet. The disadvantage of charter flights is that you are sometimes restricted to periods of 7 or 14 days.

From the USA TAP has scheduled flights to Lisbon from New York (6.5 hours), with connections to other North American cities.

By Car There are numerous entry points along the border with Spain, with little or nothing in the way of border controls. The main roads into Portugal are from Vigo to Porto, Zamora to Bragança, Salamanca to Guarda, Badajoz to Elvas and the motorway from Seville to the Algarve. From Britain, take a car ferry to Bilbao or Santander in northern Spain, from where it is a drive of about 800km (500 miles) to Porto and 1,000km (620 miles) to Lisbon.

By Rail There are regular trains to Lisbon from Madrid (10 hours) and Paris (24 hours). A train line from Vigo in Spain crosses the border at Valença do Minho to Porto and Lisbon.

TIME

Portugal is on Greenwich Mean Time (GMT), and one hour behind most of continental Europe. During the summer, from the last Sunday in March to the last Sunday in October, the time in Portugal is GMT plus one hour (GMT+1).

CURRENCY AND FOREIGN EXCHANGE

Currency The euro (€) is the official currency of Portugal. Euro coins are issued in denominations of 1, 2, 5, 10, 20 and 50 euro cents and €1 and E2. Notes are issued in denominations of €5, €10, €20, €50, €100, €200 and €500. Note: €200 and €500 notes are not issued in Portugal, but those issued elsewhere are valid.

Foreign currency and traveller's cheques can be changed at banks and exchange bureaux, as well as in many hotels. Exchange bureaux generally offer the best deal, but it pays to shop around and compare commission charges. You will need to show your passport when cashing traveller's cheques.

You can also withdraw cash from ATM machines using your credit or debit card and a PIN (personal identification number). Your bank will usually charge for this service.

Major credit cards are accepted in most resorts. When in the countryside it is advisable to have small denomination notes to hand. It is easier and no more expensive (depending on your credit card charges) to rely solely on plastic, rather than taking travellers' cheques or buying cash in advance.

In Ireland
Portuguese National Tourist Office
54 Dawson Street
Dublin 2
☎ 01 670 9133

In the USA
Portuguese National Tourist Office
590 Fifth Avenue
4th Floor
New York NY 10036-9702
☎ 646/723 0200

In Canada
Portuguese National Tourist Office
60 Bloor Street West
Suite 1005
Toronto, Ontario M4W 3B8
☎ (416) 921 7376

WHEN YOU ARE THERE

NATIONAL HOLIDAYS

1 Jan	New Year's Day
Feb/Mar	Shrove Tuesday
Mar/Apr	Good Friday/Easter Monday
25 Apr	Day of the Revolution
1 May	Labour Day
May/Jun	Corpus Christi
10 Jun	National Day
15 Aug	Feast of the Assumption
5 Oct	Republic Day
1 Nov	All Saints' Day
1 Dec	Independence Day
8 Dec	Feast of the Immaculate Conception
25 Dec	Christmas Day

ELECTRICITY

 The power supply is 220 volts AC. Sockets take two-pronged round continental plugs.

Visitors from the UK will need an adaptor, and visitors from the USA will need a transformer for 100–120 volt devices.

OPENING HOURS

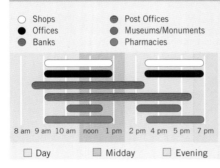

○ Shops ● Offices ● Banks ● Post Offices ● Museums/Monuments ● Pharmacies

8 am 9 am 10 am noon 1 pm 2 pm 4 pm 5 pm 7 pm

☐ Day ☐ Midday ☐ Evening

Shops Usually 9–1, 3–7. Large stores and supermarkets open 9–7 or 10 (5 on Sundays).
Banks Banks are open 8:30–3.
Post offices Mon–Fri 9–6, Sat 9–12 in cities, shorter hours in provincial areas.
Museums and churches Usually 10–12:30, 2–5, but check before visiting.
Pharmacies Usually 9–12:30, 2–7, but duty chemists will be open longer (▶ 192).

TIPS/GRATUITIES

Tipping is not expected for all services and rates are lower than elsewhere in Europe.
As a general guide:

Restaurant bill	(service not included) 10%
Taxis	10%
Tour Guides	half day E3
	full day E5
Porters	€1 per bag
Chambermaids	€2 per night
Toilet attendants	small change

DRINKING LAWS

There is no minimum age for drinking in Portugal, although the minimum age to purchase alcohol is 16. Drinking and driving laws, however, are very strict, and the alcohol limit is 0.5g per litre of blood, with hefty fines imposed if found in breach of this limit.

TIME DIFFERENCES

| GMT 12 noon | Portugal 12 noon | USA (New York) 7am | USA (Los Angeles) 4am | Spain 1pm | Sydney 10pm |

STAYING IN TOUCH

Post Stamps (*selos*) can be bought at post offices, kiosks and tobacconists.

Letters to European Union countries will arrive within five to seven days, and to the USA within 10 days.

Send urgent mail by *correio azul* and ensure that you post it in a blue postbox. Other postboxes are red.

Telephones There are public telephones on almost every street corner. They take coins, credit cards or phonecards, available from post offices, kiosks and shops displaying the PT (Portugal Telecom) logo.

International calls are cheaper between 9pm and 9am and at weekends.

Calls from hotel rooms will invariably attract a heavy premium.

International Dialling Codes
Dial 00 followed by

UK:	44
USA/Canada:	1
Irish Republic:	353
Australia:	61
Spain:	34

Mobile providers and services The coverage for mobile phones across Portugal is fairly extensive, and your mobile should pick up the local network automatically – although US cell phones may have more difficulty. Call charges will vary according to your contract. Check with your service provider before travelling.

Wi-Fi and Internet There is high-speed Internet access across Portugal, however WiFi service is sporadic. You will find WiFi, however, in most good hotels, particularly in Lisbon, Porto and the Algarve, and in some cafés and libraries, although this is still unusual. Most WiFi is offered through the mobile phone networks, and you pay for usage per minute or hour. There are Internet cafes in most beach resorts on the Algarve (expect them to be busy), and some in Lisbon.

PERSONAL SAFETY

Violence against tourists is unusual in Portugal. Theft from cars is the most common form of crime.

- Do not leave valuables on the beach or poolside.
- Always lock valuables in hotel safety deposit boxes
- Never leave anything inside your car. If you have to, lock valuables in the boot.
- Beware of pickpockets in crowded markets, around train stations and on crowded buses in Lisbon and Porto.
- Do not leave bags unattended while standing at a car hire desk or loading suitcases onto a bus.

Police assistance:
☎ 112 from any phone

There are police stations (esquadra da policia) in all towns and villages across Portugal. If your lose your passport, credit cards or any personal items you will need to fill out a crime report at a police station for insurance or replacement purposes. In 2001 Portugal decriminalised drugs for personal use.

EMERGENCY	
POLICE	112
FIRE	112
AMBULANCE	112

HEALTH

 Insurance Citizens of EU countries receive reduced-cost emergency health care with relevant documentation (European Health Insurance Card), but private medical insurance is still advised and essential for all other visitors.

 Dental Services The standard of dental care is generally excellent. Dental practices advertise in the free English-language magazines and newspapers at hotels. You have to pay for treatment, but your insurance should cover the costs.

 Weather The sun is intense at all times of year, and it is possible to burn very quickly, even on cloudy days. Cover up with high-factor sunscreen, wear a hat and drink plenty of water, especially if walking in the hills or along the coast.

 Drugs Chemists (*farmâcia*) are open Mon–Fri 9–1 and 2:30–7, and Sat 9–12.30. Some open through lunch and the late-night duty chemist is posted in pharmacy windows. Pharmacists are highly trained and can sell some drugs that require prescriptions in other countries. However, take adequate supplies of any drugs you take regularly as they may not be available.

 Safe Water Tap water is safe but its mineral content may make it taste unpleasant. Ask for sparkling (*água com gás*) or still (*água sem gás*) bottled water.

CONCESSIONS

Young People Most museums have lower admission rates for students (and entry is generally free for children) on production of a passport or valid student identity card.

Senior Citizens Senior citizens from many European countries come to the Algarve for its year-round warmth and long-stay low-season rates. Travellers over 65 are usually entitled to discounted admission at museums and reduced fares on public transport (proof of age needed). If mobility is a problem getting around can be a bit of a trial (► Travelling with a Disability, opposite).

TRAVELLING WITH A DISABILITY

Facilities for disabled travellers in Portugal are slowly improving, but many older hotels and public buildings are still inaccessible, especially in cities where hotels tend to be situated on the upper floors of apartment blocks. Cobbled streets are a particular problem for wheelchair users. There are "blue badge" car parking spaces in most town centres, and adapted toilets at airports and railway stations.

It is best to discuss your particular needs with your tour operator or hotel before booking a holiday.

CHILDREN

Hotels and restaurants tend to be child-friendly, and many coastal hotels have playgrounds and children's pools. Facilities like baby-changing rooms are improving.

TOILETS

There are public toilets in shopping centres and some of the larger beaches.

CUSTOMS

The import of wildlife souvenirs sourced from rare or endangered species may be illegal or require a special permit. Check your home country's regulations.

CONSULATES AND EMBASSIES

UK
☎ 213 924 000

USA
☎ 217 273 300

Ireland
☎ 213 929 440

Australia
☎ 213 101 500

Canada
☎ 213 164 600

USEFUL WORDS AND PHRASES

There are two distinctive Portuguese sounds: firstly, the nasalised vowels written with a til (~, like the tilde on Spanish ñ): (so "bread", *pão*, is pronounced "pow!" with a strong nasal twang; secondly, "s" and "z" are often pronounced as a slushy "sh" (so "banknotes", *notas*, is pronounced "not-ash").

GREETINGS AND COMMON WORDS

Yes/No **Sim/Não**
Please **Se faz favor**
Thank you **Obrigado** *(male speaker)*/ **Obrigada** *(female speaker)*
You're welcome **De nada/Foi um prazer**
Hello/Goodbye **Olá/Adeus**
Welcome **Bem vindo/a**
Good morning **Bom dia**
Good evening/night **Boa noite**
How are you? **Como está?**
Fine, thank you **Bem, obrigado/a**
Sorry **Perdão**
Excuse me, could you help me? **Desculpe, podia-me ajudar?**
My name is… **Chamo-me…**
Do you speak English? **Fala inglês?**
I don't understand **Não percebo**
I don't speak any Portuguese **Não falo português**

EMERGENCY! Urgência!

Help! **Socorro!**
Stop! **Pare!**
Stop that thief! **Apanhe o ladrão!**
Police! **Polícia!**
Fire! **Fogo!**
Go away, or I'll scream! **Se não se for embora, começo a gritar!**
Leave me alone! **Deixe-me em paz!**
I've lost my purse/wallet **Perdi o meu porta-moedas/a minha carteira**
My passport has been stolen **Roubaram-me o passaporte**
Could you call a doctor? **Podia chamar um médico depressa?**

DIRECTIONS AND TRAVELLING

Airport **Aeroporto**
Boat **Barco**
Bus station **Estação de camionetas**
Bus/coach **Autocarro**
Car **Automóvel**
Church **Igreja**
Hospital **Hospital**
Market **Mercado**
Museum **Museu**
Square **Praça**
Street **Rua**
Taxi rank **Praça de táxis**
Train **Comboio**
Ticket **Bilhete**
  Return **Ida e volta**
  Single **Bilhete de ida**
Station **Estação**
I'm lost **Estou perdida**
How many kilometres to…? **Quantos quilómetros faltam ainda parachegar a…?**
Here/There **Aqui/Ali**
Left/right **À esquerda/À direita**
Straight on **Em frente**

NUMBERS

0	**zero**	16	**dezasseis**
1	**um**	17	**dezassete**
2	**dois**	18	**dezoito**
3	**três**	19	**dezanove**
4	**quatro**	20	**vinte**
5	**cinco**	21	**vinte e um**
6	**seis**	30	**trinta**
7	**sete**	40	**quarenta**
8	**oito**	50	**cinquenta**
9	**nove**	60	**sessenta**
10	**dez**	70	**setenta**
11	**onze**	80	**oitenta**
12	**doze**	90	**noventa**
13	**treze**	100	**cem**
14	**catorze**	101	**cento e um**
15	**quinze**	500	**quinhentos**

DAYS

Today **Hoje**
Tomorrow **Amanhã**
Yesterday **Ontem**
Tonight **Esta noite**
Last night **Ontem à noite**
In the morning **De manhã**
In the afternoon **De tarde**
Later **Logo/Mais tarde**
This week **Esta semana**
Monday **Segunda-feira**
Tuesday **Terça-feira**
Wednesday **Quarta-feira**
Thursday **Quinta-feira**
Friday **Sexta-feira**
Saturday **Sábado**
Sunday **Domingo**

MONEY: DINHEIRO

Bank **Banco**
Banknote **Notas**
Cash desk **Caixa**
Change **Troco**
Cheque **Cheque**
Coin **Moeda**
Credit card **Cartão de crédito**
Exchange office Casa de Cámbio
Exchange rate **Cámbio**
Foreign **Estrangeiro**
Mail **Correio**
Post office **Agência do correios**
Traveller's cheque **Cheque de viagem**
Could you give me some small change, please? Podia-me dar **também din-heiro trocado, se faz favor?**

ACCOMMODATION

Are there any...? **Há...?**
I'd like a room with a view of the sea **Queria um quarto com vista para o mar**
Where's the emergency exit/fire escape? **Onde fica a saída de emergéncia/ escada de salvação?**
Does that include breakfast? **Está inclu-ido o pequeno almoço?**
Do you have room service? **O hotel tem serviço de quarto?**
I've made a reservation **Reservei um lugar**
Air-conditioning **Ar condicionado**
Balcony **Varanda**
Bathroom **Casa de banho**
Chambermaid **Camareira**
Hot water **Água quente**
Hotel **Hotel**
Key **Chave**
Lift **Elevador**
Night **Noite**
Room **Quarto**
Room service **Serviço de quarto**
Shower **Duche**
Telephone **Telefone**
Towel **Toalha**
Water **Água**

RESTAURANT: RESTAURANTE

I'd like to book a table **Posso reservar uma mesa?**
A table for two, please **Uma mesa para duas pessoas, se faz favor**
Could we see a menu, please? **Poderia dar nos a ementa, se faz favor**
What's this? **O que é isto?**

A bottle of... **Uma garrafa de ...**
Alcohol **Alcool**
Beer **Cerveja**
Bill **Conta**
Bread **Pão**
Breakfast **Pequeno almoço**
Café **Café**
Coffee **Café**
Dinner **Jantar**
Lunch **Almoço**
Menu **Menú/ementa**
Milk **Leite**
Mineral water **Água mineral**
Pepper **Pimenta**
Salt **Sal**
Table **Mesa**
Tea **Chá**
Waiter **Empregado/a**

SHOPPING

Shop **Loja**
Where can I get....? **Em que loja posso arranjar...?**
Could you help me please? **Pode-me atendar, se faz favor?**
I'm looking for... **Estou a procura de...**
I would like... **Queria...**
I'm just looking **Só estou a ver**
How much? **Quanto custa?**
It's too expensive **Acho demasiado caro**
I'll take this one/these **Levo este(s)/ esta(s)**
Good/Bad **Bom/Mau**
Bigger **Maior**
Smaller **Mais pequeno**
Open/Closed **Aberto/Fechado**
I'm a size... in the UK **Na Grã Bretanha o meu número é...**
Have you got a bag please? **Tem um saco, se faz favor?**

TOWN PRONUNCIATION GUIDE

Braga **brag-uh**
Bragança **bra-gan-suh**
Coimbra **queem-bruh**
Évora **e-vor-uh**
Faro **far-ooh**
Fátima **fa-tee-muh**
Lagos **lah-goosh**
Lisboa **leezh-boh-ah**
Marvão **mar-vow**
Porto **port-ooh**
Sagres **sar-gresh**
Tavira **ta-veer-ah**
Vila Viçosa **vee-lah-vee-soh-sah**

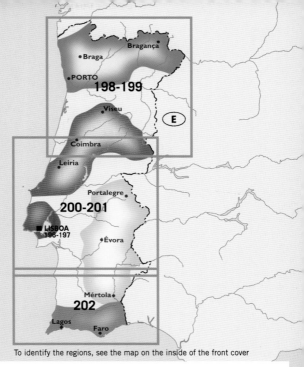

To identify the regions, see the map on the inside of the front cover

Streetplan

══════ Main/other road	▢ Featured place of interest
══════ Minor road	● Metro station
─────── Railway	𝒊 Tourist information
●──● Funicular railway	✝ Church
▓ Important building	✉ Post Office
▓ Park/garden	☼ Miradouro/viewpiont

Regional Maps

─ ·· ─ International boundary	▢ City
─── Regional boundary	▫ Town/village
══════ Major route	✈ Airport
══════ Motorway/toll motorway	▓ Built up area
══════ National road	▓ National/Natural park
══════ Regional road	▣ Featured place of interest
─── Other road	▪ Place of interest
┄┄┄ Railway	▲ Height in metres

196/197	0 ━━━━━ 150 metres
	0 ━━━━━ 150 yards

198-202	0 ━━━━━ 25 km
	0 ━━━━━ 15 miles

Atlas

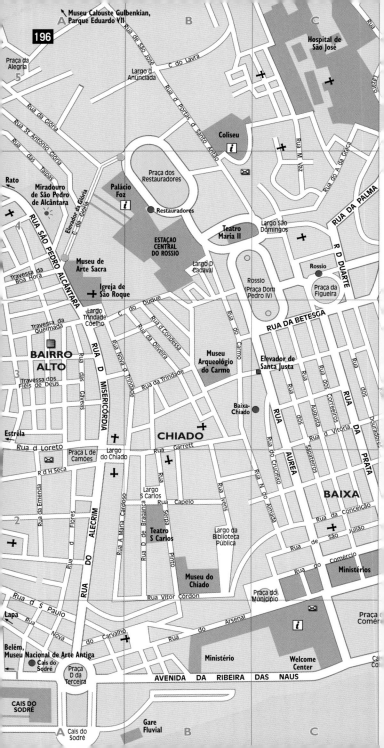

Museu Calouste Gulbenkian,
Parque Eduardo VII

A · B · C

Praça da
Alegria

5

Rua de São José

C do Lavra

Largo d
Anunciada

Rua das Portas de Santo Antão

Hospital de
São José

Rua da Glória

Rua St António da Glória

Rua das Taipas

Coliseu

i

Rua M. Vaz

Rua do A da Graça

RUA DA PALMA

Rato

Miradouro
de São Pedro
de Alcântara

Palácio
Foz

i

Praça dos
Restauradores

Restauradores

Teatro
Maria II

Largo São
Domingos

Rossio

R D DUARTE

Elevador da Glória

C da Glória

ESTAÇÃO
CENTRAL
DO ROSSIO

Largo D
Cadaval

Rossio
(Praça Dom
Pedro IV)

Praça da
Figueira

4

RUA SÃO PEDRO DE ALCÂNTARA

Museu de
Arte Sacra

Travessa da
Boa Hora

Igreja de
São Roque

Largo
Trindade
Coelho

C do Duque

Rua d Condessa

Rua d
Carmo

RUA DA BETESGA

Rua da Oliveira

Rua da Trindade

Museu
Arqueológio
do Carmo

Elevador de
Santa Justa

Rua dos
Correeiros

RUA DA PRATA

BAIRRO
ALTO

Travessa dos
Fiéis de Deus

RUA D MISERICÓRDIA

Rua das Gáveas

Rua Nova da Trindade

Baixa-
Chiado

RUA
AUREA

Rua dos
Sapateiros

Rua d Vitória

Rua dos
Dourados

3

Estrêla

Rua d Loreto

Praça L de
Camões

Largo
do Chiado

CHIADO

Rua Carrett

Rua do Crucifixo

Rua N do Almada

BAIXA

R d H Seca

Largo
S Carlos

Rua Capelo

Rua Serpa Pinto

Rua Ivens

Rua da Conceição

Rua de São
Julião

2

Rua da Emenda

Rua das Flores

RUA DO ALECRIM

Rua A Maria Cardoso

Rua D de Bragança

Teatro
S Carlos

Largo da
Biblioteca
Pública

Rua do
Comércio

Ministérios

Museu do
Chiado

Rua Vítor Córdon

Praça do
Município

Praça do
Comércio

Belém,
Museu Nacional de Arte Antiga

Rua d S Paulo

Rua Nova

do Carvalho

Rua do Arsenal

i

Lapa

Cais do
Sodré

Praça
D da
Terceira

Ministério

Welcome
Center

Cais
Col

CAIS DO
SODRÉ

Cais do
Sodré

AVENIDA DA RIBEIRA DAS NAUS

Gare
Fluvial

A · B · C

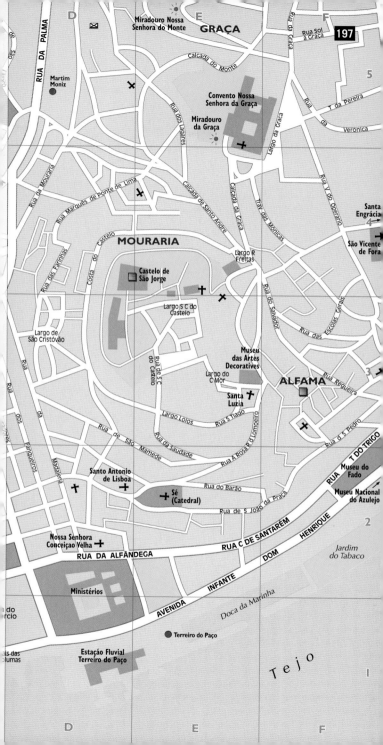

Miradouro Nossa
Senhora do Monte

Martim
Moniz

Calçada do Monte

Rua Sol
à Graça

Rua da Graça

Rua da T da Pereira

Veronica

Convento Nossa
Senhora da Graça

Rua da Mouraria

Rua Marquês de Ponte de Lima

Rua dos Lagares

Calçada de Santo André

Miradouro
da Graça

Largo da Graça

Calçada da Graça

Trav. das Mónicas

Rua V do Oseiro

Santa
Engrácia

MOURARIA

Rua das Farinhas

Costa do Castelo

Castelo de
São Jorge

Largo R
Freitas

São Vicente
de Fora

4

Rua do Salvador

Rua das Escolas Gerais

Largo S C do
Castelo

Largo de
São Cristóvão

Rua de S C
do Castelo

Museu
das Artes
Decorativas

Rua das

ALFAMA

Rua Regueira

3

Largo do
C Mor

Santa
Luzia

Rua

Rua dos

Largo Loios

Rua S Tiago

Rua A Rosa R d Tomoeiro

Rua de S Pedro

Rua da Saudade

Rua de São Mamede

Rua de S. João da Praça

Rua T DO TRIGO

Museu do
Fado

Magdalena

Santo António
de Lisboa

Sé
(Catedral)

Rua do Barão

RUA

Museu Nacional
do Azulejo

2

Nossa Senhora
Conceição Velha

RUA C DE SANTARÉM

RUA DA ALFÂNDEGA

INFANTE

DOM

HENRIQUE

Jardim
do Tabaco

Ministérios

AVENIDA

Doca da Marinha

do
ercio

is das
olumas

Terreiro do Paço

Estação Fluvial
Terreiro do Paço

Tejo

1

D

E

F

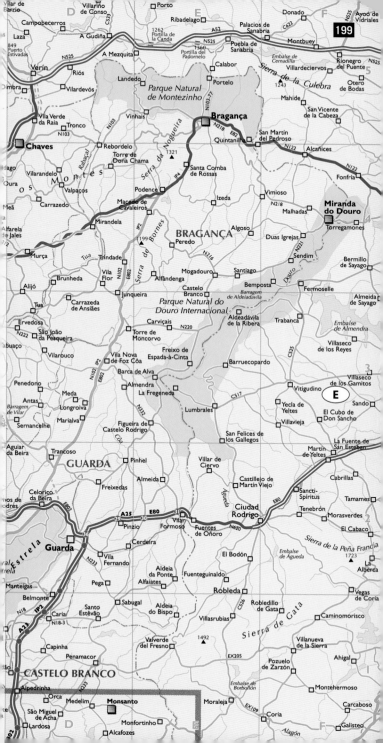

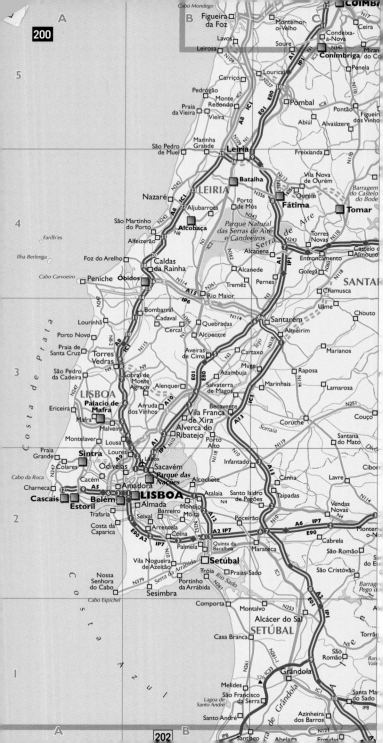

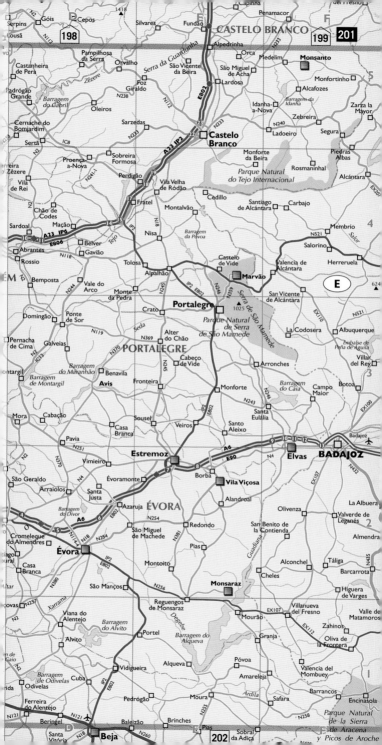

Picture credits

Bethan Court.

The Automobile Association would like to thank the following photographers, companies and picture libraries for their assistance in the preparation of this book.

Abbreviations for the picture credits are as follows – (t) top; (b) bottom; (c) centre; (l) left; (r) right; (AA) AA World Travel Library.

2(i) AA/J Edmanson; 2(ii) AA/C Jones; 2(iii) AA/M Wells; 2(iv) AA/T Harris; 3(i) AA/A Mockford and N Bonetti; 3(ii) Photolibrary Group; 3(iii) AA/C Jones; 3(iv) AA/M Wells; 5l AA/J Edmanson; 5c AA/M Wells; 5r AA/M Wells; 6/7 AA/M Wells; 9 AA/A Mockford and N Bonetti; 11 AA/A Mockford and N Bonetti; 12 AA/C Jones; 13 AA/A Mockford and N Bonetti; 14 AA/T Harris; 15 AA/A Mockford and N Bonetti; 16 AA/A Mockford and N Bonetti; 17 AA/A Mockford and N Bonetti; 18 AA/A Mockford and N Bonetti; 19t AA/A Kouprianoff; 19c AA/M Wells; 21 AA/M Wells; 22/23 Photolibrary Group; 24 AA/A Mockford and N Bonetti; 25l Photolibrary Group; 25r AA/P Wilson; 26l Getty Images/Sean Gallup; 26r Photolibrary Group; 27 AA/P Wilson; 28 AA/C Jones; 30 AA/C Jones; 31l AA/C Jones; 31c AA/M Wells; 31r AA/M Wells; 41l AA/M Wells; 41c AA/M Wells; 41r AA/M Wells; 43 AA/M Wells; 44 AA/M Wells; 45t AA/M Wells; 45b AA/A Mockford and N Bonetti; 46 AA/M Wells; 47 AA/T Harris; 48 AA/M Wells; 49 AA/M Wells; 50 The Mirror of Venus, 1870-76 (oil on canvas), Burne-Jones, Sir Edwards (1833-98)/Museu Calouste Gulbenkian, Lisbon, Portugal/Bridgeman Art Library; 51 AA/A Kouprianoff; 52 AA/M Wells; 53 AA/M Wells; 54 AA/M Wells; 55 AA/A Kouprianoff; 56 AA/A Kouprianoff; 57 AA/M Wells; 58 AA/M Wells; 59t AA/A Mockford and N Bonetti; 59b AA/M Wells; 60 AA/A Mockford and N Bonetti; 61 AA/T Harris; 62 AA/A Mockford and N Bonetti; 63 AA/A Kouprianoff; 64 AA/M Wells; 65t AA/M Wells; 65b AA/A Mockford and N Bonetti; 66 AA/A Kouprianoff; 75l AA/T Harris; 75c AA/T Harris; 75r AA/T Harris; 76 AA/T Harris; 77 AA/P Wilson; 78 AA/T Harris; 79t AA/A Mockford and N Bonetti; 79b AA/A Mockford and N Bonetti; 80 AA/T Harris; 80/81 AA/P Wilson; 82t AA/T Harris; 82b AA/A Mockford and N Bonetti; 83 AA/A Kouprianoff; 84 AA/A Mockford and N Bonetti; 85 AA/T Harris; 86/87 AA/T Harris; 88 AA/A Mockford and N Bonetti; 89t AA/A Mockford and N Bonetti; 89b AA/A Kouprianoff; 90 AA/A Mockford and N Bonetti; 91 AA/A Mockford and N Bonetti; 92 AA/T Harris; 93 AA/P Wilson; 94t AA/C Jones; 94b AA/A Kouprianoff; 95 AA/A Kouprianoff; 101l AA/A Mockford and N Bonetti; 101c AA/A Kouprianoff; 101r AA/Mockford and N Bonetti; 103 AA/A Kouprianoff; 104 AA/A Kouprianoff; 105 AA/A Mockford and N Bonetti; 106 Photolibrary Group; 107 AA/A Kouprianoff; 108 AA/A Kouprianoff; 109 Photolibrary Group; 110 AA/A Kouprianoff; 111 AA/A Kouprianoff; 112 AA/P Wilson; 113 AA/A Kouprianoff; 114 AA/A Kouprianoff; 115 AA/A Mockford and N Bonetti; 116c AA/A Kouprianoff; 116b AA/A Kouprianoff; 117 AA/Harris; 118 AA/T Harris; 119 AA/A Mockford and N Bonetti; 120 AA/T Harris; 121 AA/A Mockford and N Bonetti; 122 AA/A Kouprianoff; 127l Photolibrary Group; 127c AA/A Mockford and N Bonetti; 127r AA/A Kouprianoff; 128 AA/J Edmanson; 130 AA/A Kouprianoff; 131l AA/A Mockford and N Bonetti; 131r AA/A Kouprianoff; 132 AA/A Mockford and N Bonetti; 133 AA/A Kouprianoff; 134 AA/P Wilson; 136 AA/A Mockford and N Bonetti; 137 Photolibrary Group; 138 AA/A Kouprianoff; 139 AA/A Kouprianoff; 140 AA/J Edmanson; 141 AA/A Kouprianoff; 142 AA/A Kouprianoff; 147l AA/C Jones; 147c AA/C Jones; 147r AA/C Jones; 148 AA/C Jones; 149 AA/C Jones; 150 AA/C Jones; 151t AA/M Chaplow; 151b AA/C Jones; 152 AA/M Chaplow; 153 AA/C Jones; 154 AA/M Chaplow; 155 AA/M Chaplow; 156/157 AA/A Mockford and N Bonetti; 158 AA/J Edmanson; 159 A/C Jones; 160 AA/C Jones; 161 AA/A Mockford and N Bonetti; 162 AA/M Chaplow; 163t AA/M Birkitt; 163b AA/C Jones; 164 AA/M Chaplow; 165 AA/A Kouprianoff; 171l AA/M Wells; 171c AA/J Edmanson; 171r AA/S Day; 172 AA/A Mockford and N Bonetti; 174 AA/M Wells; 176 AA/A Kouprianoff; 178 AA/A Kouprianoff; 179 AA/T Harris; 180 AA/M Birkitt; 181 AA/P Wilson; 183 AA/J Edmanson; 184 AA/C Jones; 186 AA/M Chaplow; 187l AA/A Mockford and N Bonetti; 187c AA/A Kouprianoff; 187r AA/M Jourdan; 191t AA/M Chaplow; 191c AA/A Mockford and N Bonetti; 191b AA/C Jones

Every effort has been made to trace the copyright holders, and we apologise in advance for any accidental errors. We would be happy to apply any corrections in the following edition of this publication.

SPIRALGUIDE
Questionnaire

Dear Traveller

Your comments, opinions and recommendations are very important to us. Please help us to improve our travel guides by taking a few minutes to complete this simple questionnaire.

You do not need a stamp (unless posted outside the UK). If you do not want to remove this page from your guide, then photocopy it or write your answers on a plain sheet of paper.

Send to: The Editor, Spiral Guides, AA World Travel Guides, FREEPOST SCE 4598, Basingstoke RG21 4GY.

Your recommendations…
We always encourage readers' recommendations for restaurants, night-life or shopping – if your recommendation is used in the next edition of the guide, we will send you a FREE AA Spiral Guide of your choice. Please state below the establishment name, location and your reasons for recommending it.

_____

_____

_____

_____

_____

Please send me AA Spiral _____
(see list of titles inside the back cover)

About this guide…
Which title did you buy?

_____ **AA Spiral**

Where did you buy it?_____

When? m m / y y

Why did you choose an AA Spiral Guide? _____

_____

_____

_____

_____

Did this guide meet your expectations?

Exceeded ☐   Met all ☐   Met most ☐   Fell below ☐

Please give your reasons_____

_____

_____

_____

_____

continued on next page…

Were there any aspects of this guide that you particularly liked?

Is there anything we could have done better?

About you...

Name (Mr/Mrs/Ms)

Address

Postcode

Daytime tel no ———————————— email

Please *only* give us your email address and mobile phone number if you wish to hear from us about other products and services from the AA and partners by email or text or mms.

Which age group are you in?

Under 25 ☐ 25–34 ☐ 35–44 ☐ 45–54 ☐ 55–64 ☐ 65+ ☐

How many trips do you make a year?

Less than one ☐ One ☐ Two ☐ Three or more ☐

Are you an AA member? Yes ☐ No ☐

About your trip...

When did you book? m m / y y   When did you travel? m m / y y

How long did you stay?

Was it for business or leisure?

Did you buy any other travel guides for your trip? ☐ Yes ☐ No

If yes, which ones?

Thank you for taking the time to complete this questionnaire. Please send it to us as soon as possible, and remember, you do not need a stamp (unless posted outside the UK).